A SENSE OF MISSION

A
SENSE OF
MISSION

*Defining Direction
for the Large Corporation*

· · · · ·

ANDREW CAMPBELL and LAURA L. NASH

with Marion Devine and David Young

The
Economist
Books

Addison-Wesley Publishing Company

Reading, Massachusetts   Menlo Park, California   New York
Don Mills, Ontario   Wokingham, England   Amsterdam
Bonn   Sydney   Singapore   Tokyo   Madrid   San Juan
Paris   Seoul   Milan   Mexico City   Taipei

LIBRARY OF CONGRESS CATALOGING-IN-PUBLICATION DATA

Campbell, Andrew.
    A sense of mission: defining direction for the large corporation / Andrew Campbell and Laura L. Nash with Marion Devine and David Young.
        p. cm.
    Includes bibliographical references and index.
    ISBN 0–201–60800–6
    1. Corporate culture. 2. Employee motivation I. Nash, Laura L.
  II. Title
    HD58.7.C3463 1992
    658.3'14—dc20   92–21088
                                      CIP

First published in Great Britain by Hutchinson Business Books Limited
An imprint of Random Century Limited

Jacket design by One Plus One Studio
Text design by Lloyd Lemna Design
Set in 10-point Palacio by ST Associates, Inc., Wakefield, MA

1 2 3 4 5 6 7 8 9-MA-95949392
First printing, November 1992

Contents

Acknowledgements

This project has been a team effort. Before we explain the contributions made by all the people who helped with the research and the production of the book, we would like to clarify the roles of the four authors. Andrew Campbell led the research from its inception in 1987 and acted as integrator of the conceptual thoughts. Marion Devine challenged the concepts, refined the thinking, and compiled the evidence. David Young joined the project in the autumn of 1988 and was responsible for much of the case study work reported in Chapters 5, 7, 8, and 10. Laura L. Nash, working independently, researched and wrote the case studies in Chapters 6 and 9 and added her findings on the conjunction of corporate mission and business ethics.

The Campbell team's research effort was paid for by the Ashridge Strategic Management Centre with special sponsorship from the Boston Consulting Group. The project was approved at the first Research Committee meeting of the Centre in November 1987 by the founding members of the committee: BP, BOC, Courtaulds, ICI, Lloyds Bank, United Biscuits, and the Strategic Planning Society. Throughout its somewhat circuitous progress, it was enthusiastically encouraged and guided by the committee and the additional members—Digital, Grand Metropolitan, and Shell—which joined in 1988. Without the financial and emotional support given so generously by the committee and the Boston Consulting Group, none of this could have happened.

We also want to praise the generosity of the companies that have given precious management time to share their experiences with us and to send us their mission statements. Full lists of the companies from which we have drawn material are given on pages 15 and 245–6. Here we would like to thank six companies in particular:

British Airways, Bulmers, Dist, Inc. (disguised), Marks and Spencer, Royal US, and Johnson & Johnson. We took up substantially more of the time of people in these companies than in any others. And we want to thank all the managers and employees who went out of their way to help us.

Many people have been part of the research team over the last two and a half years. Clive Rassam, author and researcher, was involved in the early research work. He is responsible for the much-quoted and highly insightful interviews at Egon Zehnder. Kiran Tawadey, a research associate at the Ashridge Strategic Management Centre, collected mission statements and delved into the many dimensions of the literature. Her contributions to the concepts as they evolved were important and the quality of her work shines through in the review of the literature in Chapter 2. Hilary Chadwick, an MBA student at the London Business School, expertly interviewed staff at Bulmers and still describes wide-eyed the warmth and hospitality she received on her visit to Hereford. Sally Klewin, an associate of Ashridge Management College, helped with our understanding of the company we call Dist, as did John Roberts, a lecturer at Cambridge University who had interviewed Dist managers on the subject of culture change. David Clutterbuck, author and chairman of Item, did much of the interviewing at Marks and Spencer and contributed personal experiences from working with companies to develop their mission statements. Sally Yeung, administrator at the Ashridge Strategic Management Centre, organized many aspects of the project, researched particular companies, contributed valuable insights, and conjured up the disks that were sent to the publisher. We also received invaluable support from Juliet Venter and Siân Turner.

Laura Nash's research would not have been possible without the Graduate School of Business at Harvard University, which generously funded research into ethical issues in business; the Business Round Table; and the Institute for the Study of Economic Culture at Boston University.

We would like to acknowledge the important roles played by Virginia Merritt of Ashridge, Carolyn White of The Economist Books, Lucy Shankleman of Hutchinson Business Books, and John Bell of Addison-Wesley. They spurred us into writing the book by enthusiasm, by setting deadlines, and by their belief that the book touches a chord with a broad audience of people involved with business.

Finally, we want to give prominence to Michael Goold, director of the Ashridge Strategic Management Centre, and Stephen Bungay, Barry Jones, and colleagues at the Boston Consulting Group. The rigor of our conceptual thinking is mainly due to their refusal to let woolly ideas pass and to their penetrating contributions.

Those woolly ideas that still exist in the following chapters, and the errors or omissions that you may find, are entirely our responsibility. The insights, the inspiring examples, and the practical advice that we hope you will discover are in the main due to the long list of people who have helped us in this project.

Foreword

One of the activities that has given me great pleasure over the last nine years has been directing the annual management development program for two large companies. It is a privilege to be locked away for two weeks with a dozen or so managers earnestly interested in improving themselves and their companies. Much of the time is spent discussing and analyzing the company and, at an appropriate moment, the chief executive is put on stage to answer questions.

One question that almost always comes up is about where the company is going and what it stands for. The question may be asked simply: "What do you think the company will be like in the year 2000?" It may be asked indirectly: "What management qualities do you think we will need to make the company successful over the next 20 years?" Or, "Do you think that our current culture is appropriate as we face the globalization of our market?" And I have even heard it asked in a threatening fashion: "Why do you think you are the right person to lead this company?"

With the amount of practice that chief executives get, you would think that they would be very good at answering this question. But they are not. Their answers rarely get close to the concern that gave rise to the question; managers are frequently left unsatisfied. What managers are searching for is a sense of purpose and a sense of identity, something that we are going to call in this book a "sense of mission." They want more from their organizations than pay, security, and the opportunity to develop their skills. They want a cause that is personally satisfying.

Psychologists would no doubt provide useful descriptions of this phenomenon, labeling it the dependency syndrome or something similar. They might say that people are always looking for their

leaders to answer the unanswerable and that the feelings of dissatisfaction are normal in a boss–subordinate relationship of this type.
Yet I have had one or two experiences in these classrooms that make
me hopeful that managers do not need to be dissatisfied after asking
the question and that chief executives do not have to make jokes
about what else they would be doing if they could see into the
future.

One experience sticks in my memory. It concerns a manager
from a small clothing manufacturer who was a participant in one of
these development programs. Throughout the two weeks the manager bubbled with enthusiasm about his company and led us to
believe that most of the other managers in the company were
equally excited by the business. He was eager to tell us about how
they had improved quality standards, about how they keep in close
touch with the buying public, about almost everything the
company did. Even when faced with colleagues who knew something to criticize, he was undaunted. "Of course everything is not
perfect," he would protest, "but we are working on it and it's
already better than it was."

His enthusiasm was partly infectious and partly threatening (or
as one "threatened" manager put it, "naïve verging on the obnox-
ious"). His contributions were not always supportive of the messages of the course. He believed that too much analysis and thinking
could get in the way. To him, what to do was simple. The hard part
was doing it.

After the chairman's visit, when the group was at the bar
expressing their feelings of dissatisfaction with the chairman's
response to one of the "where is our company going" questions,
this manager took on his colleagues:

> The reason why you are all moaning is because you don't have any
> commitment to your own businesses. If you focused on getting your
> own companies sorted out and created some commitment to the busi-
> ness as we have, you wouldn't be worrying about what people at head-
> quarters are doing or where they are going. To us they are just a minor
> irritant. Hardly worth thinking about.

This manager had a sense of mission about his business. He was
getting all the fulfillment he needed from it. His business was his
cause to the point where he was hardly interested in the larger
organization to which he belonged. His colleagues, on the other

hand, lacked a cause. They had no sense of mission about their businesses or about the larger whole.

Some readers will question the benefit of creating managers as passionate as this man. It can be argued that business needs calm, rational, clearheaded managers who can be dispassionate and caring about their companies. Managers who fall in love with their business are dangerous. Moreover, in larger organizations these passionate managers can create divisiveness and cultural conflict that hinders smooth operating.

In this book we are going to argue that the opposite is true. Most organizations, we believe, have become depersonalized to the point where energy levels are low, cynicism is high, and work fails to fulfill or excite. Our observation is that committed employees perform many times more efficiently than apathetic ones do, and this is even more true for teams.

When I worked at McKinsey & Co. as a consultant, Tom Peters, the coauthor of *In Search of Excellence* and at that time a principal of McKinsey, used to talk about the power of the turned-on team. "A turned-on team does not perform 20 percent better or even 50 percent better," he explained, "it performs ten times better or 50 times better."

We believe that individuals with a strong sense of mission are more effective at their jobs and that they make their organizations more successful in fulfilling the needs of all the stakeholders: customers, shareholders, suppliers and employees. In this book we define what we mean by mission and by a sense of mission; we examine the writings of others, such as Peter Drucker and Tom Peters; we look at the benefits of a sense of mission; and we give advice to leaders and managers seeking to create a mission and develop employees with a sense of mission. But before describing the content of the chapters that follow, I want to explain how these insights came about.

Developing Understanding

The research that lies behind this book began in November 1987. It was launched because a number of the corporate members of the Ashridge Strategic Management Centre were in the process of trying to write mission statements. The research was designed to examine the use and misuse of mission statements. Some managers seemed to think that a mission statement is an essential management tool. Others considered them to be vacuous and unnecessary. The research team hoped to resolve the differences.

With my classroom experiences of middle management's hunger for clarity of direction and purpose, I was a keen supporter of mission statements without having any clear idea of what they should contain. I felt that a clear mission statement would help the chief executive give a good answer to the "where is our company going" question and it would be a useful supporting document. Michael Goold, my colleague and codirector at the Strategic Management Centre, was more skeptical. Coming from the rational school of strategic analysis, he had little warmth towards the concept of mission statements and suppressed a slightly nauseous reaction to the word "mission," a reaction that we recognize is shared by a large number of managers.

Fortunately, we had had the experience of working from opposite starting positions on previous research projects, and the pressure of these opposing views proved to be a positive benefit, creating the first insight. I found it hard to disagree with Michael that mission statements are frequently worth little more than the paper they are written on. Having collected more than 100 statements, it was apparent that some were not intended as documents of great consequence. One, for example, had been drafted by a communications consultant in order to add body to a recruitment brochure. It was hard for me to argue that this mission statement was important. Yet I knew from experience that some managers have an added zest and commitment to their work. And it was then that we came up with the concept of a "sense of mission." Companies, we reasoned, should not be trying to write mission statements. They should be trying to create a sense of mission among their employees. A statement might be something that would help them do so.

This concept of a sense of mission fitted well with our experience. We could immediately identify companies where at least a portion of employees and managers have, like the manager in the clothing manufacturer, a sense of mission about their work. Moreover we could also identify noncommercial organizations, like the Boy Scouts, where members also have a sense of mission about their work. We realized, therefore, that before we could research mission statements we needed to research a "sense of mission."

On the surface, this seemed to be a simple task. We could go and talk to managers in companies that we believed had a sense of mission. But we had a problem. We had no definition of the word "mission." The prerequisite for creating a sense of mission among managers was presumably to have a company with a mission.

It was about this time that I had started research interviews at Egon Zehnder, an international partnership of executive search consultants. It was immediately apparent that these people had a sense of mission. And it was from these interviews that we developed our second most important insight. In response to questions such as "What is your mission?" the Egon Zehnder interviewees did not mention goals like size or profit per partner; and they did not talk about the importance of helping industry by finding the right people. They talked about things much closer to home. They talked about the importance of cooperation and the one-firm concept. They talked about the systematic approach that they use for assignments. They talked more about the way they do business than about the business services they offer, their goals, or their clients. We came to realize that members of an organization sense the mission of the organization through the way the organization operates—through its behavior standards and its values. Sense of mission seemed to be about an identification with the culture of the organization more than about identification with the goals.

I can remember at this point arguing that, if sense of mission comes from an identification with culture, then the mission of the company must be the creation and maintenance of a satisfying culture. But this definition was contrary to almost all the other definitions we had been considering. The most common definition of mission used by managers is "the business we are in and the competitive positioning we choose within that business."

In early 1988 a company much in the news was the TI Group, an international engineering business based in Britain. It had been completely restructured around a new mission. The annual report stated: "TI's strategic thrust is to become an international engineering group concentrating on specialized engineering businesses, operating in selected niches on a global basis. Key businesses must be able to command positions of sustainable technological and market share leadership." This articulation of TI's purpose, people argued, was a mission statement. Mission, they argued, is about identifying the business you are in.

This line of thinking fitted well with Michael Goold's views, and so we found ourselves again in a period of conflict. The Egon Zehnder interviews were telling me that mission is about culture, while common sense and experience were telling Michael that mission is about business definition and strategy.

The impasse was finally solved by Michael and colleagues at the Boston Consulting Group who came up with the diagrammatic representation illustrated in Figure 1.1 (page 19). Mission, we realized, is about culture *and* about strategy. In fact, a mission exists when strategy and culture are mutually supportive. An organization has a mission when its culture fits with its strategy.

With this definition of mission, we were able to explain the Egon Zehnder interviews. We could readily apply our definition of mission to Egon Zehnder. It is an international executive search firm aiming to be positioned as the most professional firm in its industry. This business definition and positioning fits well with its professional working methods and "one-firm culture," a concept that encourages its consultants around the world to collaborate with one another. The Egon Zehnder consultants were, therefore, talking about mission when they were describing the one-firm culture and the cooperative spirit. They were emphasizing the values element of mission rather than the strategic element. It is not surprising that people talk more about values than about strategy, because they attach themselves much more easily to values than to abstract strategic concepts.

We began to realize (and this was confirmed by other interviews) that a sense of mission occurs when the values of the company are attractive to the employees—that is, when the employees find their work fulfilling because they are using it to act out some deeply held values. In one of our later interviews a British manager working in the United States explained this link. He described the reason for his commitment to his company. "The integrity thing is very big for me. My father was a policeman, so I had already signed up for straight dealing and treating people well. I am a supporter of the philosophy because Harry [the chief executive] obviously communicates it from the heart and his behavior supports it. It is really a commitment to Harry as much as anything else."

The definitions that we developed for "mission" and "sense of mission" are described in Chapter 1. Chapter 2 examines the views of other writers and shows how their concepts link in with our concept of a sense of mission. We took care to look at the writings of academics from a variety of fields—strategy, culture, motivation, and leadership—because we perceived that mission is a subject that spans many aspects of business. We were rewarded by finding references to the concept of a sense of mission in all these fields.

In Chapter 3 we explain why a sense of mission is so valuable. Not only does it improve decision-making but it raises energy levels, reduces the need for supervision, promotes constructive behavior, and increases satisfaction.

Making It Useful

Once we understood the difference between mission and sense of mission, we became excited about the implications. If leaders define clear missions for their organizations and share these missions with their employees, then surely all employees could feel as enthusiastic about their organizations as the manager at the clothing manufacturer and the consultants at Egon Zehnder.

So how do leaders define clear missions and, more importantly, how do they "share" these missions with employees so as to create a sense of mission? And, returning to our original question, what is the role of the mission statement? Chapter 4 answers these questions and is supported by five detailed case studies (Chapters 5 through 9). We identified companies that had been through a process of defining mission and, in particular, we identified a few companies that had made major changes around a new mission.

Defining mission is essentially a creative process. You cannot arrive at a mission by analysis or by following a process of management meetings and workshops. It comes from insight and understanding. In this sense mission is no different from strategy. A strategy is a commercial concept that will enable you to outperform your competitors. For example, your strategy may be to offer better service by employing more customer service staff and encouraging the organization to think about customers. The extra money you spend will, you hope, be more than offset by higher prices or greater volume or both. This strategy may or may not be based on thorough analysis. It may or may not have been discussed with multiple layers of management. And it may or may not be successful.

Nevertheless, it is a strategy and such strategic thoughts can only be developed creatively. Mission is the same. As a combination of strategy and values, mission must also be developed creatively, even inspirationally. As a result, there are no rules or regulations about how it should be done.

Some leaders are lucky. They have discovered a mission either from experience or because it has sprung almost fully formed into their heads. It is so obvious to them that they cannot understand why others cannot see what they see. Other leaders have to work harder. They draw on the mission of one of their team or build a mission out of different ideas from across their teams. Still others discover a mission the hardest way; each piece of it falls into place only after years of experimentation.

The vast majority, however, discover no mission because they are not looking for one. Our most valuable advice to managers is that they should be looking. They should be searching for more than a good strategy. They should be searching for a set of values that fits the strategy and can help to create a mission for their company and a sense of mission among employees.

Finally, our research did address the issue of mission statements. Once we understood mission and how leaders can create a sense of mission, we were able to see the role of mission statements more clearly. A mission statement is the articulation of a company's mission. It can help to clarify detailed issues; it can serve as a symbol of the common cause shared by the people in the company; and it can help individuals who get "led astray" by events to pull themselves back to the original mission. Seen like this, a mission statement for a company has a role similar to that of the Bible for Christians or the Constitution for Americans. The Bible and the U.S. Constitution are statements of what Christians and Americans believe are the most important principles that guide their behavior. In a company, a mission statement should be seen as a document that captures what employees believe to be the most important principles that guide behavior in the company.

The Bible and the Constitution are useful documents only to those who believe in them, those who are committed to follow their doctrine or their rules. A mission statement is the same. It is useful only to those committed to follow its principles. Therefore a mission statement is most valuable to those who have a sense of mission. To use another analogy, a mission statement is like writing down your New Year's resolutions. The statement of your resolutions is of no value in itself. You are either committed to the resolutions or you are not. Writing them down will not help greatly. But it may help a little, especially if you are already resolved. The statement can be useful to refer back to, a document that strengthens your resolve. How would you feel if someone else wrote your New Year's resolutions for you and sent you a copy? Unless they were nearly identical to the ones you had written already, you would be unlikely to pay much attention.

This is not how the majority of leaders perceive mission statements. They view mission statements as a vehicle for disciplining and motivating the company. In our view, mission statements are not useful for this purpose. Only management behavior can discipline people, and motivation comes from a sense of mission, not from a mission statement. Mission statements do not create a sense of mission; it is rather the other way round. A mission statement has meaning only to someone with a "sense" of the mission being described. We therefore see mission statements as being most useful after a sense of mission has been created, not before.

To underline our view about mission statements, Chapter 11 identifies ten standards by which you can measure the quality of a mission statement. These standards are demanding. It is hard for a statement to meet the standards unless it is written by the leader of an organization that already has a sense of mission. Managers who write statements that do not meet these standards will be better advised to abandon the task and devote more energy to fostering a sense of mission.

As we see it, mission statements frequently do more harm than good because they imply a sense of direction, clarity of thinking, and unity that rarely exists. Most often they describe values and behavior standards that are unrealistic and certainly not part of employees' normal behavior. Instead of uplifting employees with elevating ideals, they encourage cynicism. "If this is what the leaders think we should be believing and doing, then they are more stupid or out of touch than we thought," say the employees. Naïveté or hypocrisy are obvious to those in the front line, and they are seen as more serious weaknesses than uncertainty or indecisiveness.

This understanding of mission statements brought us to the end of what turned out to be a remarkable research expedition. As with all research, the route to the destination was unpredictable. But the outcome has been wholly satisfying. The word *mission* may still make some people cringe. The way we use it in this book, however, describes the very essence of organizational cohesiveness, identity, and effectiveness. It is a central, and frequently overlooked, part of leadership and management.

What Is Mission?

A corporate mission is much more than good intentions and fine ideas. It represents the framework for the entire business, the values which drive the company and the belief that the company has in itself and what it can achieve.

COLIN MARSHALL
Deputy Chairman and Chief Executive
British Airways

. . . .

In this chapter, we describe the components of mission. We pull together previously unrelated views of mission, creating a more robust and comprehensive approach. By doing so, we believe that we have produced a definition of mission that enables managers to analyze and discuss a subject that has until now remained vague. We also throw new light on a neglected area of management—the interface between mission and employee motivation and behavior.

Many managers misunderstand the nature and importance of mission, while others fail to consider it at all. As far back as 1973, Peter Drucker observed: "That business purpose and business mission are so rarely given adequate thought is perhaps the most important cause of business frustration and failure."[1] Sadly, his comment is as true today as it was then.

The reason for this neglect is due in part to the fact that mission is still a relatively uncharted area of management. Most management thinkers have given mission only a cursory glance, and there is little research into its nature and importance. What research there is has been devoted to analyzing mission statements and attempting to develop checklists of items that should be addressed in the statement.[2] Indeed, a major problem is that mission has become a meaningless term—no two academics or managers agree on a definition. Some speak of mission as if it were commercial evangelism, others talk about strong corporate cultures, and still others talk about business definitions. Some view mission as an esoteric and somewhat irrelevant preoccupation that haunts senior managers, while others see it as the bedrock of a company's strength, identity, and success—its personality and character.

Despite the diversity of opinion about mission, it is possible to distinguish two schools of thought. Broadly speaking, one approach describes mission in terms of business strategy, while the other expresses mission in terms of philosophy and ethics.

The strategy school of thought views mission primarily as a strategic tool, an intellectual discipline that defines the business's commercial rationale and target market. Mission is something that is linked to strategy but at a higher level. In this context, it is perceived as the first step in strategic management. It exists to answer two fundamental questions: "What is our business and what should it be?"

The strategy school of mission owes its birth to an article, "Marketing Myopia," which appeared in the *Harvard Business Review* in 1960.[3] The author, Ted Levitt, a professor of marketing at Harvard, argued that many companies have the wrong business definition. Most particularly, companies define their businesses too narrowly. Levitt reasoned that a railroad company should see its business as moving people rather than railroading, an oil company should define its business as energy, and a company making tin cans should see itself as a packaging business. Managers, Levitt argued, should spend time carefully defining their business so that they focus on customer need rather than production technology.

More recently, it has become common for companies to include a statement of what their business is in the annual report. The cover of the 1988 annual report of Redland, a roofing, aggregates, and construction materials company, is an example. It reads:

Spanning the

Roofing

World with

Aggregates

Construction

Bricks

Materials

The first page of the annual report of British Telecom, a large telecommunications business, reads: "British Telecom's mission is to provide world class telecommunications and information products and services and to develop and exploit our networks at home and overseas."

Corning Glass states:

> We are dedicated to the total success of Corning Glass Works as a worldwide competitor. We choose to compete in four broad business sectors. One is Specialty Glass and Ceramics, our historical base, where our technical skills will continue to drive the development of an ever-broadening range of products for diverse applications. The other three are Consumer Housewares, Laboratory Sciences, and Telecommunications. Here we will build on existing strengths, and the needs of the markets we serve will dictate the technologies we use and the range of products and services we provide.

In contrast, the second school of thought argues that mission is the cultural "glue" that enables an organization to function as a collective unity. This cultural glue consists of strong norms and values that influence the way in which people behave, how they work together, and how they pursue the goals of the organization. This form of mission can amount to a business philosophy that helps employees to perceive and interpret events in the same way and to speak a common language. Compared with the strategic view of mission, this interpretation sees mission as capturing some of the emotional aspects of the organization. It is concerned with generating cooperation among employees through shared values and standards of behavior.

IBM seems to subscribe to the cultural view of mission. The computing giant describes its mission in terms of a distinct business philosophy, which in turn produces strong cultural norms and values. In his book, *A Business and Its Beliefs*, Thomas J. Watson, Jr., described these beliefs, many of which were established by his father, and insisted that they have been the central pillar of the company's success. Watson asserted: "The only sacred cow in an organization should be its basic philosophy of doing business." For IBM, "the basic philosophy, spirit and drive of the business" lies in three concepts: respect for the individual, dedication to service, and a quest for superiority in all things. The importance of other factors that contribute to commercial success, such as technological and economic resources, is "transcended by how strongly the people in the organization believe in its basic precepts and how faithfully they carry them out."[4]

Is it possible to reconcile these two different interpretations? Are they conflicting theories or are they simply separate parts of the same picture? We believe these two theories can be synthesized into a comprehensive single description of mission. We also believe that some of the confusion over mission exists because of a failure to appreciate that mission is an issue that involves both the hearts (culture) and minds (strategy) of employees. It straddles the world of business and the world of the individual.

The central aim of this chapter is to outline a framework that defines mission. The value of this framework is that it helps managers to think clearly about mission and, more importantly, to discuss mission with their colleagues. Previously, managers have had an intuitive understanding of mission. Intuition is not, however, enough. Mission needs to be managed and it can be managed better if it is clearly defined.

Building a Definition of Mission

We have developed our theory of mission both through an intellectual, top–down process and through direct talks with employees. Through this approach, we have tried to build an understanding of mission that is firmly grounded in the day-to-day realities of corporate life.

During the last three years, the Ashridge research team approached 53 companies that had expressed an interest in the research project on mission. These companies are listed in Table 1.1. Initially, we asked them how they had developed and used their mission statements. However, we soon discovered that a number of the companies in our sample had a strong sense of purpose, or a strong culture, or both.

We therefore identified from the original group of companies five businesses that seemed to have a strong sense of purpose supported by a strong sense of culture. These companies were: Bulmers, manufacturers of cider and soft drinks; Egon Zehnder, the Swiss-based international executive search consultancy; Dist, Inc. (disguised), a distributor of white goods and industrial controls based in the United States and Europe; Marks and Spencer, the international retailing business; and Royal US, the American arm of

Table 1.1 **Companies Involved in the Research**

Existing case material examined	Detailed interviews carried out
ASICS (Onitsuka Corporation)	Bulmers
Borg-Warner	Dist (disguised)
Disney	Egon Zehnder
Dow Corning	Marks and Spencer
Honeywell Information Systems	Royal US
Komatsu	
Richardson Sheffield	Full case studies developed
Securicor	
Wacoal	British Airways
	Dist (disguised)
	Ind Coope Burton Brewery
	Shell UK Refining

Personal experiences discussed	
Akzo	Mars
Ashridge	McKinsey & Co.
BBA	Metropolitan Police
BOC	Northern Ireland Electricity
The Body Shop	Portsmouth & Sunderland
British Petroleum	Newspapers
BUPA	Price Waterhouse
Burmah Oil Co	Prudential
Burson Marsteller	Rank Xerox
Courtaulds	Richard Lochridge Associates
First Chicago Bank	Royal UK
Ford	Shell International
Gencor	W. H. Smith
Grand Metropolitan	Tarmac
Hanson	TI Group
ICI	Trusthouse Forte
LIG	Wellcome
Lloyds Bank	Valmet

a British insurance company. In addition, for this book Laura Nash examined two corporations with missions that had been codified in writing for many years: Johnson & Johnson, the pharmaceutical manufacturer; and the Jewel Companies, a supermarket and retailing concern.

Finally, we examined five cases where senior managers had set
about developing a new mission and philosophy. One of these
cases, Shell UK Refining, has been well documented by a variety of
different researchers and we have relied on their evidence. We have
also relied on published data for Borg-Warner, a diverse multi-
national corporation, because the company's efforts to create a mission have been developed into a Harvard Business School case. The
story of Burton Breweries was described in a book, *By GABB & By
GIBB*, published and edited by former managing director David
Cox, and we have tested its evidence through a number of interviews with employees. In the other two companies, British Airways
and Dist, we interviewed many directors and employees at different locations.

The managers we interviewed in companies with a strong sense
of purpose and a strong culture brimmed with stories about why
their companies were special. At Marks and Spencer, a retailer
known for its high quality and value for money, employees talked
about quality and value. They described the high standards they
demanded of themselves and their suppliers. One manager
commented:

> The M&S standards were much higher than those I had worked with
> before. It appealed to me and I became hooked. Before I had set my
> standards to conform with the group of people with whom I associated.
> I was fairly lazy. I found at M&S I had to work harder than I had ever
> worked at school, but it was attractive because the standards that were
> set were so high and to fall short of them would be letting myself down.

They enthused about good human relations and visible management:

> I have had 27 years in Marks and Spencer. What was it that appealed to
> me when I joined? It was that the senior levels were real people and
> real personalities, even for me in a relatively low position. It wasn't that
> I spent a lot of time with them but rather it was the apocryphal stories
> that were handed down to me that made me feel I had met them. The
> organization had a strong personality and I could identify with the
> policies, people and practices of the business. The Board have enough
> visibility so that I have a good idea of what they want from me.

At British Airways, staff spoke of the new pride and professionalism among employees as the result of the effort in the 1980s to

build a service culture: "I feel proud to work for BA," said one individual. "People outside BA recognize the achievement, especially when they travel on the airline."

Pride and dedication are also evident in Egon Zehnder, an executive search firm. Consultant after consultant spoke of concepts and values that the company holds dear: the primacy of the client's interest, teamwork, and the "one-firm" concept. Mark Weedon, former managing director of the London office, explains: "We are not a group of separate profit centers. The objective is to maximize the whole. We shy away from measuring productivity. You're selling the firm not the individual or the office. We are very different from the average search firm. It's a sort of subjugation of self." Said another consultant: "There are very few arguments here. Because? Because we all depend on each other. We're not selfish in generating work. . . . We recognize each others' skills and we'll switch assignments or work as a team."

An employee in a large manufacturing company speaks of emotional commitment and sense of purpose. For her, the company's high standards of behavior are epitomized by the chairman's example. She comments: "He believes that all people are equal. He's a bit paternalistic for my way of thinking but he insists on human decency and he is consistent. . . . The company believes in treating people like human beings. There is too little of that in my life—look at the way people push past you in the street. . . ." To this woman, working for her company is one way of supporting "human decency," a concept she values strongly.

In these companies the commitment and enthusiasm among employees seem to come from a sense of personal attachment to the principles on which the company operates. Employees are clear about what is important and are happy to follow the standards and behaviors their companies ask of them. From this flows pride and enthusiasm. Employees are not simply conforming to peer pressure or suffering from corporate indoctrination—they are giving their personal endorsement and commitment to these standards and behaviors.

We began to feel that the link between personal and corporate values was a crucial aspect of mission. We tried to push interviewees to articulate this link by asking: "Why are you attached to these standards? Why is the one-firm concept important to you?

Why is treating people well so important to you?" The answers were the same—in the blunt words of a director of Bulmers, the UK brewery and liquor business, "Because it's right." Interviewees were making strong value judgments, arguing that the values and practices of their companies are morally correct. In other words, they make a connection between their own personal values and the beliefs of their companies. When these reinforce one another, people feel a deep satisfaction.

But the sense of rightness these employees feel is not restricted to a personal and moral realm. When pushed to explain themselves, some also articulate a commercial rationale. They assert that their behavior is more effective than that of their competitors, that their way of working is not only more personally satisfying but also superior.

A consultant at Egon Zehnder explained the commercial rationale behind the company's philosophy: "The philosophy means you're more dedicated to the client. One has a different attitude from what you might have in another search firm. . . . The firm bends over backward to encourage sharing, giving advice, helping other offices around the world. . . . In the long term, the approach produces better-quality search work."

Another consultant from Egon Zehnder reinforced the link between the commercial rationale and moral rationale, showing how the two can become intertwined:

> When you first come here, you are exposed to a lot of strong hype and ethics. At first it seems a bit heavy. . . . Then you start to believe it, and that worries you, until you realize that you have to have it because of the way we try to present ourselves and our belief in quality, in confidentiality, the process of dealing with the client—that's all funda- mental to ensure that you operate efficiently. . . . I was interviewing this morning and I found myself becoming Messianic about the firm because you really believe it. I do believe it because I need it.

We were hearing managers talk primarily about the standards and behaviors in their companies and why these are important to them. On the one hand, they like the company's standards because, to them, they are worthwhile and elevating. On the other hand, they support the company's standards because they can see the practical good sense behind them; they can see that the standards add up to a superior business strategy.

Figure 1.1 **The Ashridge Mission Model**

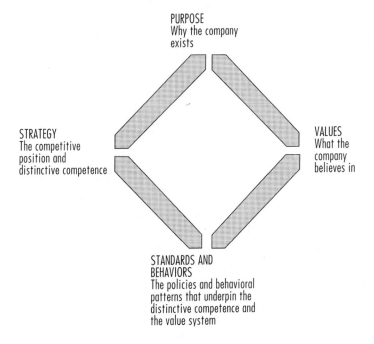

PURPOSE
Why the company
exists

STRATEGY
The competitive
position and
distinctive competence

VALUES
What the
company
believes in

STANDARDS AND
BEHAVIORS
The policies and behavioral
patterns that underpin the
distinctive competence and
the value system

We have attempted to make sense of these responses by developing a definition of mission. Our definition, which is illustrated in Figure 1.1, includes four elements—purpose, strategy, behavioral standards, and values. A strong mission, we believe, exists when the four elements of mission link tightly together, resonating and reinforcing each other.

Purpose

What is the purpose of the company? For whose benefit is all the effort being made? Why should a manager or an employee do more than the minimum required? For a company, these questions are the equivalent of a person asking "Why do I exist?" The questions are deeply philosophical and can lead boards of directors into heated debate. Indeed, many companies do not even attempt to reach a conclusion about the nature of their overall purpose.

However, where there does appear to be an overall idea of purpose, companies fall into three categories. The first type of company claims to exist for the benefit of its shareholders. Its purpose is to maximize wealth for the shareholders. All decisions are assessed against a yardstick of shareholder value. Hanson, a conglomerate focused on Britain and the United States, is one example. Lord Hanson repeatedly states, "The shareholder is king." Unlike many companies whose chairpersons claim to be working primarily for the shareholders, Lord Hanson believes what he says and manages the business to that end. Hence Martin Taylor, a director, feels quite free to say: "All of our businesses are for sale all of the time. If anyone is prepared to pay us more than we think they are worth, we will sell. We have no attachment to any individual business."

Most managers, however, are not as single-minded as Lord Hanson. They don't believe that the company's only purpose is to create wealth for shareholders. They acknowledge the claims of other stakeholders such as customers, employees, suppliers, and the community. Faced with the question, "Is your company in business to make money for shareholders, make products for customers, or provide rewarding jobs for employees?" they will answer "yes" to all three.

The second type of company, therefore, exists to satisfy all its stakeholders. In order to articulate this broader idea of purpose, many of these companies have written down their responsibility to each stakeholder group. Ciba-Geigy is an example. It has published the company's business principles under four headings—the public and the environment, customers, employees, and shareholders. Under the heading of the public and the environment, it has five paragraphs describing principles such as: "We will behave as a responsible corporate member of society and will do our best to cooperate in a responsible manner with the appropriate authorities, local and national." For customers there are three paragraphs, for employees eight paragraphs, and for shareholders five.

A less detailed statement of a company's commitment to its stakeholders is given by Monsanto: "Monsanto's continuing success requires customer enthusiasm for our products, employee dedication and skill, public acceptance of our social behavior, and shareowner confidence and investment. Our goal is to merit their collective support and, in so doing, share with them the rewards that a truly great worldwide company can generate."

Dist, a distributor of white goods and industrial controls, has not only defined its responsibilities but also explicitly addressed the conflict that can arise between shareholders and employees. A company document states: "We will exercise responsibility in our dealings with all our stakeholders and in the case of conflict balance the interests of employees and shareholders on an equal basis over time."

In practice it can be argued that the multiple-stakeholder view of purpose is more a matter of pragmatism than arbitrary choice. In a competitive labor market, a company that totally ignores its employees' needs will soon find its labor costs soaring as it fights to stem the tide of rising employee turnover. But what is important is the psychology of statements of purpose. Lord Hanson is saying that he is expecting his managers to put the allegiance of employees after the interests of shareholders in their list of priorities. Dist is saying they have equal priority. For employees, this makes each company very distinct.

Managers in the third type of company are dissatisfied by a purpose solely aimed at satisfying stakeholder needs. They have sought to identify a purpose that is greater than the combined needs of the stakeholders, something to which all the stakeholders can feel proud of contributing. In short, they aim toward a higher ideal. The planning director in one company, operating in a depressed region of Britain, explained: "I don't get excited about making money for shareholders. I like to help businesses succeed. That's something I can get excited about. I believe our future depends on it—I don't just mean this company, it's about the future of the nation, even the international community—it's about world peace and that sort of thing."

At Marks and Spencer, Britain's most successful clothing retailer, one manager described the company's purpose as "raising standards for the working man." This rings true for many others in the company who felt, particularly in the early days of M&S and after the war, that they were improving the standard of clothing available to the average person because they were able to retail high-quality goods at affordable prices.

At The Body Shop, a retailer of cosmetics, managers talk about "products that don't hurt animals or the environment." At Egon Zehnder, the purpose is to be the worldwide leader in executive search. Whether these companies have an almost moral crusade, like Marks and Spencer or The Body Shop, or whether they just aspire to be the best, like Egon Zehnder, they have all reached beyond the stakeholder definition of purpose. Each stakeholder, whether shareholder, employee, or supplier, can feel that doing business with the company supports some higher-level goal.

As will become clearer in the next two chapters, we believe that leaders will find it easier to instill employees with a sense of mission if they choose a purpose aimed at a higher ideal. We have met individuals with a sense of mission aimed at shareholders or at the broader definition of stakeholders, but we believe that it is harder for this commitment to grow. Purposes expressed in terms of stakeholders tend to emphasize their different selfish interests. Purposes aimed at higher ideals seek to deny these selfish interests or at least dampen their legitimacy. This makes it easier to bind the organization together. In Chapter 11, which discusses mission statements, we examine how some companies have developed statements of purpose that reach beyond the selfish interests of stakeholders.

Strategy

To achieve a purpose in competition with other organizations, there must be a strategy. Strategy provides the commercial logic for the company. If the purpose is to be the best, there must be a strategy explaining the principles around which the company will become the best. If the purpose is to create wealth, there must be a strategy explaining how the company will create wealth in competition with other companies.

Strategy will define the business that the company is going to compete in, the position that the company plans to hold in that business, and the distinctive competence or competitive advantage that the company has or plans to create.

The Dist strategy provides a good example of these three elements. Dist seeks to be in any distribution business where there is an opportunity to predominate through quality. In these businesses Dist wants to hold the position as the quality leader, giving more reliable delivery and shorter delivery times as well as a friendlier and more helpful approach. Dist's distinctive competence is its service-oriented culture supported by policies of good human relations and training.

Egon Zehnder provides another example of a strategy that explains how the firm will achieve its purpose. It wants to be the most professional, although not necessarily the biggest, international executive search firm. Its competitive advantage comes, it believes, from the methods and systems it uses to carry out search assignments and from the "one-firm," cooperative culture it has so carefully nurtured.

Marks and Spencer's strategy in textiles is a third example. In its clothes retailing business, Marks and Spencer seeks to offer the best value for money by providing a broad range of classic quality clothes. The company's competitive advantage comes from its dedication to quality through managing suppliers, its high levels of service, and the low overheads generated by high sales per square foot.

Strategy is, therefore, an important part of mission because it links purpose to behavior.

Policies and Behavioral Standards

Purpose and strategy are empty intellectual thoughts unless they can be converted into action, into the policy and behavior guidelines that help people to decide what to do on a day-to-day basis.

British Airways provides a good example of how a company's purpose and strategy have been successfully converted into tangible standards and actions. It promotes itself as the "world's favorite airline" and its mission statement declares as its aim "To be the best and most successful company in the airline industry." The strategy to achieve this is based on providing good value for money and service that overall is superior to its competitors and having friendly, professional managers who are in tune with its staff. These strategic objectives have been translated into policies such as the need for in-flight services to be at least as good as those of competing airlines on the same route, and the requirement that managers and employees should be helpful and friendly at all times.

By translating purpose and strategy into actionable policies and standards, senior managers at British Airways have dramatically changed the performance of the airline. Central to this effort was the training and behavioral change connected with the slogan "Putting People First."

The Body Shop has as its purpose the development of cosmetics that are not harmful to animals or the environment. Its strategy is to be more environmentally conscious than its competitors, hence attracting the "green" consumer and the "green" employee. Within the company, environmental consciousness has been translated into policies and behavioral standards, one of which was almost unique when first introduced. All employees have two waste bins: one for recyclable products and one for ordinary garbage. Employees receive training in what can be recycled and what cannot. In the last year or two a number of other companies have introduced similar policies.

Egon Zehnder provides another example of the link between strategy and policies. Their strategy is to be more professional than other executive search consultants. In conjunction with this, it has formulated a set of policies about how consultants should carry out assignments, called the "systematic consulting approach." One of the policies is that consultants should not take on a search assignment unless they believe that it will benefit the client. Another policy is that there should be a back-up consultant for every assignment in order to ensure a quality service to the client. Supporting this systematic approach are behavioral standards about cooperation. These are ingrained into the culture rather than written on tablets of stone. Egon Zehnder consultants willingly help each other either within their own offices or from other offices around the world. Philip Vivian, a consultant, explained this behavioral standard:

> Collaboration and cooperation are very important and it is unusual in this industry. It is essential that we recognize each other's skills and switch assignments or work as a team. It is also critical for international work. We have one Japanese assignment that is being coordinated from Tokyo, Milan, Paris, London, and Frankfurt. So we have to work as a team. It doesn't always work out perfectly because of the inevitable problems of communication. But the "one-firm" concept helps. We all know we are working for the same firm—no office is going to lose out if it helps another.

The logic for the cooperation as described by Vivian is a commercial logic. The firm wants to be the best. This means being better at cooperation than its competitors. As a result, it needs a behavioral standard that makes sure consultants help each other. This commercial logic is the left-brain logic of the firm.

Human beings are emotional, however, and are often driven more by right-brain motives rather than left-brain logic. To capture the emotional energy of an organization, the mission needs to provide some philosophical or moral rationale for behavior to run alongside the commercial rationale. This brings us to the next element of our definition of mission.

Figure 1.2 **Two Reasons for Action**

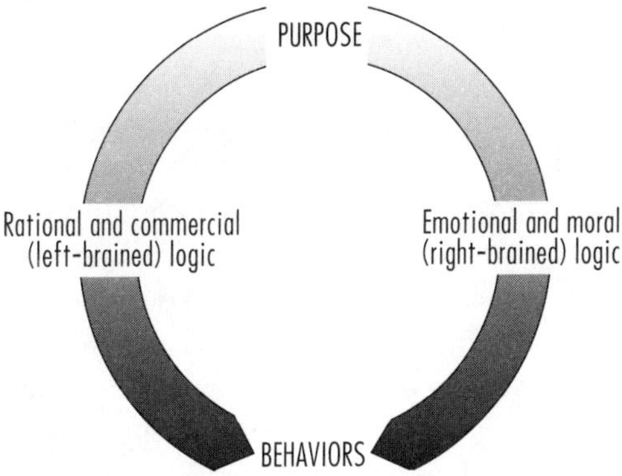

PURPOSE

Rational and commercial
(left-brained) logic

Emotional and moral
(right-brained) logic

BEHAVIORS

Values

Values are the beliefs and moral principles that lie behind a company's culture. Values give meaning to the norms and behavioral standards in the company and act as the right brain of the organization. Figure 1.2 illustrates how strategy and values constitute the left and right brain of companies with a mission.

In many organizations, corporate values are not explicit and can be understood only by perceiving the philosophical rationale that lies behind management behavior. For example, Egon Zehnder consultants believe in cooperative behavior because they are committed to the firm's strategy. But they also believe in cooperative behavior because they feel that it is "right." Egon Zehnder employees are naturally cooperative. They have been selected for that quality. They believe that people ought to be cooperative. "It makes a nicer place to work and it suits my style," explained one consultant. "And it's a better way to work," he added with the faintest implication of a moral judgment.

Egon Zehnder consultants can also be moral about certain aspects of the systematic approach. The policy of not taking on an assignment unless the consultant believes it is good for the client highlights a moral as much as a commercial rationale. Other executive search companies will take on any assignment, they argue. But Egon Zehnder puts the interests of the client first and will advise the client against an assignment even if that means lost revenues to the company. It is a professional code of behavior. As professionals, they feel a moral duty to advise the client to do what is best for the client rather than what is best for Egon Zehnder. There is a commercial rationale for this behavior, but the moral rationale is stronger.

The same is true at British Airways. There is a good commercial reason for "Putting People First," but there is also a moral reason: We are all people and life would be better for all of us if we took a little more care of each other. This moral rationale was put high on the agenda when 35,000 BA staff participated in the "Putting People First" training programs. The new behaviors described by the trainers were presented as a philosophy of life as much as a way of improving British Airways. Participants were asked to consider how they greeted their families when arriving home as well as how they handled customers.

A third example of the way in which values can provide an additional logic for behavior comes from Hewlett-Packard (HP). *The HP Way* describes a behavioral standard made famous by Tom Peters in *In Search of Excellence:* "Management by Wandering Around" (MBWA). Hewlett-Packard's strategy has been to succeed in high-value niches of the electronics industry by being better at innovation and product development. To implement this strategy, HP needs to attract and retain the best engineers and product managers. These high-quality individuals do not like to be closely controlled or hierarchically managed. HP, therefore, developed the MBWA policy as a management approach suitable for these kinds of high achievers. The MBWA behavior standard is based on good commercial logic.

But MBWA has also become a crusade of its own. Managers believe it is the right way to manage not only high achievers but all personnel. MBWA is good behavior not only because it is good strategy but also because it is something everyone should be doing. It acknowledges the innate creativity of individuals and underlines the manager's respect for people. It has been imbued with values.

The objective observer can easily identify situations, such as captaining a ship, where MBWA would be totally the wrong style of management. Yet for managers committed to *The HP Way*, it is almost sacrosanct. Like the systematic approach at Egon Zehnder, or "Putting People First" at British Airways, MBWA in Hewlett-Packard is not only good strategy but "the right way to behave."

Figure 1.3 **A Sense of Mission Comes From a Values Match**

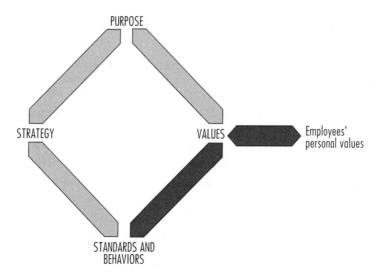

These three examples show how values can provide a rationale for behavior that is just as strong as strategy. It is for this reason that the framework in Figure 1.3 has a diamond shape. There are two rationales that link purpose with behavior. The commercial rationale—the left-brain reasoning—is about strategy and what sort of behavior will help the company outperform competitors in its chosen arena. The emotional, moral, and ethical rationale—the right-brain reasoning—is about values and what sort of behavior is ethical: the right way to treat people, the right way to behave in our society.

Our definition of mission includes both these rationales linked together by a common purpose.

Creating a Strong Mission

A strong mission exists when the four elements of mission—purpose, strategy, behavioral standards, and values—reinforce each other. This is most easily perceived by looking at the links between the strategy and the value system and whether both can be acted out through the same behavior standards. Are the important behavior standards central to both the strategy and the value system?

At Egon Zehnder, British Airways, and Hewlett-Packard they are. We looked at only one or two behavioral standards for each company, but we would find much the same reinforcement of both strategy and values if we examined other behavioral standards. Hewlett-Packard's commercial strategy depends on attracting and keeping high-quality committed employees. This means it has to demonstrate a set of values that desirable employees will find attractive. So, for example, it has an "open door" policy that encourages dissatisfied employees to approach senior managers; a policy of high integrity and open communications with stakeholders; a belief in informality and in decentralization; a policy of promoting from within; and a commitment to teamwork. Each of these policies and behavioral standards has a rationale both in the company's strategy and in its value system. They work cumulatively to create a strong mission.

Marks and Spencer is another company where the most important behavioral standards are essential pillars of both the strategy and the value system. One of the platforms of Marks and Spencer's philosophy is good human relations. As one manager explained: "Marcus Sieff [the former chairman] gave many presentations both in the company and outside. But he only ever gave one speech, about good human relations." Part of Marks and Spencer's strategy is to have employees who take more care, particularly in relation to customer service. By caring for employees, Sieff would argue, the company will create employees who will care for the company and its customers. As a result, Marks and Spencer is famous for its services and support for employees, from the quality of the toilets to benefits like dental care. Supporting the policy of good human relations is a standard of management behavior referred to by one manager as "visible management." Almost identical to Hewlett-Packard's standard of MBWA, visible management requires that managers, even at the highest level, spend time visiting stores and talking to staff and customers. As one board member explained: "In a normal week, the 12 board members will probably between them visit about 25 stores. These are not red letter days. We will just go in and talk with some of the management, supervisors and staff. It's about getting out and listening to the organization."

In companies like Egon Zehnder, Marks and Spencer, and Hewlett-Packard, the management philosophy and value system dovetail with the strategy so that each company's policies and

behavioral standards reinforce both the strategy and the philosophy. The whole has integrity. These companies have strong missions. Strong missions come, therefore, from a clear fit between the
four elements in the framework.

A Sense of Mission: The Emotional Bond

A sense of mission is an emotional commitment. Some people feel
this strong sense of mission, but even in companies with very
strong missions there are many people who do not feel an emotional commitment. We were told, for example, that even at the
height of Hewlett-Packard's success an employee survey revealed a
notable minority of employees who did not have a strong belief in
the capabilities of the senior management team, implying that they
lacked a sense of mission.

In Chapter 3, "Mission Fuels Success," we give quotes and
examples of individuals who feel an emotional commitment to their
organizations. At this point, however, we need to be clear only
about what a sense of mission is and how it occurs. A sense of
mission occurs, we believe, when there is a match between the
values of an organization and those of an individual. Because
organizational values are rarely explicit, the individual senses them
through the company's behavioral standards. For example, if the
behavioral standard is about cooperative working, the individual
will be able to sense that helpfulness is valued above individual
competition. If the individual has a personal value about the importance of being helpful and cooperative, then there is a values match
between the individual and the organization. The greater the link
between company policies and individual values, the greater the
scope for the individual's sense of mission.

We see the values match, as illustrated in Figure 1.3, as the most
important part of a sense of mission, because it is through values
that individuals feel emotional about their organizations. Commitment to a company's strategy does not, on its own, constitute a
sense of mission. It is not unusual for groups of managers to discuss
their company's purpose and strategy and reach an intellectual
agreement. However, this intellectual agreement does not necessarily translate into an emotional commitment and hence the strategic plan does not get implemented. The emotional commitment

comes when the individual personally identifies with the values and behaviors lying behind the plan, turning the strategy into a mission and the intellectual agreement into a sense of mission.

As we will argue in the next chapter, the source of the emotional commitment created by a values match is subtle. Each of us is searching for meaning and for an opportunity to transcend the ordinariness of day-to-day existence. Values give meaning, and living up to our values or joining a group of people successfully following these values helps us feel a sense of transcendence. Work becomes more fulfilling because it is imbued with greater purpose. Work helps us achieve something that is personally important and that, therefore, gives us intrinsic satisfaction.

Consider a fastidious individual who has a personal bias towards tidiness and perfection and who works as a proofreader. If the organization believes fervently in accuracy and error-free work, the individual will, in all likelihood, find satisfaction in rooting out the minutest blemish or error. He or she will also feel valued. If the organization applies these principles to other areas of the business, the person may begin to feel a warmth for the organization that gives further personal satisfaction. The employee will see the organization as a "good" company. If, on the other hand, the organization is driven by deadlines and allows too little time for proofreading, causing books to be published with errors, the proofreader will feel frustrated, unappreciated, and angry.

Working with a "good" organization does not guarantee that employees will have a sense of mission. Consider the person who is responsible for the parking lot of the Boy Scouts' headquarters. The organization has an elevating purpose. It has a clear strategy. It has strong values and well-grooved policies and behavioral standards. It is also highly successful, with more than 17 million members worldwide. In other words, the Boy Scout movement has a strong mission. Yet the organization's parking lot attendants may or may not feel a sense of mission. It will depend on their personal values and the values and behavioral standards by which they are managed. Each individual is making a judgment: "Does this organization care about the sort of things I care about?" If it does, then there is the potential for developing an emotional commitment. If not, then support from the individual is grudging, based on a contract of so much work for so much pay.

It is important to recognize the individual nature of a sense of mission. It is a personal, emotional feeling created by the individual relationship that the person has with the organization. If the parking lot attendants are gregarious and believe more in making people happy than in dirt-free cleanliness, they are more likely to feel a sense of mission about the Boy Scouts if the office workers stop to chat and involve them in the office events. If the parking lot supervisor is a tidiness fanatic, these same attendants are going to feel uncomfortable and will be unlikely to develop an energetic commitment to the organization.

Recognizing the personal nature of a sense of mission has two important implications. First, no organization, unless it is very small, can possibly hope to instill all of its employees with a sense of mission. People are too varied and have too many individual values for it to be possible for a large organization to achieve a values match for all its employees. Second, careful recruitment is essential. People's values do not change when they change companies. By recruiting people with compatible values, companies are much more likely to foster a sense of mission.

We have pointed out that, even in companies with a strong mission, many people lack a sense of mission. This may be because they have few strong values and, therefore, feel very little for the company. It may also be because their values conflict with those of the company. These individuals may not be poor performers or disruptive, but their motivation is more self-interested and their attitudes are likely to be more cynical. These individuals may give good service to the company but, as we point out in Chapter 3, there are benefits to a company that come only through having individuals with a sense of mission.

Mission and Vision

In talking about mission with audiences of managers and academics, we have been asked to explain the difference between mission and vision. Also, since the publication of an article in the *Harvard Business Review* by Gary Hamel and C. K. Pralahad called "Strategic Intent,"[5] we have been asked to explain the difference between mission and strategic intent.

Warren Bennis and Burt Nanus, authors of *Leaders: The Strategies for Taking Charge*, identify vision as a central concept for their theory of leadership.

> To choose a direction, a leader must first have developed a mental image of a possible and desirable future state of the organization. This image, which we call a vision, may be as vague as a dream or as precise as a goal or mission statement. The critical point is that a vision articulates a view of a realistic, credible, attractive future for the organization, a condition that is better in some important ways than what now exists.[6]

As long as the word vision has a meaning in business language, this quote from Bennis and Nanus captures its distinguishing features as well as its vagueness.

A vision and a mission can be one and the same. A possible and desirable future state of the organization can include all of the elements of mission—purpose, strategy, behavioral standards, and values. But vision and mission are not fully overlapping concepts. Vision refers to a future state, "a condition that is better . . . than what now exists," whereas mission more normally refers to the present. Marks and Spencer's mission "to raise the standards of the working man" was being achieved throughout the 1950s and 1960s and is still being achieved today. It is a timeless explanation of the organization's identity and ambition. When a vision is achieved, a new vision needs to be developed. But a mission can remain the same and members of the organization can still draw strength from their common and timeless cause.

A vision is, therefore, more associated with a goal whereas a mission is more associated with a way of behaving. We believe that mission is the more powerful concept and we take issue with Bennis and Nanus for using the word "vision" without separating the two concepts. Vision is valuable because goals are valuable. But it is the clarity of mission rather than vision that we believe is the strength of a great leader. We say more about Bennis and Nanus's ideas in the next chapter.

In times of change, a new mission will be difficult to distinguish from a vision because the new mission will be a mental image of a desirable future state. Hence our difference of opinion is not, in practice, a serious one. Nevertheless, we have two concerns with vision as a concept. First, a vision begins to lose its power when it is achieved. It is no longer a driving force for action and the organization can begin to lose direction. This can happen to companies that strive for market leadership. Once achieved, the ambition that drove the company drains away, leaving it directionless. Second, if a vision is so ambitious that it is unlikely to be achieved in the next five or ten years, it loses its power to motivate and stimulate. It becomes too ambitious and unrealistic.

Mission is concerned with the way the organization is managed today (behavioral standards) and its purpose. Both of these are timeless concepts and can supply an unbounded source of fulfillment and energy.

Strategic intent is another concept that overlaps with vision and mission. Hamel and Pralahad comment:

> On the one hand strategic intent envisions a desired leadership position and establishes the criterion the organization will use to chart its progress. Komatsu set out to "Encircle Caterpillar," Canon sought to "Beat Xerox," Honda strove to become a second Ford, an automotive pioneer. All are expressions of strategic intent.
>
> At the same time strategic intent is more than just unfettered ambition. (Many companies possess an ambitious strategic intent yet fall short of their goals.) The concept also encompasses an active management process that includes: focusing the organization's attention on the essence of winning; motivating people by communicating the value of the target; leaving room for individual and team contributions; sustaining enthusiasm by providing new operational definitions as circumstances change; and using intent consistently to guide resource allocations.[5]

Strategic intent is a concept that draws from both vision and mission. It includes a desired future state, a goal defined in competitive terms that is more a part of vision than of purpose. It also includes a definition of strategy that is fundamentally the same as the use of strategy within mission. Strategic intent is, therefore, closest in concept to the traditional definition of mission—"What business are we in and what strategic position do we seek?"

We see strategic intent as suffering from the same problem as vision, in that once the intent has been achieved the organization is liable to lose direction. The problem with goals is that they have to be reset as they are achieved. Purpose has the advantage of being everlasting.

We also see strategic intent as being a left-brain concept. Hamel and Pralahad argue that intent should motivate people "by communicating the value of the target." We have not found many managers who are motivated by a target, unless it is a short-term objective or milestone.[7] The managers we spoke to were motivated more by the current organizational values than by some distant ambition. Strategic intent is, in our view, a less powerful concept than mission because it fails to include values and behavioral standards, the keys to longstanding employee commitment and enthusiasm.

Review

In this chapter we have defined the terms "mission" and "sense of mission" at some length. We have been at pains to draw a distinction between these two concepts because we believe managers are frequently confused by them.

Mission is an intellectual concept that can be analyzed and discussed unemotionally. Like strategy, mission is a set of propositions that can be used to guide the policies and behaviors of a company. However, mission is a larger concept than strategy. It covers strategy and culture. The strategy element of mission legislates what is important to the commercial future of the company. The values element of the mission legislates what is important to the culture of the company. When the two are in tune, reinforcing each other and bound by a common purpose, the mission is strong. When there are contradictions and inconsistencies, the mission is weak.

Sense of mission is not an intellectual concept; it is an emotional and deeply personal feeling. The individual with a sense of mission has an emotional attachment and commitment to the company—to what it stands for and what it is trying to do.

A company with a clear mission does not necessarily have employees with a sense of mission. Some individuals may have a sense of mission with varying degrees of intensity; many will not. Over time, the number of employees with a sense of mission will increase as the policies of the mission become implemented and embedded in the company culture. But even at a company like Hewlett-Packard, which has had a clear mission for more than 30 years, no more than half of its employees will have what we would recognize as a sense of mission.

Mission is, we believe, a more powerful concept than vision or strategic intent. Mission contains a purpose that is timeless, avoiding the need to reassess the organization's direction every time its objectives are achieved. Mission is also grounded in an understanding of employee commitment. It recognizes that employees are stimulated more by the beliefs and values that the organization uses today than by dreams of glory and success in the future.

NOTES

1. Peter Drucker, *Management: Tasks, Responsibilities, Practices* (New York: Harper & Row, 1973), p. 78.

2. The main academic work on the contents of mission statements has been done by Fred David and Jack Pearce. See J. A. Pearce II and F. R. David, "Corporate Mission Statements: The Bottom Line," *Academy of Management Executive* 1, no. 2 (1987); D. Cochran and F. R. David, "The Communication Effectiveness of Organizational Mission Statements," *Journal of Applied Communication Research* (1987); Fred R. David, "How Companies Define Their Mission," *Long Range Planning* 22, no. 1 (1989).

3. Ted Levitt, "Marketing Myopia," *Harvard Business Review* (July-August 1960), pp. 45–56.

4. Thomas J. Watson, Jr., *A Business and Its Beliefs: The Ideas that Helped Build IBM* (New York: McGraw-Hill, 1963).

5. Gary Hamel and C. K. Pralahad, "Strategic Intent," *Harvard Business Review,* (May-June 1989), p. 64.

6. Warren Bennis and Burt Nanus, *Leaders: The Strategies for Taking Charge* (New York: Harper & Row, 1985), p. 89.

7. Michael Goold has researched the impact of strategic objectives and milestones as used by companies in their control systems. He argues that short-term objectives—milestones—are necessary if the control system is to motivate managers to reach for higher levels of performance; see Michael Goold with John J. Quinn, *Strategic Control: Milestones for Long-Term Performance* (London: The Economist Books/Hutchinson, 1990. US edition forthcoming, Economist Books/Addison-Wesley, Reading, Mass., 1993).

The Emotional Organization

. . . .

In the previous chapter we have defined mission as the combination of purpose, strategy, values, and behavioral standards. A strong link between these four elements amounts to a strong mission. An individual feels a sense of mission when the organization has a strong mission and its values are attractive to the individual. Sense of mission is an individual feeling. Some employees may feel it and some may not. It occurs when an employee finds meaning in work, when the organization's values match the employee's values.

Much of what we are saying is not new: The importance of values has been underlined in the writings on culture; the role of a clear purpose has been noted by researchers into leadership; the link between strategy and values has been suggested by consultants; and the opportunity to satisfy the spiritual needs of employees through developing a moral rationale for work was argued as long ago as 1938.

Our contribution is to bring all these relationships together into one model around the concept of mission, and to recognize that behavioral standards are most meaningful when they are explained by both a commercial rationale and a moral rationale. The writers whose mental models most closely relate to ours are early leadership theorists such as Chester Barnard and Philip Selznick. Surprisingly, it is the motivation theorists Herzberg, McGregor, and Maslow whose ideas seem to be furthest from ours.

Early Leadership Theorists

Chester Barnard is one of the fathers of leadership theory. After a long career in industry, which culminated in Barnard becoming president of New Jersey Bell Telephone Company and president of the Rockefeller Foundation, he moved to Harvard and wrote a book on *The Functions of the Executive*.[1] Published in 1938, it was the first analytical book on leadership that recognized the noneconomic dimensions of managing an organization. Barnard was among the first writers to acknowledge the importance of what he called organizational philosophy or "morality." Executives need to manage two aspects of organization philosophy: They need to help employees cope with conflicts that arise between their personal morality and the organization's collective morality; and they need to create an inspiring philosophy or morality to which employees can attach themselves.

In his work, Barnard shows how every individual's behavior is influenced by several moral codes, such as loyalty to certain religious ethics, a code of family obligations, and adherence to professional or work norms and values. Problems arise when these codes conflict in some way. One of three outcomes may occur, says Barnard:

> Either there is paralysis of action, accompanied by emotional tension, and ending in a sense of frustration. . .uncertainty. . .loss of decisiveness and lack of confidence, or (2) there is conformance to one code and violation of the other, resulting in a sense of guilt, discomfort, dissatisfaction or a loss of self respect, or (3) there is found some substitute action which satisfies immediate desire. . .yet conforms to all other codes. . . .such a solution frequently requires imaginative and constructive ability. (p. 264)

Business leaders have to not only overcome these conflicts in their own working lives (moral choices becoming increasingly complex as they progress through the organization) but also help resolve these conflicts for others. Barnard calls this the "judicial function." "There is no escape from the judicial process in the exercise of executive functions. Conflicts of codes in organizations are inevitable" (p. 280), he says. It is the responsibility of the leader to help employees find an answer that is acceptable to an employee's personal morality and the morality of the collective whole. Such a task is a "severe test" of a leader's moral responsibility and ability.

Barnard rates as even more important the leader's responsibility to create an inspiring philosophy or morality for employees. This should give them "faith in the ultimate satisfaction of personal motives, faith in the integrity of objective authority, faith in the superiority of common purpose as a personal aim of those who undertake it" (p. 259). Such a morality will ensure that people subordinate their individual interest and the "minor dictates of personal codes" to the good of the cooperative whole.

Barnard calls these two functions of leadership moral creativeness, "the highest expression of responsibility." He argues that it creates among employees something close to a sense of mission— common meaning, common purpose, personal conviction, and "a spirit that overcomes the centrifugal forces of individual interests or motives" (p. 283).

Barnard undoubtedly recognizes the need for organizations to provide spiritual fulfillment for employees through a match of the organization's values and the individual's values, and the advantage of having a mission for the organization that is inspiring and elevating. However, he does not suggest that leadership is only about creating a morality. Much of his book is devoted to advice on the formulation of objectives, recruitment, motivation, and organizational structure. But he distinguishes these maintenance roles of the executive from the leadership roles that are concerned with inspiring people. He sees the leadership role as being the creation of moral codes for employees:

> Organizations endure, however, in proportion to the breadth of the morality by which they are governed. This is only to say that foresight, long purposes, high ideals are the basis for the persistence of cooperation.
>
> Executive responsibility, then, is that capacity of leaders by which, reflecting attitudes, ideals, hopes, derived largely from without themselves, they are compelled to bind the wills of men to the accomplishment of purposes beyond their immediate ends. Even when these purposes are lowly. . .the transitory efforts of men become a part of that organization of living forces that transcends man unaided by man; but when these purposes are high and the wills of many men of many generations are bound together they live boundlessly.
>
> So among those who cooperate the things that are seen are moved by the things unseen. Out of the void comes the spirit that shapes the ends of men. (p. 282)

Philip Selznick was a pioneer in the academic study of leadership. He wrote a book called *Leadership and Administration: A Sociological*

Interpretation.[2] Published in 1957, it builds on the experience-based insights of Chester Barnard. In Selznick's view, the primary task of leaders is to "institutionalize" a business so that it becomes infused with values and meaning and becomes a source of fulfillment to its members. "To institutionalize is to *infuse with value* beyond the technical requirements of the job at hand. The prizing of the social machinery beyond its technical role is largely a reflection of the unique way in which it fulfills personal or group needs. . . . From the standpoint of the committed person, the organization is changed from an expendable tool into a valued source of personal satisfaction" (p. 93).

Selznick bases his theory on a distinction similar to that of Barnard: the distinction between organizations and institutions. The former describes rational instruments engineered to do specific tasks. Leaders of organizations are mainly concerned with administrative efficiency and policy and procedures that ensure a "smooth running machine." Institutions, however, are a product of social needs and are more akin to responsive, adaptive organisms. Institutional leaders are concerned with developing a more comprehensive view of their enterprise. In particular, they want to understand how and why people work and they also want to have a wider perspective of the organization itself and its changing aims and abilities.

Institutional leadership is the key both to developing this larger perspective and to increasing employee motivation, Selznick believes. Leaders can help their organizations evolve into institutions through two methods. The first is to define the "mission of the enterprise," a task that gives a wider perspective of the institution. This involves hard intellectual labor as the leader needs to identify the business's purpose and goals and "attendant claims and responsibilities." This process may therefore involve resolving differences of opinion about the mission of a business both in and outside the organization.

The second task of institutional leadership is to infuse values into the institution, thereby giving greater fulfillment to its members. The institutional leader is "primarily an expert in the promotion and protection of values." He or she must offer "a guiding hand to a process that would otherwise occur more haphazardly" and ensure that these values are truly accepted in the institution. When this happens, the organization begins to symbolize certain values and aspirations of its people and therefore assumes an identity of its own.

Both Selznick and Barnard make a distinction between the task of running an organization and the task of infusing an organization with values. In the language that we have developed in the previous chapter, they distinguish between the rational, commercial side of leadership and the emotional, moral side.

The ideas of Barnard and Selznick reemerged in the 1980s, popularized in books such as *In Search of Excellence* by Tom Peters and Robert Waterman.[3] More recently two academics, Joseph Badaracco at Harvard and Richard Ellsworth at Claremont, have examined these ideas of leadership and have compared them with other theories.[4] They analyzed three philosophies of leadership—political leadership, directive leadership, and values-driven leadership:

> Each starts with a different view of human nature and these lead to very different patterns of action. Political leadership holds that man is motivated by self-interest and by search for power, wealth and coherence in the face of self-interested behavior by others. While not rejecting these realities, directive leadership argues that they are too limited for explaining people's motivation. Directive leadership believes that man is also a competitive creature driven to achieve. People want to take personal responsibility for their decisions and have the satisfaction of knowing they have won through their own efforts. Man has a strong, innate drive to realize his own potential or, in psychological terms, to self-actualize. As Maslow has said, 'What man can be, he must be.' As they strive for higher levels of attainment, people meld self-interest with corporate interest.
>
> The values-driven leader takes the directive leader's view one step further and believes that people need to find meaning in life through their work. Meaning is derived from creativity in the service of worthwhile purposes. Creating something of value is the ultimate expression of one's individuality. Values-driven leadership holds that energy, commitment and creativity are unleashed when a company harnesses these motives. (p. 95)

Like Barnard and Selznick before them, Badaracco and Ellsworth recognize the difference between the rational, commercial side of leadership and the emotional, moral side. And they have also concluded that leaders must bind the two parts together. Whereas we talk about the need for a leader to have a mission, Badaracco and Ellsworth talk about the need for leaders to develop their own philosophies or "set of predispositions and prejudices" that meld together the three philosophies of leadership and create an "integrity" for the manager such that "his behavior should be consonant with his personality, beliefs, and judgments" (p. 199).

Badaracco and Ellsworth see the leader's personal values as an essential part of his personal philosophy. Values-driven leadership is "not simply an alternative to the other two. Rather it transcends both of them" (p. 66).

The Importance of Values

The study of values and their role in organizational management was one of the growth businesses of the 1980s, sparked by three books published in 1981 and 1982.

In *Corporate Cultures*,[5] Terence Deal, a Vanderbilt professor, and Alan Kennedy, a McKinsey & Co. consultant, explain the link between values and culture. Like Barnard before them, they were trying to underline the importance of the soft side of management—the emotional dimension. "Rational managers," they complain, "rarely pay much attention to the value system of an organization." Yet they believe that "shaping and enhancing values can become the most important job a manager can do"; "In fact we think that often companies succeed because their employees can identify, embrace, and act on the values of the organization" (p. 21).

Deal and Kennedy have a balanced understanding about the role of values in business. Much of their analysis is devoted to the benefits of values as a control mechanism: "In broad terms, they [values] act as an informal control system that tells people what is expected of them" (p. 53). Nevertheless, they also recognize that values can be a motivator that gives meaning to work: "The power of values is that people care about them."

William Ouchi, a professor at the University of California at Los Angeles and an equally important author on the subject of values, focuses mainly on the control benefit of values. Coming from an academic background studying control systems, Ouchi published a book in 1981 called *Theory Z*, which explained that some organizations, such as the U.S. military and IBM, control decisions through a value system or what he calls a "clan culture."[6]

The type Z organization is similar to many Japanese companies. It makes decisions based as much on values as on facts. "In a type Z organization, the explicit and implicit seem to exist in a sense of balance. While decisions weigh the complete analysis of facts, they are also shaped by serious attention to questions of whether or not this decision is suitable, whether it fits the company" (p. 72).

To Ouchi, a value system is a governance mechanism. He compares type Z organizations with bureaucracies and with markets. He points out that in type Z organizations and in markets individuals are encouraged to act selfishly, to do whatever they most want to do. The market mechanism is one way of ensuring that the selfish acts of individuals combine toward a common good. The socialization of individuals into a value system is the other way of ensuring that "individuals will naturally seek to do that which is in the common good." He argues: "Only the bureaucratic mechanism explicitly says to individuals, 'Do not do what you want, do what we tell you to do because we pay you for it.' The bureaucratic mechanism alone produces alienation, anomie, and a lowered sense of autonomy" (p. 85).

The third influential book published at the beginning of the 1980s is called *The Art of Japanese Management* by Richard Pascale and Anthony Athos.[7] Like Ouchi, the authors recognize that many Japanese companies have an ingredient that is missing from Western companies. Unlike Ouchi, they examine the benefit these Japanese companies give to their employees—"a deeper meaning." Pascale and Athos focus more attention on the way values provide fulfillment for employees than do either Ouchi or Deal and Kennedy. Pascale and Athos note that organizational values can become "superordinate goals [that] tie the purpose of the firm to human values." They become the "spiritual fabric" of the organization and are "probably the most underpublicized 'secret weapon' of great companies."

The problem with most Western companies is that managers and leaders feel shy of spiritualism."By an accident of history, we in the West have evolved a culture that separates man's spiritual life from his institutional life. This turn of events has had a far-reaching impact on modern Western organizations. Our companies freely lay claim to mind and muscle, but they are culturally discouraged from intruding upon our personal lives and deeper beliefs" (p. 192). "What is needed in the West is a non-deified, non-religious spiritualism that enables a firm's superordinate goals to respond truly to the inner meanings that many people seek in their work—or, alternatively, seek in their lives and could find in their work if only that were more culturally acceptable" (p. 193).

Pascale and Athos recognize the attention that some companies in the late 1970s were giving to corporate responsibility, mission, and mission statements. But they conclude that these efforts were insufficient. "The trend has been toward expanding the notion of corporate purpose. Nevertheless, recognition of an organization's role in serving higher-order human values still awaits full-scale acceptance" (p. 192).

These three books were the beginning of a tidal wave of writings on culture and the importance of values. This has not been limited to academics and consultants: Managers of great companies have also been arguing the importance of values. Some of the more telling quotations from chief executives have been captured by Badaracco and Ellsworth. Walter Wriston, former chief executive of Citicorp, sees shared values as essential to smooth functioning. He explains:

> A lot of leadership is being able to articulate your value system and where you are going in ways people understand. I spend a lot of time trying to hold out before people the concepts of excellence, honesty and integrity.
>
> In the corporation, as in your life, you have to have some bench-marks by which to operate. . . . A corporation is a collection of individuals. Without a framework, you don't know what you are doing. The only thing that draws our different cultures together is our common value system. For example, collegial management is a value. You have to have trust between people, and that's based on a common set of values and a common set of procedures. (p. 76)

James Burke, chief executive of Johnson & Johnson, sees values as a way of tapping into people's moral yearning:

> It is very hard to keep people pulling together if you have a real entre-preneurial environment. The very nature of the people that run our business—as well as the businesses themselves—is to go off on their own. "To hell with all that crap in New Brunswick [Johnson & Johnson's headquarters]. Who needs the Executive Committee? We know how to do it." People are also somewhat egocentric.
>
> How do we keep them all together? We try to do it by an overall set of principles and the fundamental moral precepts of the credo, which everyone buys into and responds to. At some level, everybody is a moral creature, whether they want to admit it or not. (p. 85)

William Weiss, chairman and chief executive officer of Ameritech, writes about the importance of linking employee values and company values. In an article "Minerva's Owl: Building a Corporate Value System,"[8] Weiss appeals to Minerva, the goddess of wisdom, to help him form a value system for Ameritech, which in 1986 had been set up only 18 months earlier to run part of Bell Telephone. He sees a value system as a critical part of leadership: "I am saying that a corporation can create a moral environment, a distinct set of values and standards, to which it holds its people accountable. If a person's individual values are significantly different, he will soon find he is in the wrong place. It is a key responsibility of corporate leadership to set the pattern and tone of this conscience."

Thomas Watson, Jr., of IBM was probably the first of the leaders of U.S. companies to stress values. He wrote a much-quoted book, *A Business and Its Beliefs*,[9] that explains IBM's value system.

It is not only American business leaders who have argued the case for values. Most Japanese leaders consider it such an obvious part of management that it is hard to find quotations that refer explicitly to the management of the value system. Konosuke Matsushita, former chairman of Matsushita Electric, is probably the most outspoken on the subject. Like Watson, he wrote a book about his company's values, called *Not for Bread Alone*.[10]

Even European managers, normally more reserved about the emotional side of management, have been speaking up. Jan Carlzon, chairman of the Swedish airline SAS, wrote about the contribution values management made to the dramatic change of fortunes at SAS in a book called *Moments of Truth*.[11] At a recent conference in Chicago he underlined his commitment to emotional management:

> You don't hear much about love in discussions of management philosophy, or human resources for that matter. But if love is defined as the will to nurture growth in other human beings, then it is the appropriate term. Or you can call it respect for the individual, respect for his feeling of responsibility and his desire to do a good job. Allowing an individual to share your vision gives that person greater understanding and motivation. That, to me, is strategic leadership.[12]

In recognizing the importance of values in our model of mission, we have done no more than acknowledge the weight of academic, consultant, and management opinion that values can both motivate employees to behave in a desired way and provide employees with the meaning that can make work fulfilling and worthwhile.

The Strategy–Values Link

Ouchi and others have studied the link between values and behaviors; Deal and Kennedy and also Weiss have commented on the link between corporate values and employees' values; and Pascale and Athos have emphasized the link between values and purpose. Between them, these authors have effectively explained the emotional, moral side of our definition of mission.

One area that has received very little attention is the link between strategy and values—the link between commercial logic and moral logic. The consultants McKinsey & Co. have the most well-developed understanding of this link. They developed a model of organization called the 7S model. It has been presented in many formats, but the format in Figure 2.1, with strategy, skills, and shared values as the lead Ss, was the one most frequently used at McKinsey in the mid-1980s. Pascale and Athos used another format of the model in their book *The Art of Japanese Management.*

The central message of the 7S model is that organizations are most effective when their seven different elements fit well together: when the strategy fits the values and all the other Ss reinforce the strategy and the values. Consultants at McKinsey use it as a diagnostic tool for understanding organizations that are ineffective and for managing change. When managing change, the model is a useful guide to ensure that change is balanced and is aimed at moving toward a future state of "fit." The value of the model is that it discourages the belief that organization is just about structure or management systems. These "hard" elements of organization are important, but they are not the whole story. "Softer" elements such as shared values, management style, and skills are also critical to the effective running of an organization. Managers must act on all Ss in parallel if they want to maintain balance and fit.

With further rearranging, it is possible to argue that our definition of mission is little different from the 7S model. Systems, structure, style, staff, and skills can all be viewed as forming part of what we have called policies and behavioral standards (see Figure 2.2).

Figure 2.1 **The McKinsey 7S Model**

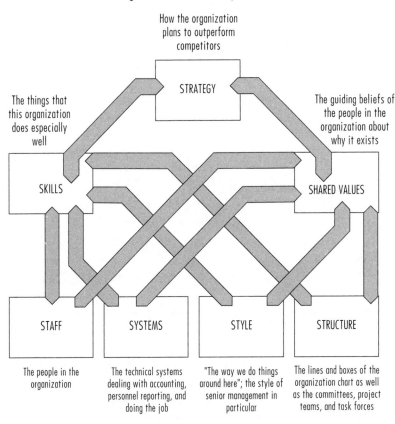

How the organization
plans to outperform
competitors

STRATEGY

The things that
this organization
does especially
well

The guiding beliefs of
the people in the
organization about
why it exists

SKILLS

SHARED VALUES

STAFF	SYSTEMS	STYLE	STRUCTURE
The people in the organization	The technical systems dealing with accounting, personnel reporting, and doing the job	"The way we do things around here"; the style of senior management in particular	The lines and boxes of the organization chart as well as the committees, project teams, and task forces

With this representation, the only element missing from the 7S model is purpose. Interestingly, in the earlier format used by Pascale and Athos the label "superordinate" goals was used instead of shared values; and in their discussion of superordinate goals they bring in elements of what we would call purpose. We do not feel the need to apologize for the overlap between our definition of mission and the McKinsey 7S model. It is no surprise that there is little in our definition that is dramatically new. What we have done is to pull together previous insights in a new way and to draw out some new implications as a result.

While the 7S model emphasizes the need for fit, particularly between strategy and values, it misses the importance of three relationships in our mission definition that we feel are vital to a

Figure 2.2 **The 7S Model Rearranged in the Format of Our Model of Mission**

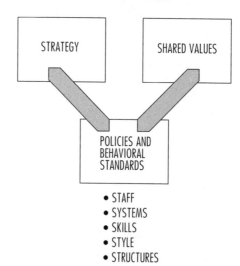

- STAFF
- SYSTEMS
- SKILLS
- STYLE
- STRUCTURES

deeper understanding of the nature of organization management. First, the 7S model does not recognize the importance of the link between the private values of employees and the shared values of the organization. Through the concept of "staff," the model acknowledges the need to have people who fit well with the other Ss; but like Ouchi, it sees only the control and behavioral benefits for the organization and misses the fulfillment and feelings of worth that values can ignite in the employee.

Second, the 7S model does not emphasize the importance of behavioral standards. We have argued that policies and behavioral standards are the bottom line of mission. By creating some behavioral standards that capture the essence of both the strategic logic and the moral logic in the organization, leaders can ensure that the values fit the strategy. The behavioral standards are the means of fitting values with strategy. The 7S model has no such powerful integrating thought. It relies on a loose concept of fit that encourages managers to eliminate obviously incongruent elements in their organizations. We are more demanding. We are asking leaders to search for behavioral standards, like British Airways' "Putting People First" or Hewlett-Packard's "Management by Wandering Around" (MBWA), that will act as the integrating mechanism for the mission.

Third, as we have already pointed out, the 7S model gives little attention to purpose. We view purpose as the cornerstone of mission. Forming a purpose is full of pitfalls because managers are trying to sort out the relationship between competing constituencies: shareholders, employees, customers, suppliers, and the community. The 7S model sidesteps this area. However, other writers have addressed purpose.

Purpose

Philosophers and economists have written at length on the role of business in society. Before the creation of the corporation, the purpose of work and the purpose of an individual's existence were closely connected and closely tied to religion. A Lutheran believed that people had a predetermined fate to which they must submit. Hence work was an act of submission to be borne with a glad heart because it was part of living out the Almighty's wish.

During the Reformation, the Protestant work ethic was born. In Max Weber's words: "For everyone, without exception, God's Providence has prepared a calling, which he should profess and in which he should labor."[13] People were seen to be working for the "divine glory," using their talents to the maximum. Like the parable of the talents, people were expected to work to maximize their contribution to the world.

During the Industrial Revolution, capitalists built companies. It became hard to view these industrial capitalists of the late eighteenth and early nineteenth centuries as leaders of a divine calling. The religious connection with work became less relevant and was replaced by work as a social duty. People were expected to work as members of society to contribute to the well-being of society. Business was also seen in this context: the purpose of business was to produce goods to help society.

In the years since the Industrial Revolution the role of work and the purpose of business have become much less clear. Work has become for many a way of achieving success, of accumulating wealth and gaining independence. For others it has become a creative activity. Like the artist, employees are fulfilling some inner need to express themselves. Work has become a much more selfish activity connected with personal gratification. This has left a philosophical void. The role of business in society has become unclear. If businesses contain groups of people pursuing selfish ends, then what is the role of business in society?

Three views of business have evolved. The first is that business is an association of stakeholders, each pursuing selfish ends and joining together in an association purely because they find it easier to achieve their ends through business. Each stakeholder group—shareholders, employees, suppliers, customers—has equal importance in the association. Each has the right to bargain for the maximum split of the cake that can be made available to each without unbalancing the established relationships. The company is a vehicle of convenience for self-interested groups. It is a form of controlled marketplace.

The second view of business that has developed is associated with Milton Friedman.[14] Railing against the mood in business for what was called in the 1970s "corporate social responsibility," the need to do charitable deeds for the benefit of the community, Friedman argues that the purpose of business is to create wealth and this can best be done by maximizing profits. The capitalist system is designed so that the unremitting pursuit of profits by business will result in the greatest overall contribution to the system.

The third view of the role of business is that it should maximize the public good and promote social harmony. This is a particularly Japanese view promoted by leaders such as Konosuke Matsushita. Companies make products for the public good. The public rewards the company with loyalty and support, making sure that all the stakeholders are well rewarded for their efforts.

Edward Freeman and Daniel Gilbert, professors at the University of Virginia and Bucknell University, have captured much of the confusion about the role of business in their book *Corporate Strategy and the Search for Ethics*.[15] They define seven possible purposes for business:

1. The "stockholder strategy," based on the property rights of stockholders.
2. The "managerial strategy," which recognizes that managers have the power to pursue their own ends.
3. The "limited stakeholder strategy," which focuses on satisfying the needs of two or three stakeholder groups.
4. The "unrestricted stakeholder strategy," which recognizes that all claimants on the business need satisfying.

5. The "social harmony strategy," based on a positive view of the public good rather than a satisfactory view.
6. The "Rawlsian strategy," which argues for equality among social groups unless inequality helps to raise the level of the worst-off.
7. The "personal projects strategy," which views business as a vehicle for all stakeholders to pursue their personal projects.

Choosing between these purposes is obviously an important management task. Moreover linking purpose with strategy and with values is also important. The authors conclude a chapter titled "The Revolution in Management" with the following words:

> Corporate strategy is about purpose and so is ethics. Purpose is a person-based justification for action, shaped through interdependent bargaining among multiple parties. Ethics not only parallels strategy, through a common concern with purpose, but also provides a framework for reasoning through the thornier aspects of strategy as purpose. By explicitly acknowledging the connection, we can make some real intellectual and practical progress in the study of corporate strategy. (p. 20)

And, the authors could have added, in the study of mission.

The importance of purpose has also been documented by the leadership theorists. We mention only the work of Warren Bennis and Burt Nanus. In their book *Leaders: The Strategies for Taking Charge*,[16] they argue that one of the most important roles of the leader is to grab the attention of the organization by creating a vision of the future that can serve as a motivating purpose. Bennis and Nanus were not concerned about the philosophical issues underlying purpose. They had recognized the link between purpose and motivated behavior. A clear purpose is one of the tools that leaders can use to energize the organization:

> When the organization has a clear sense of purpose, direction and desired future state and when this image is widely shared, individuals are able to find their own roles both in the organization and in the larger society. . . . This empowers individuals and confers status upon them because they see themselves as part of a worthwhile enterprise. They gain a sense of importance, as they are transformed from robots blindly following instructions to human beings engaged in a creative and purposeful venture. (p. 90)

And the authors recognize the linking role of values. Values act to bind the emotions of employees to the purpose. By articulating a purpose,

> the leader operates on the emotional and spiritual resources of the organization, on its values, commitment and aspirations. . . . Great leaders often inspire their followers to high levels of achievement by showing them how their work contributes to worthwhile ends. It is an emotional appeal to some of the most fundamental of human needs—the need to be important, to make a difference, to feel useful, to be part of a worthwhile enterprise. (p. 93)

Motivation Theory

Throughout this chapter we have shown that our definition of mission includes little that is completely new. All the relationships within our definition have been explored by other authors. We therefore turn finally to the motivation theorists. Our view of mission argues that employees can develop an emotional attachment to their work and their organization when their values match the values of the organization. Surprisingly, we find almost no acknowledgement of this relationship among the early motivation theorists. The motivation giants such as Herzberg, Maslow, and McGregor say little about an individual's search for meaning and the potential of finding meaning and fulfillment through commitment to an organization. We have to examine the work of organization psychologists such as Edgar Schein to find the search for meaning as a powerful source for motivation.

Frederick Herzberg, professor of management at the University of Utah, is one of the best-known professors of motivation theory. His status was reinforced a few years ago by the republication as a *Harvard Business Review* classic of an article titled "One More Time: How Do You Motivate Employees?"[17] In the article Herzberg addresses the perennial problem of management: "How do I get employees to do what I want them to do?" He points out that many of the traditional methods of getting things done fail to motivate employees. He illustrates this well: "I have a year-old Schnauzer. When it was a small puppy and I wanted it to move, I kicked it in the rear and it moved. Now that I have finished its obedience training, I hold up a dog biscuit when I want the Schnauzer to move." In both cases, Herzberg points out, it is he who is motivated, not the dog. The Schnauzer does not want to move; it is purely responding to a stimulus given by Herzberg. So how does a manager get an employee to want to do something?

Herzberg distinguishes between intrinsic and extrinsic motivators. Extrinsic motivators are like those he used to get his dog to move. Intrinsic motivators, such as "achievement, recognition for achievement, the work itself, responsibility, growth and advancement," give employees the internal desire to do something.

The solution to the original question of how to get employees to do what is required is, in Herzberg's view, job enrichment. By "bringing the job up to the level of challenge commensurate with the skill that was hired," managers can reap a "return in human satisfaction and economic gain that would be one of the largest dividends that industry and society have ever achieved through better personnel management." Herzberg says nothing about values or about sense of mission as a motivator.

Dr. Abraham Maslow is another titan in the motivation field with his hierarchy of needs theory. In *Motivation and Personality*[18] he describes a model that charts the progression from basic physiological needs, such as food and shelter; to social needs, such as safety and self-esteem; to the highest need, the search for self-actualization. The latter is "the desire for self-fulfillment, namely the tendency for [man] to become actualized in what he is potentially." Such individuals have satisfied their basic needs, have achieved social stability and have a healthy measure of self-esteem. They do not feel "the pangs of loneliness, of ostracism, of rejection, of friendlessness, of rootlessness."

Maslow's assertion that every person seeks "self-actualization" has powerful implications for motivation at work. Maslow clearly states that fulfilling the highest human need yields powerful results: People live more healthy and stress-free lives and achieve "more profound happiness, serenity, and richness of the inner life." Self-actualization also enables people to develop their individuality and enjoy better relationships with others. Because "the higher the need the less selfish it must be," people who achieve self-actualization are more likely to work toward an unselfish cause.

Maslow's self-actualization only touches on the motivation that can come from a sense of mission. He recognizes that people search for meaning, "for knowledge, for understanding, for a life philosophy, for a theoretical frame of reference, for a value system." But he does not translate this into a concept that is equivalent to a sense of mission. Our view of mission implies that there is a need at a higher level than self-actualization—a need to contribute to something worthwhile, a need for a sense of mission.

Edgar Schein, professor of organization psychology and management at MIT, does recognize the importance of mission in employee motivation. He acknowledges that academics have not yet developed a complete theory of human behavior, particularly behavior at work. He suggests that behavior is dependent on inherited traits, learned routines and perception of the situation. Values are important because they influence perception.

Referring to the work of Etzioni and others, Schein describes a number of perceived relationships or psychological contracts between individuals and organizations: the coercive relationship, such as that existing in custodial institutions; the utilitarian relationship, where the individual is involved to the extent of doing a fair day's work for a fair day's pay; and the normative relationship, "which means that the person intrinsically values the mission of the organization and his or her job is personally involved and identified with the organization."[19]

Unfortunately, even Schein does not recognize the implication that this categorization has for business. He does not challenge Etzioni's original assumption that business organizations will inevitably have utilitarian relationships with their employees. Organizations with normative relationships are deemed to be noncommercial: hospitals, religious groups and voluntary organizations.

It is this blindness to the opportunity for business organizations to develop missions that are intrinsically valued that has left a hole in motivation theory. The culture writers, such as Pascale and Athos, recognize the opportunity from studying Japanese companies and some American companies such as IBM. The reason motivation theorists have given so little attention to this area is that so few of their ideas have been based on empirical fieldwork. Motivation studies are frequently carried out in the sterile atmosphere of the laboratory, an environment where sense of mission is absent by definition.

Review

In this chapter we have shown that none of the relationships central to our definition of mission is new. All of them have been exposed by other writers, some of the wisest of whom were writing as long ago as the 1930s. We have deliberately left one book out of our analysis, *In Search of Excellence* by Tom Peters and Robert Waterman. It became the best-selling business book of all time because of its gleeful recognition of the emotional side of organizations. It champions the human being in organizations, arguing that people are the difference between good and bad organizations.

In a chapter of their book entitled "Man Waiting for Motivation," Peters and Waterman carry out a review of the literature in a similar fashion to this chapter. They point out that man is "quite strikingly irrational. He reasons by stories, assumes himself to be in the top 10 percent judged by any good trait, and needs to stick out and find meaning simultaneously" (p. 86). The authors examine psychologists, philosophers, and many practical studies of behavior and conclude that people yearn for transcendence. "Perhaps transcendence is too grand a term for the business world, but the love of product at Cat, Bechtel, and J&J comes very close to meriting it. Whatever the case, we find it compelling that so many thinkers from so many fields agree on the dominating need of human beings to find meaning and transcend mundane things" (p. 76). It is this observation that makes it possible for an organization to help an employee develop a sense of mission. And it is the opportunity to create employees with a sense of mission that makes mission so important.

NOTES

1. Chester I. Barnard, *The Functions of the Executive* (Cambridge, Mass.: Harvard University Press, 1938 and 1968).

2. Philip Selznick, *Leadership in Administration: A Sociological Interpretation* (Berkeley: University of California Press, 1957).

3. Thomas J. Peters and Robert H. Waterman, *In Search of Excellence: Lessons from America's Best Run Companies* (New York: Harper & Row, 1982).

4. Joseph L. Badaracco, Jr. and Richard R. Ellsworth, *Leadership and the Quest for Integrity* (Boston: Harvard Business School Press, 1989).

5. Terence Deal and Alan Kennedy, *Corporate Cultures* (Reading, Mass.: Addison-Wesley, 1982).

6. William Ouchi, *Theory Z: How American Business Can Meet the Japanese Challenge* (Reading, Mass.: Addison-Wesley, 1981).

7. Richard T. Pascale and Anthony G. Athos, *The Art of Japanese Management* (New York: Simon & Schuster, 1981).

8. William L. Weiss, "Minerva's Owl: Building a Corporate Value System," *Journal of Business Ethics* 5 (1986, Kluwer Academic Publishers).

9. Thomas J. Watson, Jr., *A Business and Its Beliefs: The Ideas that Helped Build IBM* (New York: McGraw-Hill, 1963).

10. Konosuke Matsushita, *Not for Bread Alone: A Business Ethos, A Management Ethic* (Tokyo: PHP Institute, 1984).

11. Jan Carlzon, *Moments of Truth* (New York: HarperCollins, 1989).

12. Jan Carlzon, speech given at AMA Human Resources Conference, Chicago, April 20, 1988.

13. Max Weber, *The Protestant Ethic and the Spirit of Capitalism*, rev. ed. (New York: Macmillan, 1980).

14. Milton Friedman, *Capitalism and Freedom* (Chicago: University of Chicago Press, 1962).

15. Edward Freeman and Daniel Gilbert, *Corporate Strategy and the Search for Ethics* (Englewood Cliffs, N.J.: Prentice-Hall, 1988).

16. Warren Bennis and Burt Nanus, *Leaders: The Strategies for Taking Charge* (New York: Harper & Row, 1985).

17. Frederick Herzberg, "One More Time: How Do You Motivate Employees?" *Harvard Business Review* (January–February 1968).

18. Abraham H. Maslow, *Motivation and Personality* (New York: Harper & Row, 1970).

19. Edgar H. Schein, *Organizational Psychology*, 3d ed., (Englewood Cliffs, N.J.: Prentice-Hall, 1980), p. 45.

CHAPTER
3

Mission Fuels Success

· · · · · · · · · · · · · ·

We have argued that leaders will benefit from having a sense of mission and that under certain circumstances employees can develop a sense of commitment to a company's mission. Throughout this book we have been implying that mission and sense of mission are positive assets that help organizations to succeed. In this chapter we explain why. We explore why a management team with a mission is likely to outperform a management team with no mission. We also show why a company that has many employees and managers with a sense of mission (an emotional attachment to the mission) will outperform a company that has only a few employees with a similar form of attachment.

In this chapter we hope to explain why Thomas Watson, Jr., stated in the introduction to his book *A Business and its Beliefs:*

> This, then, is my thesis: I firmly believe that any organization, in order to survive and achieve success, must have a sound set of beliefs on which it premises all its policies and actions.
>
> Next, I believe that the most important single factor in corporate success is faithful adherence to those beliefs.
>
> And finally, I believe that if an organization is to meet the challenges of a changing world, it must be prepared to change everything about itself except those beliefs as it moves through corporate life.[1]

Today, Watson's words are even more important because the world has become more competitive. Mission is no longer a subject that a company can turn to when it has achieved reasonable success and stability. The competition is too intense. Companies that are unclear about their strategies and values and that have not won the commitment of their important employees will be overtaken by those that have. A French researcher reviewing the evolution of the concept of mission among French companies explained:

> Previously people were able to adapt to impersonal companies; the huge growth in the economy meant that there was something for everyone; passion was not necessary. . . . When you can promise booty to all your soldiers, you can make do with an army of mercenaries. But now, with the flood of new industrialized companies, the battle has changed. There is no longer room for everybody. An era of crusaders is on the way. Those who know why they are fighting will win over those who don't.[2]

At this point many readers will be feeling uncomfortable. Is it necessary to have a crusade? Surely all that businesses need is a sound strategy? If we are going to demonstrate that mission and sense of mission can contribute to success, we must be able to explain what they add over and above clear strategy. Because we are asking managers to become more conscious of the emotional and moral side of their companies, we must therefore show why this attention will lead to better performance.

Benefits come from two sources: from the clarity of direction that results from defining a mission and from the commitment and loyalty that come from individuals with a sense of mission.

The Benefits of Defining Mission

A management team capable of defining a clear mission will have advantages over a team that has defined only its strategy. The mission team will have values as well as strategic concepts to guide it through important decisions; the strategy team will have commercial logic only. Business decisions and people decisions are often hard to take, particularly on a consistent basis. The financial analysis rarely proves that one option is clearly superior to another because the financial analysis depends on estimates of the future, and the future is uncertain. Moreover, people decisions are nearly always hard. Issues of performance become confused with issues of potential and these are further clouded by issues of politics and loyalty. In these two areas—business decisions and people decisions—senior managers need as much support as possible. A clearly defined set of values reinforcing the strategy gives this extra support.

Better Strategic Thinking

Making strategic decisions is one of the most difficult tasks for senior managers because they are dealing with ambiguous and complex issues where no clear right or wrong is involved. After considering all the research and analysis available, managers are normally faced with a choice that can be made on the basis of personal judgment and instinct. Inevitably, corporate values will strongly influence the manager's thinking and, as a result, a clear and sound value framework can improve these personal judgments and help keep them consistent. This process is also helped if managers have a clear understanding of their organization's purpose. By perceiving the links between both strategy and purpose and values and purpose, leaders are more easily able to stay on course when making important strategic decisions.

An example from our research illustrates the way in which values help to improve decisions. David Sainsbury, a director of the British supermarket chain Sainsbury's, told us of the company's important decision in 1963 not to follow other supermarket chains in offering customers Green Shield stamps, a type of trading stamp that was very popular at the time in the United Kingdom and was used to attract additional customers. It was a difficult decision that needed to be extensively debated by the board. Choosing not to offer the stamps would cause Sainsbury to lose some market share and face a short-term decline in profits. Moreover, the long-term effects were difficult to estimate.

The directors decided not to offer stamps, a decision based on their beliefs about the company's values and purpose. They realized that the additional cost of the stamps would inevitably lead to price rises because all the supermarket chains were copying each other. This meant that the stamps would prevent the company from pursuing its central goal of providing the customer with quality food at reasonable prices—hence its treasured slogan "Good food costs less at Sainsbury." A company booklet on the history of Sainsbury's describes the strength of management's views:

> In 1963 came one of the most dramatic and successful interventions made by Sainsbury's into the "politics" of retail trading. In that year, trading stamp companies made a very strong effort to establish themselves among the multiples of the retail food trade. They were opposed by many traders and emphatically by Sainsbury's. Alan Sainsbury, by

his forthright condemnation of stamp trading, was one of its leading opponents. Together with Mr. Malcolm Cooper, Chairman of Allied Suppliers, he became Joint Chairman of the Distributive Trade Alliance, which was set up to fight the spread of trading stamps.

The trading stamp companies expected acceptance on a scale comparable to that which had been given this kind of promotion in the United States; they were amazed at the success that the Alliance had in opposing it.

Sainsbury's regarded stamp trading with such hostility that they were prepared to fight it all the way. The whole family, united solidly behind Alan Sainsbury, treated the threat very seriously indeed and emerged successful from the battle with many valuable lessons learnt.

In the event the decision proved right for the company's long-term success and helped to position Sainsbury's as a champion of customer value. But the most important lesson from Sainsbury's experience was that it was not the commercial analysis but the clarity of mission among the company's directors that led them to make the decision.

Other researchers have also defined the importance of values in decision making. In *Theory Z*,[3] William Ouchi describes a difficult decision faced by Hewlett-Packard management, who were considering the opportunity presented by the fast-expanding digital watch industry. Hewlett-Packard already manufactured some of the critical electronic components at the heart of digital watches and the financial analysis promised very good rewards should they go into the business.

As at Sainsbury's, numbers are not allowed to dominate Hewlett-Packard. The more important question was whether a new business in digital watches would fit with the company philosophy. The view of senior managers was that it would not. *The HP Way* defines the features of HP-type products as "engineering excellence," "lasting value," and the potential to offer "best after sales service." Against these criteria, digital watches for the mass market did not seem to fit.

The digital watch proposal, however, had been put forward by a young general manager with a proven record for success. HP senior managers also had a strong philosophy of decentralization, support of successful employees and freedom to act. They were afraid that turning down the project would discourage initiative. Senior managers were caught between two pillars of the HP value system: a preference for high added-value products and a belief in innovation and autonomy.

The result, not surprisingly, was a compromise. Senior managers persuaded the general manager to draw up a more modest proposal that focused on the higher added-value technical end of the watch market. Once this was done, they approved the project. As it turned out, the new business was initially highly successful as the digital watch industry took off. However, when prices eventually fell and competition became fierce, HP was able to avoid the losses that companies such as Texas Instruments, the electronics company, were experiencing. In the process of gradually winding down its digital watch business, HP was also able to salvage technical advances and marketing ideas.

In making their decision, managers at Hewlett-Packard relied much more heavily on their corporate mission—their business definition and management philosophy—than on simple financial analysis. Given the uncertainty surrounding the watch industry at that time and the mistakes made by many other companies, observers have judged that, with hindsight, HP's initial decision was excellent.

The HP story is also a useful example of how a strong mission encourages consensus at the top of organizations. Almost without exception, senior management teams have found that the process of discussing mission helps them to clarify their common beliefs and expose misunderstandings, pinpointing areas of disagreement or confusion.

Better Recruitment and Promotion Decisions

Companies with clear missions are more choosy about the people they hire and promote. They use a broader range of criteria than the traditional measures of education, experience, skill level, and leadership qualities. This is because they have a clearer idea of what sort of company they want to be and what sort of people are likely to do well in the culture. By defining the values that form the organizational culture, managers with a clear mission are better able to judge who will fit with the culture and who will not.

Anita Roddick, founder of The Body Shop, a cosmetics retailing business, places the utmost importance on the values and attitudes of potential new recruits. She believes that basic business skills can be acquired by training but that the right attitude and values cannot.

"We have the back-up to teach almost anyone to run a Body Shop outlet," she says. "What we can't control is the soul." To this end, the strict screening process that all applicants must pass is balanced by seemingly offbeat questions such as How would you like to die? Who is your heroine in poetry?—all questions that give Roddick a feel for whether the applicant is someone she can work with comfortably.

At Borg-Warner, the manufacturing and services multinational, the company's former chief executive, Robert Ingersoll, was well known for his emphasis on exploring the values and attitudes of potential recruits. According to a company document: "When he interviewed someone for an upper level job . . . he often started the interview with a thoroughly unexpected question: 'What is your philosophy of life?' He was looking for honesty and a sense of dedication to company and customer, rather than followers of the old tradition of 'make a buck any way you can.'" Ingersoll's attention to values and beliefs was an important symbol within Borg-Warner at a time when the company was struggling to formalize and clarify its ethics and standards of behavior.

Egon Zehnder goes to great lengths to assess whether a consultant will fit its culture and values. The firm emphasizes its mission continuously and, in keeping with the "one-firm" concept, tends to introduce applicants to as many consultants as possible to see if they will be able to work with them effectively. An applicant can have as many as 18 interviews in four different offices around the world.

This incredibly time-consuming and drawn-out interview process ensures that the firm and the new recruit get a good long look at each other before both agree to work together. An individual with an incompatible personality or working style is unlikely to survive the process. Yet by involving many consultants in the interviewing process the firm ensures that new appointments are not all clones of the senior consultant in the office.

The lengthy interview process and clearly espoused values also help to encourage self-selection. Individuals who do not have compatible values are unlikely to feel that they still want to join the firm after the long, exhausting interview process, especially after hearing yet another interviewer explain the way in which Egon Zehnder likes to work.

This self-selection process also applies to individuals already working for a company. A director of Marks and Spencer pointed out to us that the company's strong culture can push out people who are unlikely to fit. He said:

> I think [the mission] I have just described is not for everybody. There is a strong underlying sense of paternalism in the M&S approach. In exchange for adhering to M&S's way of doing things, you know that the company will look after you and support you. In M&S you are asked to conform in a way that is not everybody's cup of tea. Some suddenly realize it's not for them. The number of times I have heard people say they enjoyed working with M&S but that it's not a company that suits them.

Various other businesses we talked to spoke of people who had fought against the mission and then eventually parted company. First Chicago Bank spoke of the departure of several senior managers who could not accept the bank's emphasis and belief in "team-playing and group decision-making." The case study of Dist in Chapter 8 reveals how the chief executive had to work hard to get his managers to subscribe to a new set of values and philosophy and how one senior manager in particular disagreed so strongly that he subsequently resigned. An employee at Bulmers similarly described the abrupt departure of a relatively new manager who had unsuccessfully tried to ignore the brewery's time-honored tradition of extensive employee consultation. A more stark example of how mission weeds people out is the decisive way in which the new head of British Airways eased out of the organization approximately 70 managers because he felt they would be unable to adapt to the new culture.

In some cases, this process of self-selection will lead to organizations losing some very bright and creative people. This result cannot be avoided in companies with a mission. At some point or other, these organizations will be forced to make a trade-off between the quality of an individual and his or her fit with the culture. If the mismatch between the individual's values and those of the organization is causing considerable friction, allowing the person to stay could do more harm than good. Such is the difficult dilemma that companies with a mission sometimes have to face.

Training and Development
Companies with a mission use their training to establish further the skills, values, and behaviors they need to continue being successful. The most outstanding example of this is the competency-based

Figure 3.1 **British Airways' Competency-based Appraisal System**

IMPORTANCE TO THE JOB								PERFORMANCE											
NR* Low					High			Very low										Very high	
0	1	2	3	4	5	6	Strategic awareness	0	1	2	3	4	5	6	7	8	9	10
0	1	2	3	4	5	6	Business awareness	0	1	2	3	4	5	6	7	8	9	10
0	1	2	3	4	5	6	Establishing objectives	0	1	2	3	4	5	6	7	8	9	10
0	1	2	3	4	5	6	Planning and organization	0	1	2	3	4	5	6	7	8	9	10
0	1	2	3	4	5	6	Judgment and decision-making	0	1	2	3	4	5	6	7	8	9	10
0	1	2	3	4	5	6	Commitment	0	1	2	3	4	5	6	7	8	9	10
0	1	2	3	4	5	6	Initiative/flexibility	0	1	2	3	4	5	6	7	8	9	10
0	1	2	3	4	5	6	Knowledge	0	1	2	3	4	5	6	7	8	9	10
0	1	2	3	4	5	6	Communication/influencing	0	1	2	3	4	5	6	7	8	9	10
0	1	2	3	4	5	6	Interpersonal skills	0	1	2	3	4	5	6	7	8	9	10
0	1	2	3	4	5	6	Team management	0	1	2	3	4	5	6	7	8	9	10
0	1	2	3	4	5	6	Individual subordinate management	0	1	2	3	4	5	6	7	8	9	10

*Not relevant

appraisal and training program for managers at British Airways. Through extensive research on the range of leadership skills likely to be needed by future generations of senior managers and through talks with the existing senior executives about the strategic direction of the company, British Airways has identified constellations of "abilities, personal qualities, values, and drives" that distinguish the type of people BA want both now and in the future (see Figure 3.1).

The company's training program is based around competencies that reflect these ideal profiles. It uses psychometric tests, self-assessment, and reports from line managers and senior executives to select potential future leaders. These candidates are then put through an extensive development program. There, BA's new-found mission is reflected in the emphasis it puts on such skills as the ability to "promote open and constructive relations" across the organization and the ability to develop a "large organization perspective," which is "an appreciation of and sensitivity to the complex interdependencies" that exist in an organization like BA.

The training provided by The Body Shop is unique to the company and reflects clearly its strong values and philosophy. The company has its own training school, which concentrates on business and retailing skills such as product knowledge, customer care, communication, and presentation skills. But, in addition, the company teaches its staff to think about wider social and environmental issues. Says Anita Roddick:

> The courses do not simply tell our people how to keep a customer or stock up shelves. We have courses on the chemistry of cosmetics covering issues such as skin biology and aging in society. We have courses on acid rain, for example, where franchises and staff are invited to take part in environmental campaigns. We have lectures from design people who discuss values and aesthetics. . . . We therefore run in the opposite direction to the rest of the cosmetic industry. They train for a sale. We train for knowledge.

These two examples show how mission enables companies to formulate training strategies that not only concentrate on technical skills but also clarify the managerial style, behaviors, and values that they wish their staff to adopt. Like the famous Hamburger University at McDonald's or the training of cast members at Disney, training and development in these companies have an important socialization and behavior modification role that goes well beyond traditional skill-building.

The Benefits of a Sense of Mission

Employees with a sense of mission will be more committed, more disciplined, and more open to change than other employees. Their contribution will still depend on their individual ability, but, given equal ability, employees with a sense of mission will make a higher-quality contribution.

Before giving our research results, we would like to highlight a major research project that provides empirical evidence to support many of our assertions. This consists of a nationwide survey of 1,500 U.S. managers in 1985 by Barry Posner, James Kouzes, and Warren Schmidt[4] of the University of Santa Clara. The three attempted to gauge the importance of the link between personal and organizational goals and to see if it really did make a difference to business success. The link between personal and organizational values is, of course, an essential dimension of a sense of mission.

Respondents were asked about the compatibility of their personal goals with those of their organizations and to estimate the extent to which organizational expectations forced them to make compromises. Responses to these questions were grouped in three categories of "value congruence": low, moderate, and high. The rest of the questionnaire focused on the manager's feelings about career success, job stress, concern about ethical issues, commitment, and understanding of others' values.

The three authors concluded from the study: "The findings clearly reveal that efforts to clarify and merge personal and corporate values can have a significant payoff for both managers and their organizations." The study's most important discoveries include the following:

1. *Success:* Managers reporting greater compatibility between personal and corporate values scored significantly greater feelings of success in their lives and increased confidence about achieving their ambitions. Those with the least overlap of values were twice as likely to express doubt about fulfilling their ambitions.

2. *Commitment:* Managers with compatible values were significantly more confident that they would remain with their current employers for the next five years. They were also much more likely to be willing to work long hours for their employer.

3. *Ethical behavior:* Managers reporting shared values tended to believe their organizations acted ethically and accordingly acted in the same way themselves. They also tended to try to avoid taking advantage of the organization. Managers with low congruence were more likely to act unethically if requested by their bosses.

4. *Stress:* Managers in the low shared values category reported higher levels of job-related anxiety spilling into their personal lives.

5. *Corporate goals:* Managers with shared values placed more importance on internal corporate goals, such as productivity, reputation, and morale. There was no difference between this group and the other managers in their ratings for external goals, such as growth and value to the community.

6. *Organizational stakeholders*: Respondents with shared values attached more importance to stockholders, owners, and customers. Compared with respondents in the other two categories, managers with weak shared values viewed their bosses and managers as less important.

Posner, Kouzes and Schmidt conclude:

> Strong shared values provide individuals with a sense of success and fulfillment, a healthy (less cynical) assessment of the values and ethics of their colleagues, subordinates and bosses, and a greater regard for organizational objectives. . . . Shared values do make a difference to organizational and personal vitality. Companies with strong corporate cultures (and high degrees of shared values) underscore the conclusion of Pascale and Athos that "great companies make meaning."

Our research interviews definitely support Posner's conclusion. But, because of the more general nature of our interviews, we were not able to separate out the different kinds of benefit to the same level of detail. We perceived two kinds of benefit.

1. Loyalty and Commitment

A sense of mission is the energy, commitment, and enthusiasm that employees feel about their companies. As we have said in earlier chapters, this form of emotional commitment leads to a greater dedication and willingness to sacrifice personal interests to the good of the whole. This emotional commitment is also a valuable aid to retaining key employees at a time when many industrialized economies have highly skilled work forces that are more than willing to vote with their feet if they believe they can get better pay and benefits elsewhere.

Employees with a sense of mission are more unlikely to say, "It's someone else's problem," "It's not my job," or "It's 5 p.m., it'll have to wait until tomorrow." Their ability to identify personally with the company means that anything that reflects badly on the company reflects badly on them and vice versa.

At Bulmers, a distribution manager describes how the company's drivers have this sense of identification. "If they don't do it right, they're letting the company down. The company has an identity, character, and style in the way it's grown up. It is so personalized that there is no distinction between letting it down and letting other people down." A trade union official and former Bulmers driver gives an example of this extra dedication: "The drivers help the company in a number of ways. For example, a load went too soon to a customer in the northeast of England. The customer didn't require the goods and couldn't take them. The driver rang and suggested he go to another customer in the same area so as not to come back with a full load. What do the drivers get out of it? Satisfaction; it's aggravating not to do the job right."

A favorite anecdote told by Marks and Spencer's Lord Sieff vividly illustrates the extra dedication that some employees show.

> I got a letter . . . from a Mrs. Williams, a part-time stockroom assistant at our Chatham store who writes telling me that she knows that Chatham area is in a bit of a depression, that the store catalogue is poor. Now she serves on the floor on a Saturday. She said last Saturday she had to refuse within five minutes three customers for lines which she knew are overall in the catalogue but Chatham does not have them. It cost us £100 in sales.
>
> Now remember, this lady gets no commission, she's on a flat rate. And she said it's really not good enough: "Do you know that we get customers at Chatham from the Isle of Sheppey to, I think, the Isle of Grain, and you've got the whole thing wrong!"
>
> I couldn't go down so I sent my personal assistant, who came back with the report that the range at Chatham was poor. We improved that range and the increase of sales in Chatham within a space of three weeks was dramatic.
>
> We gave Mrs. Williams a little cash gift and she wrote me a letter: "Dear Chairman, I was overwhelmed when Mr. Adam (that's the Manager) gave me the gift. But the most important thing is what is happening at Chatham." And she says: "Do you know that last Saturday, on the floor, customers came up to me and said, oh we didn't know you had this in the catalogue. How nice!" She said the morale of the whole of the staff at Chatham has changed. She then went on to say that Chatham is on the way back. Nobody is going to stop Chatham now.

This anecdote illustrates the way in which employees with a sense of mission can become, in Marks and Spencer's words, "the ears, eyes, and brains" of an organization. It also illustrates the way in which employees often have a strong sense of loyalty to their companies, with the result that many stay with their employers for several years. Long-term employment is in fact a strikingly common characteristic of companies where employees have a sense of mission. This phenomenon probably accounts in part for the ability of these companies to maintain over the years a shared and coherent vision of the company's values and goals.

Many interviewees told us of their affection for their companies, commonly likening them to an extended family. They often confessed that they had stayed with the company far longer than they ever intended to or expected. The comments of this Marks and Spencer staff manager are typical: "I have been with the company all my working life; I think most of us have. It's hard work and demanding work, but it's satisfying and you know the company will look after you better than anyone else. I really don't think I'd have had a better career with anyone else."

At Egon Zehnder, in particular, the tendency to stay with the consultancy for several years is a remarkable phenomenon in an industry with such rapid staff turnover. Indeed, 70 percent of the consultants who have ever worked for Egon Zehnder are still doing so, and the company has no hesitation in asserting: "Continuity is a major asset for our clients and our firm. We have a loyal and happy team, with rewards geared towards seniority and long-term careers with the firm."

Employees echoed similar opinions about working for Egon Zehnder: "The consultancy does care about keeping its people and if you have committed people you are going to be a success," said one young consultant. Another consultant said he joined the firm because "I saw that I liked pretty well all the people I'd met— agreeable, interesting and lively. I thought if this business can keep these guys happy it will do the same for me." An office manager commented: "Our purpose is to attract the right people into the environment where they are happy, well compensated and enjoy what they are doing so that it is almost a family."

A newly arrived consultant also uses the simile of a family: "I organized the Christmas party and sent everybody an 'I love Egon Zehnder' bear. I sent one to Egon, too, and he phoned me that day. Everybody here feels part of a family. A friend of mine in another office recently said to me, 'I'm still trying to find the skeleton in the cupboard—and I can't find anything.'"

Bulmers is another outstanding example of a company with long-serving, loyal employees. Much of this loyalty derives from the fact that the company has managed to retain its family atmosphere, stemming from the days when the Bulmers family first founded the cider-making business over 100 years ago. A production manager who has worked for the company for 36 years describes how Bulmers's chairman helped to maintain a family atmosphere:

> He made people feel they belonged, that he and the company were interested in them. For example, he was a great motorcyclist and one day he walked up to one of the boys who worked here and asked him if he'd like to ride his motorcycle—just went up and asked him, knew he wanted to. Well, the boy couldn't wait to come into my office and say he'd been on the chairman's motorcycle.

2. Additional Guidance for Behavior

Because companies with strong missions have strong norms and cultures, employees have recourse to clear behavioral standards. These standards encourage cooperation between employees, ensure that clients are treated in a consistent way by everyone in the organization, and help mold managerial styles and behaviors. As Deal and Kennedy say in *Corporate Cultures:* "Managers and others throughout the organization give extraordinary attention to whatever matters are stressed in the corporate value system—and this in turn tends to produce extraordinary results."[5]

A sense of mission often helps create a positive and cooperative work environment where employees respect one another and search for a solution that is in the interests of the organization rather than individual departments. This truism is almost tautological: If people acknowledge a common cause, they will be much more likely to cooperate. Also, if they share certain values, they will find it easier to trust their colleagues and overcome the usual work rivalries and suspicions. This type of trust is hard to create even in the most favorable environments. While a sense of mission will not overcome all the problems of "not invented here," power games, and emotional incompatibility, it will certainly help to reduce or defuse them to manageable levels.

A manager in ICI found that, once converted, employees cannot help but work towards achieving the mission. A senior manager spoke of his experiences during a time when the subsidiary office he was managing was trying to clarify its values and introduce certain internal changes. He said:

> If you have enough conversations about where you are going and why and the values involved, then people will trust and commit themselves to what you are doing even if it is a strong step. Our managers knew we were going in the right direction and trying to do the right things in the environment we were in. As a result they couldn't disassociate themselves from helping to make it happen.

Creating an open, trusting environment where people are free to use their skills is something that is close to the heart of ICI's former chairman, Sir John Harvey-Jones. He describes ICI as "a community—a community with an ethos, beliefs, feelings, and relationships." His vision for the company was to create a "federation of free people collaborating through their own enthusiasm toward a common purpose . . . a society which is motivated and self-driven."[6]

Egon Zehnder's values and philosophy also strongly influence how consultants behave to each other. Although each individual is an autonomous unit (independence seems to be as highly valued as teamwork, a duality that seems to stem from the Swiss culture on which the consultancy was founded), each person is accustomed to put his or her colleagues first. The phrase "the one-firm concept" is referred to again and again. Cooperative behavior among staff is highly prized, as the firm believes it leads to better quality of service to the client.

A consultant describes the type of collaboration that commonly occurs among consultants: "I got a call the other day, and gave the work to another colleague. I recognized that I did not have the relevant expertise. So we recognize each other's skills and [if necessary] switch assignments or work as a team."

Another strong behavioral standard among consultants is the importance of putting the client's interest first every time. In some cases, this can result in consultants giving advice that the client may not like or want and even declining business. A consultant explains:

> We try to understand the reason for the need to go outside in the first place. We get the brief absolutely clear and reflect it back to the client in writing and, if necessary, we have a dialogue with them if we disagree with their perception. Many other search firms will take on an assignment without asking all these questions because they want the

business. But this is what we mean by the "primacy" of the client—if we don't think we can help them, we say so. Similarly, if we think they are mistaken in their requirements, then we say that too.

The impact of organizational values on individual behavior has been studied by Jeanne Liedtka,[7] an assistant professor at Simmons College in Boston. She interviewed 18 managers in two firms and used questionnaires to assess both the organization's and the individual's values. She identified 31 "difficult situations." These were decisions faced by individuals that they had difficulty making.

Liedtka was studying these situations to understand how individuals cope with ethical dilemmas. Her work also sheds light on how values guide behavior. In all 31 situations, the individual made a decision based on what he or she perceived to be the values with the strongest influence. Where the organization's values and the individual's values were aligned (the condition where the individual is most likely to have a sense of mission), the difficult situations were easy to resolve. But, even in situations where the individual's values were in conflict with the perceived organizational norms or where the individual was ambivalent, the difficult situations were most frequently resolved in line with organization values. In other words, if the organizational values are clear and large numbers of employees support the values, behavior will be dictated by those values even for employees who feel ambivalent or actively in conflict with them.

Liedtka gives the example of one manager who was torn between her desire to treat people fairly and the organization's belief in quality. She had a quality problem in her section, but she had not been able to determine which shift or which worker was responsible. Under pressure to improve quality, she felt she had to take an extreme measure—to give all six workers a verbal warning even though she knew that five of them were probably innocent. Liedtka explains the dilemma faced by the manager and shows how the organization's values helped her make the decision:

> This is a difficult decision for Laura, and one that she is uncomfortable with, given the high value she places upon being fair. As Laura explained: "Being fair runs into my personal success. The conflict is that the production floor is a representation of me—it reflects my reputation. Versus, how fair can I be to the supervisors?"

Laura describes the choice she makes as a last resort, as it forces her to choose between two highly regarded values—her own perfectionism and regard for quality versus being fair to her subordinates. Laura sees the stance of the organization as unequivocally behind fixing the problem. She says: "As long as my idea works, it will be seen as a success. If it doesn't work, it won't be." (p. 809)

The organization's value of high quality above all else helped Laura make her decision. It helped her choose between two conflicting good ways of behaving.

Risks and Pitfalls

The strength of an organization's values and behavioral norms can be a disadvantage as well as a benefit. Because strong values can be a powerful influence over behavior, it is important that they are the right values and, so far as possible, that they are timeless values.

The story of the British motorcycle industry is a story of strongly held but inappropriate values and behavioral standards. Between 1930 and 1960 British motorcycles dominated much of the world market and were widely regarded as the biker's bike. Names like Triumph, Norton, and BSA were world brands among the motorcycle community. The bikes were associated with a style of engineering and a particular noise, and it was part of the experience regularly to have to tune the engine and adjust the chain drive.

The values associated with this kind of motorcycle were strongly held by both the manufacturers and their biking customers. When Japanese bikes became available based on a different, low-maintenance engineering philosophy and a different engine noise, they were sneered at by the British manufacturer and the traditional biker. These new bikes were attractive to a new range of customers who had previously ignored motorcycles because they were noisy and needed too much maintenance. Seeing Japanese bikes being ridden by these less sophisticated customers confirmed their second-class status in the eyes of the traditionalists.

Gradually, the size of the traditional market began to shrink and Japanese motorcycle sales began to grow and eventually surpass the sales of local manufacturers. In response, the traditional manufacturers merged together and redoubled their efforts to manufacture and market the traditional motorcycle with traditional values. The strength of their culture made it impossible for them to change sufficiently to cope with the Japanese threat. Finally, the industry collapsed when Norton, Villiers, and Triumph, the only surviving manufacturer, filed for bankruptcy.

However, the loyalty of the work force to the industry and to the values it stood for was so great that they refused to allow the liquidator to close the largest factory at Meriden. The "sit-in" at Meriden became a national issue and the government agreed to fund a cooperative formed by the work force to continue manufacturing motorcycles.

Nevertheless, the values still dominated. A visitor to the plant commented that he was amazed to see a worker hand painting the speed lines on the fuel tanks. But to the cooperative this type of behavior was not surprising. Motorcycles were works of art loved by those who made them and those who owned them. As such they deserved the attention and artistry of the hand painter. Not surprisingly, the cooperative never made money and despite further government support finally collapsed.

The story of the British motorcycle industry illustrates both the power and the pitfalls of strong organizational values and employees with a sense of mission. Against all the evidence over dozens of years and in the face of strong external pressure from bankers and the government, the British motorcycle industry stuck to its traditional values and behaviors. Even at the bitter end when Norton, Villiers, and Triumph had filed for bankruptcy, the leaders of the Meriden cooperative were unable to see the behavioral change that was needed. Their many years of socialization in the traditional ways of working and their personal and highly emotional commitment to the British motorcycle blinded them, driving them to reinforce rather than reexamine their values.

In our research we came across similar examples of a strong commitment to values that caused a reduction in performance or a resistance to change. In Marks and Spencer, managers identified two areas where the value system had delayed decision making. The first one was connected to the importing of garments. Marks and Spencer had for many years been committed to supporting Britain and British manufacturers. The company frequently claimed that more than 90 percent of its clothes were manufactured in

Britain. It was an important platform of the company's image and, because Marks and Spencer had a high share of the British market, the policy had saved many jobs in the industry. Customers and governments praised the company, arguing that others should do the same.

However, manufacturers in Hong Kong, South Korea, and China were becoming increasingly competitive as their management skills and technology began to make the best use of their colossal usage differentials. During the 1980s, Marks and Spencer's rivals were becoming more and more competitive as their imported clothes rose in quality and fell in price. Inevitably, the company's commitment to buying British caused it to delay taking advantage of the developing Far East manufacturers. In actuality the delay was not costly. When Marks and Spencer did decide to improve its supplies from the Far East, there were plenty of importers and multinationals such as Courtaulds willing to help.

A more costly decision was the delayed investment in sophisticated information technology in the late 1970s and early 1980s. The company had prided itself on minimal reporting procedures, low levels of bureaucracy, face-to-face management, and having store managers who knew what was selling because they "walked the store." As other retailers experimented with stock control systems and point of sale stock recording, building large inventory-handling departments, Marks and Spencer stuck to its traditional face-to-face, close-to-the-customer management approach. When the company finally did decide to use the new technology that was available in the mid-1980s, it found that it was a long way behind competitors and needed to move fast if it was to avoid becoming uncompetitive.

We found similar examples in other companies of the disadvantage of having inappropriate values or strong values that become difficult to change. The managing director of Bulmers, for example, explained that when he had joined Bulmers from Pedigree Petfoods, a Mars subsidiary and a company known for its strong values, he found that the employees at Bulmers had just as strong values and were just as committed. "The difference was that some of the standards at Bulmers were much lower than those at Mars," he explained. The Bulmers values were not as demanding as the Mars values.

Resistance to change and inappropriate behavior due to inappropriate values are not the only pitfalls of having employees with a sense of mission. Strongly shared values can lead to an insularity that becomes xenophobic. In *Theory Z* William Ouchi notes their tendency to fear outsiders and deviant behavior.

> The clan form in industry possesses a few potentially disabling weaknesses. In the words of the president of one major Type Z company: "We simply can't bring in an outsider at top levels. We've tried it, but the others won't accept him. I consider it to be one of our biggest problems." In other ways, too, the Type Z resists deviance in all forms. Because the glue that holds it together is consistency of belief rather than application of hierarchy, it tends indiscriminately to reject all inconsistency. The trouble is that it is difficult, perhaps impossible, to discriminate in advance between a deviant idea that is useful and adaptive and one that is simply stupid and immoral. (p. 88)

Organizations with very strong cultures, particularly those where large numbers of employees have a sense of mission, are those in which people hold strong opinions about what is right and wrong and what is the right or wrong way to do things. If these opinions are misguided, the organization will suffer, like the British motorcycle industry. If the opinions are well founded, the organization will be highly successful, like Hewlett-Packard or Marks and Spencer.

There are, therefore, two ways to avoid the risks: avoid creating clear values and discourage employees from becoming emotionally committed to them; or formulate a well-founded mission with values that are timeless and a strategy that can be sustained for decades.

The first way of avoiding the risks is appropriate when an organization faces extreme and temporary uncertainty. In these circumstances it may be better to wait and see how events unfold before developing a mission. An example of this might be a workers' cooperative in Albania in 1992. The change in political philosophy, the potential of freer trade with the West, and the lack of policy about how the government will seek to control industry make it an inappropriate time to develop a new mission. The future environment in which the business will operate is too uncertain to make the exercise useful. Moreover, in 12 months everything is likely to become much clearer, making it possible, even advisable, to develop a strategy and build a new organization, a new mission, around it.

For all other organizations, the pitfalls are best avoided by developing a timeless mission with values that need not change in fundamental ways. IBM, Hewlett-Packard, Marks and Spencer, Matsushita, Egon Zehnder, and Johnson & Johnson all have values that have stood the test of time. They had well-founded missions. Adjustments have had to be made along the way. *The HP Way* has been rewritten at least four and probably as many as ten times. At each rewrite some elements have been updated and some issues played down. For example, one of the leading objectives in the early versions was "No borrowing." Bill Hewlett and Dave Packard believed that by borrowing management would lose the flexibility to invest in research in times of hardship. The need to service the debt would interfere with the commercial need to develop new technology. However, in the 1989 version of *The HP Way* the principle has been dropped.

The same has been true of Marks and Spencer, even though the company has no formal written mission statement. The policy of buying British has reduced in importance. It is still company policy and senior managers still expect staff to buy locally where possible, but the company has now set up a large office in Hong Kong to help cultivate sources in the Far East. The acquisition of Brooks Brothers in the United States as well as initiatives to retail in the Far East have made the policy and its associated values less important.

At Johnson & Johnson the corporate credo is continually being reconsidered by teams of managers. Yet these wide-ranging discussions have not altered the values around which the document was written. Instead, executives come away from the discussion meetings with a renewed commitment to company values, having examined them at length and having heard the top officers of the corporation and their peers express commitment to ethics.

The strength of the missions of these three companies is that the core values have not needed to change. Marks and Spencer's principles of good human relations and visible management, and Hewlett-Packard's principles of encouraging creativity and MBWA have proved to be as philosophically sound in their business as "love thy neighbor" has in Western society. As a drug manufacturer, Johnson & Johnson relies on consumers' trust, and its internal organization reflects the same emphasis on trusting each other.

In Chapter 11 we define the qualities of a good mission statement. Managers who develop their missions around these quality criteria will be more likely to create a well-founded mission with values that will last decades rather than years.

Summary

We have tried to show that mission and a sense of mission are important to business success because they help organizations to move in a united direction, make consistent decisions and strategies, and harness the skill and commitment of the work force. We have also emphasized that this area of management is not without risks. If wrongly formulated, mission can become a straitjacket that prevents a company from moving forward. To avoid these pitfalls, company leaders need to create well-founded missions with values that can stand the test of time. As events change, values can be adjusted and priorities reordered, but the core values should be as everlasting as those of a religion.

NOTES

1. Thomas J. Watson, Jr., *A Business and Its Beliefs* (New York: McGraw-Hill, 1963), p. 5.

2. Although no research has been done on the percentage of companies in France with mission statements, our impression is that mission is more popular currently in France than in either the United States or Britain.

3. William Ouchi, *Theory Z: How American Business Can Meet the Japanese Challenge* (Reading, Mass.: Addison-Wesley, 1981), p. 73.

4. B. Posner, J. Kouzes and W. Schmidt, "Shared Values Make a Difference: An Empirical Test of Corporate Culture," *Human Resource Management* 24, no. 3 (Fall 1985), pp. 293–309.

5. T. Deal and A. Kennedy, *Corporate Cultures* (Reading, Mass: Addison-Wesley, 1982).

6. Unpublished interview with Sir John Harvey-Jones.

7. Jeanne M. Liedtka, "Value Congruence: The Interplay of Individual and Organizational Value Systems," *Journal of Business Ethics* 8 (1989), pp. 805–15.

CHAPTER
4

Mission Can Be Managed

. . . .

The next six chapters (Chapters 5–10) are case studies of companies where the senior managers tried to develop a new mission by creating a major change in philosophy and strategy, or to renew a mission by making changes in company traditions. These cases were chosen because they provided the maximum diversity of situation readily available to the research team.

In 1963 the management of Shell UK Refining set about developing a new philosophy of management with the intention of transforming labor relations and improving the performance of the business. In 1975 the president of Johnson & Johnson, James Burke, began a process of reviewing and renewing the company's well-known mission statement. The results helped carry the company through the Tylenol tampering crisis seven years later, and the review program continues today. In 1978 Harry Smith, chief executive of the company we call Dist, recognized that the group of companies over which he presided was getting too big to be managed personally. To ensure continuity as he lessened his involvement in the individual businesses, he instituted a program to codify and institutionalize the values and philosophy that he and his senior managers felt were essential to Dist's success. The philosophy met its greatest challenge when Dist tried to implant it in a new subsidiary that distributed industrial controls. In 1980 Wes Christopherson became chairman of the Jewel Companies and initiated an update of the company's stated management philosophy. This document remained primarily an internal matter and was challenged when the corporation became the target of a takeover bid. In 1981 James Beré, chief executive of Borg-Warner, launched a project to develop a statement of the company's beliefs. Previous efforts to define the philosophy of the organization stretch back to the *Borg-Warner Creed* documented in 1970. In 1983 Colin Marshall became chief executive of British Airways and set about making that company into an organization dedicated to customer service.

In all six cases there were explicit efforts to document the new mission in some form of mission statement. One of the cases is more than 20 years old, providing good data on the longevity of new missions; in two others, the mission statements have their roots in the first half of this century though the renewal process occurred within the past 20 years. Two of the cases are generally viewed as major successes; one is documented as being a failure; and the other results are mixed. Three cases concern the mission for a multibusiness company; the others are more focused. Two cases are about manufacturing, two about distribution, and two about service. This degree of diversity provides an excellent base from which to develop some general rules about how companies should set about managing mission.

How Not to Manage Mission

A surprisingly large number of companies treat mission in a simplistic and inappropriate way, mainly because they have an unrealistic view of the value of mission statements. Each company's approach is different, but we have encountered some common patterns.

The process starts with the chief executive or the board deciding that a mission statement will help clarify issues and foster commitment within the business. This idea sometimes comes from an external stimulus such as a consultant, who tells the chief executive that a mission statement is needed to help unite the company. A typical example is the corporate identity consultant; faced with the problem of developing an identity that can be communicated and translated into a logo and family of letterheads, the corporate identity consultant is forced to try to construct a mission. The questions that this individual asks and the ensuing attempts to write the mission down demonstrate to senior management that they have some gaps in their thinking. Developing a clear mission statement seems like the obvious answer.

The desire to develop a mission statement can also come from other external stimuli. The chief executive may read about the importance of mission, vision, or a clear corporate culture in a book on leadership or the *Harvard Business Review*. Pressure also comes from the financial community, which frequently encourages companies to clarify their strategy and management approach. The current vogue for this type of focus makes analysts and financial commentators harsh critics of managers who lack strong rationales for their company's activities and management style, or who find it hard to articulate a clear identity. As a result, there is a growing trend for publishing a mission statement or a mission-like management commentary in the annual report.

In the cases we have examined, however, it has been more often the case that something inside the company triggered off the idea of producing a mission statement. There are three typical triggers. First, the internal audience, usually middle management, may create a groundswell of noise about the need for a clearer statement of where the company is going and what it stands for. The most common place for this groundswell to start is during management development programs. When 15 or more managers spend one or two weeks learning about strategy and discussing their company, they invariably come to the conclusion that the company's mission is not clear enough and that their leaders ought to have a better-articulated mission. Gradually the pressure on the executive committee builds up until they are forced to start developing a mission statement.

The second trigger may be the executive committee itself. The desire to have a mission statement often emerges from a planning retreat. The discussion during the retreat may have brought to light some fairly deeply held differences of opinion about the future of the company or its management style. The chief executive sees a need to resolve these differences and asks the planning manager to draft a statement that clarifies the issues.

The third trigger can be the chief executive. He or she may see a clear need to change strategy and culture and may decide to use a statement of the new mission as a method of telling the organization about the new regime. Or, in the case of a mission update, the chief executive may be the one manager powerful enough to suggest that a hallowed company tradition needs change.

Whether the stimulus is internal or external, the starting point for most companies that treat mission inappropriately is a desire to develop and communicate a mission statement. With this starting point, the scenario we are about to describe will be immediately recognizable to many managers who have been involved in developing a mission.

The first event is the production of a draft statement. The executive committee may organize a special retreat to "thrash out" a draft; or the planning manager may produce a draft and circulate it for comments; or the chief executive may write the first draft over the weekend. However it is done, the first draft is produced quickly. The chief executive's desire to have a mission statement is acted on promptly.

The next step is the development of the final statement. This proves much harder than management had expected and there are long haggling sessions over particular words or sentences, over the order of paragraphs, and over the inclusion and exclusion of potentially key elements. Nevertheless a deadline will have been set, probably a management conference in six weeks' time or the publication of the annual report. As the deadline looms, compromises are made and the consensus statement emerges. No one is fully satisfied with it, but the executive committee members will each have contributed, at least to the extent of vetoing parts that offended them or their part of the organization.

The next step is to communicate the statement. In some companies, the new mission is publicized by being included in the annual report or by being turned into plastic, wallet-sized folders or desktop paperweights that are circulated to all employees. In other companies, managers recognize that, if the organization is going to feel any ownership for the statement, employees should be involved in discussing it and even editing it. So a series of management meetings, department meetings, feedback sessions, and discussion sessions are held.

The result is normally something of an anticlimax for the enthusiastic members of the executive committee and a secret triumph for the cynics. Employees and managers appear to be unmoved by the statement. Where energy is generated, it is devoted to disagreeing with the statement or lobbying to include additional elements. Nevertheless, after an agonizingly long time during which the executive committee begin to agree that too much management time is being spent on mission, a final statement is beautifully printed and converted into a videotape, with the chief executive explaining each of the main messages of the mission.

The videotape is shown to all staff in further meetings and discussions and, without voicing it, the executive committee is now firmly of the opinion that "we went overboard on this mission thing." Imperceptibly, they are individually giving off signals to their subordinates that enough is enough. And this feeling is communicated like lightning through the organization. Far from the executive committee, employees are debating not the contents of the mission but whether the effort was a good idea or not. Some see it as another demonstration of senior management's incompetence and lack of willpower, others see it as further evidence of management's manipulative intentions, and others as another willful attempt by the cynics to subvert the best of management intentions.

While it would be invidious to name individual companies that have mismanaged mission in the way that we have described, there are many examples and most managers will have personal experiences that are not dissimilar. The Shell case study in Chapter 10 has some of these features, and there is one publicly documented example that we can quote, the Metropolitan Police in London.

When Kenneth Newman became commissioner of the Metropolitan Police in 1983, the organization was being widely and publicly criticized. An independent report by Lord Scarman on the reasons for riots in Brixton, London, during the hot summer of 1980, recommended changes in the way the force was managed as well as changes to policing methods. Newman responded to Lord Scarman's recommendations by concluding that the force needed to recapture some of its old "bobby-on-the-beat" values and behaviors. He felt that the front-line police officer, the constable, had lost some of the values of professionalism and helpfulness that were part of the force's heritage and documented in *Primary Objects of the Police* written in 1829 by Commissioner Sir Richard Mayne. The constable, Newman felt, needed a reinforcement of these values in today's more modern context. Moreover, he wanted to stamp out racist, sexist, and unethical behavior among constables.

Newman's main vehicle for encouraging new values and behaviors was to produce a mission statement aimed at the constable. It was called *The Principles of Policing and Guidance for Professional Behavior* and is a blue 60-page hardcover book. It is a moving document, describing in the most explicit and emotional terms the purpose of the force and the job of a constable. For example: "The primary aims and duties of the Metropolitan Police are to uphold the Rule of Law, to protect and assist the citizen and to work for the prevention and detection of crime and the maintenance of a peaceful society, free of the fear of crime and disorder." And the constable has a responsibility to society:

> By acknowledging always that you are a friend, a guide, and a servant of your fellow citizens, and never their master, by adopting an appropriately firm but conciliatory and helpful manner to everyone you meet, and by acting always in ways which are manifestly fair and lawful, so naturally attracting public acceptance of police activity, you and your service colleagues can help to sustain our democratic way of life and build up a store of public goodwill to be drawn on in the future.

In essence, the book describes the following nine duties in a code of professional duties:

1. To prevent and detect crime; to keep the peace.
2. To uphold the rule of law.
3. To show compassionate respect for the dignity of the individual.
4. To show both resolution and restraint if faced with violent resistance, and to use with consummate skill, only such force as is necessary to accomplish a legitimate purpose.
5. To befriend and assist the citizen by giving sympathetic guidance.
6. To be brave and selfless in the face of danger.
7. To act always for the general public good.
8. When exercising police powers:
   to avoid being peremptory
   to weigh carefully all surrounding factors
   to be humane
   to be prudent
   to avoid equally undue zeal
   to be, and be seen to be, unfettered by obligation
9. To guard the good reputation of the force.

As a mission statement, it was an excellent document. In Chapter 11 we describe the qualities of a good mission statement; *The Principles of Policing* has most of these qualities.

Once produced, the book was circulated to everyone in the force, and each department and section was expected to discuss its principles. Newman hoped the book would touch everyone in the force at the same time and stimulate a change in attitudes and values. But it did not work. A report on the force in 1989 by consultants Wolff Olins, called *A Force for Change*, concluded:

> The employees of the Met do not share a common sense of purpose. There is no consistency of views on the overall mission of the Met, nor how each individual contributes to the whole. . . .
>
> The Met is uncertain of its role. This uncertainty manifests itself in a wide divergence of views on what is proper police work. Is it crime detection, or crime prevention, or are police officers social workers in uniform?
>
> The lack of clarity about mission and purpose is exacerbated by internal division.

People we interviewed claimed that the book was discredited and ridiculed by constables and administrative departments alike. For many, the book was seen to have done more damage than good.

The problem appears to have been that the book espoused values and behaviors that were perceived as unrealistic in the eyes of many constables and irrelevant for most of the administrative functions. Constables were faced with deciding either that their existing behavior was wrong or that their leader had lost touch with reality. Without strong reinforcement from the line of command, or major changes in the support systems or operating procedures, they were quick to conclude that Newman was out of touch and seized on parts of the book to make fun of. They picked particularly on the examples of ethical dilemmas in the book. These included issues such as whether constables should become Freemasons, or how they should react to seeing people smoking marijuana at a party. The constables viewed these as petty issues compared with the frequent dilemmas they faced, such as being confronted with aggressive youths on the streets, or the difficulty of catching known criminals while at the same time ensuring that all rules to protect the innocent were fully upheld. In 1987, for example, 4,534 officers were injured in the course of duty.

Newman's mistake, one that has been made by many chief executives, was to launch a new philosophy on an unreceptive organization. Senior force members believe that much of what Newman was trying to do was right, especially his focus on the constable and the need to change the constable's behavior. His list of behavioral standards is also viewed as valuable, and the current commissioner, Peter Imbert, is still promoting these.

Much of Newman's mission, therefore, was right. The intellectual thinking—the purpose, strategy, values, and behavioral standards—was reasonably good. His failure was in the way he tried to create change, or, in our language, in the way he set about managing the mission. He focused on producing and communicating a mission statement, instead of on helping constables to behave differently. He should have focused on finding ways to shape their behavior: to "manipulate" them into behaving in the way he believed to be appropriate. Moreover, he should have realized that many members of the force do not have personal values that match the values he was declaring in *The Principles of Policing*. It is not possible to change the behaviors of these individuals without changing their personal values. Small changes in personal values, particularly of younger members, may be realistic. For the rest, the only long-term solution is to get them out of the force, or to create a mission around values they can subscribe to.

The main lesson, therefore, to be drawn from the experience of the Metropolitan Police and other organizations that devote considerable energy to developing and communicating mission statements, is that they are focusing on the wrong activity. There is an important intellectual task in creating mission: choosing a purpose, a strategy, some values, and some behavioral standards that reinforce each other and make practical sense from both the commercial and the moral point of view. However, where many managers seem weak, and where Newman totally failed, is in the task of managing mission. This task is about demonstrating commitment to behavioral standards and values, visible leadership, socialization, shaping behavior and finding ways to edge out those managers or employees whose values are so different that their behavior will never sufficiently adjust.

Employees feel a sense of mission only when there is a match between their personal values and those of the organization. A leader determined to win support for the mission must confront this issue head on.

Successfully Developing a New Mission

In the previous section, we analyzed a common mistake managers make: excessive focus on developing and communicating a mission statement. This is a particularly common mistake among companies that use what we have come to call the *intellectual* approach to managing mission. The intellectual approach contrasts with the *founder* approach, where the mission is crafted and evangelized by the founder or his or her successors, and the *operational* approach, where a mission grows out of efforts to improve performance.

In all three cases, the objectives are to develop a mission (i.e., a clear commercial and philosophical rationale linking behavior to purpose) and then to manage the implementation of the mission in a way that wins the support of a large number of managers as well as a portion of employees (i.e., to give these individuals a sense of mission about the company).

It is important that the reader does not confuse these two objectives. Creating a mission is inevitably, at least in part, an intellectual process because mission is an intellectual concept. It is about the logic that links behavior to purpose. Converting individuals to the mission is about socialization; it is an emotional process. The individuals are buying into something. It can happen suddenly and visibly, or it can happen gradually without the individual being conscious of it. Managing mission is about both of these objectives.

Although we believe that the intellectual approach has pitfalls, there are companies that have used the intellectual approach successfully. Dist is one example. Others we identified include Borg-Warner, Ford Motor Company, Royal US, and Xerox. Moreover, we were told by the Japanese office of the corporate consultancy Landor Associates that a number of Japanese companies such as Sony, Matsushita, and Wacoal have recently been through an intellectual approach to redefine their missions, or as they call it to create an "inner identity."

The essential ingredient of the intellectual approach is the determination to define a fully formed mission as a guide for changes in behavior and decision making. The top team, often in conjunction with a wider group of managers, forms a mission task force. They work through the problem discussing all the issues until the job is complete. They then use the mission they have developed to guide future decisions and initiatives. Individual employees become converted to the mission as a result of the consistency of the top team's decision making, gradual socialization, and the hiring and promoting of like-minded people.

As we have shown in the example of the Metropolitan Police, the intellectual approach can lead to a view of mission that is out of

touch with the organization. The process of discussion and definition can clarify issues in the minds of the leaders, but it does
nothing for the followers. As a consequence, when the new mission
emerges, it can fall flat or create hostility. It is, however, possible to
avoid these pitfalls. Companies that do so have the following
characteristics.

First, if the values in the new mission are not radically different
from the previous values of the company, the danger of rejection is
reduced. Most people in a company can readily support the new
mission because it differs little from the old philosophy, and the
changes in behavior that it implies are either slight or easily accom-
plished. If the new mission is similar to the old, it becomes a
refinement of what people are already doing and helps to create
unity and a common view. In Royal US, the *Royal Vision* became a
reaffirmation of what most employees already believed in. It gave
backbone to the committed members of the company in taking
action against the cynics. The same was true for Borg-Warner. The
company had been working on its beliefs for more than ten years
before James Beré finally documented *The Beliefs of Borg-Warner*. By
1982 the *Beliefs* were not calling for a radical change in thinking. As
a result, they did not conflict with the existing culture.

At Wacoal, a Japanese textile company, a two-year program of
discussing the company's philosophy resulted in a strengthening
and extension of the company's creed rather than a dramatic
change. The creed previously read: "We the employees and management of Wacoal will maintain a proud corporate culture, based
on mutual trust, and will strive together to build a truly international company, to serve customers and society throughout the
world." The new creed was relabeled the corporate concept. It
stated: "Wacoal strives to promote the creation of feminine beauty
and to improve the culture of living. Wacoal will develop the true
human group, which is based upon a spirit of mutual trust. Wacoal
strives to realize coexistence and coprosperity with all the people in
the world." The company's principles of management were similarly altered and reworded, but overall the new mission was little
different in value terms.

In Shell UK Refining, however, the new philosophy was radically different from the old. It was intended to be, because it was
part of a bold attempt to change a situation that had become

intolerable. Inevitably, however, the new philosophy did conflict with the existing culture, creating concern and disbelief among those who could not see how it would work and hostility among those most threatened by the proposed changes.

In summary, the intellectual approach has a better chance of success when the leaders are seeking to refine and consolidate, not to dramatically change, the mission.

The second characteristic of companies that successfully use the intellectual approach is that a part of the organization is already demonstrating the effectiveness of any new behaviors that may be needed. One of the problems with the intellectual approach is the ivory tower thinking that can creep into discussions and debate. Normally, senior management form a task force to define the mission. Yet senior management are the furthest removed from the front line. Moreover, the process of debate can cause impractical thinking to become accepted before it has been tested in the field.

If one part of the organization is already demonstrating the practicality of the new behaviors and values, there is less danger of an unrealistic mission being foisted on the company. Moreover, it becomes much easier to convert individuals to the new order. A working model of it exists, making change much less threatening. At Dist, the *Our Principles* statement that emerged was largely based on the values and behaviors already in place in the white goods distribution business. This business provided proof that the new behaviors were not only possible but also realistic and commercially viable. We noted another example of this process in the Price Waterhouse partnership in Europe. The problem facing Price Waterhouse and most professional accounting firms in the 1980s was the need to shift from an auditing culture to a business service culture. Not only did the clients want their auditors to be more helpful, but the growth areas were in consulting and audit-related business services. Attempts had been made by the leadership to articulate a new, service-oriented mission for the partnership with little success. It was not until one of the audit groups in London demonstrated the effectiveness of the new mission that change began to occur. Price Waterhouse in Europe is now seen as one of the most client-sensitive professional accounting firms.

The third common feature among successful companies is that mission is not developed against a deadline but is continuously worked on and helped to evolve. Dist managers spent almost four years discussing their mission before it became agreed policy. The issues were worked on and worked on until they were resolved. Differences were not papered over and the departure of one senior manager was an important step in the process of reaching consensus. Royal US spent more than a year developing and refining its mission through staff workshops and discussions with every member of the organization. For Royal, the mission implied little change, yet it still took a year to develop. For Dist, the mission involved greater change, and hence the issues took much longer to resolve. Companies following the intellectual approach need to take whatever time is necessary to reach a consensus.

The fourth characteristic is that the mission is not hyped. Senior management do not try to thrust it down the throats of employees. They calmly declare that these are the principles by which the company will be managed and start making decisions accordingly. At Dist, the *Our Principles* document was not officially communicated to more than a few layers of management. Each business could choose how far down the organization to share the thoughts. Sam Calvert, Dist's vice president of strategic planning, explained: "We call this the trickle down concept. We let the message trickle out at its own pace. Each layer of management needs to be convinced before it makes sense to push it further." At Xerox, management launched a planning and decision-making process that pushed every department into reassessing its role and activities. The attitude in both companies was "now we have agreed on the principles, let's get on and manage the business by them."

At Royal there was more hype, but that may have been possible because the mission involved little change. In companies where the new principles suggest big changes there is no benefit in hyping them. Once the principles are agreed upon, what is needed is management action.

The founder approach to managing mission appears to be the most successful. In companies such as Johnson & Johnson, Jewel, The Body Shop, Bulmers, Disney, Egon Zehnder, Hewlett-Packard, Honda, IBM, Marks and Spencer, Matsushita, Sainsbury's, and many others, the mission has grown up with the company. The founders knew intuitively what they were trying to create. The company was an extension of their beliefs and their personality. By choosing people with similar values, managing consistently in line with those values, and enthusing people around them with their personal sense of mission and integrity, they built an organization with a mission.

Bill Hewlett, Robert Wood Johnson, Konosuke Matsushita, Egon Zehnder, Sir John Sainsbury, and Anita Roddick all tell the same story. "We did what we thought was right and what came naturally to us. We believe strongly in some key principles and we have worked hard to stamp these on the company. We believe the principles we have been following are the most important part of our business."

All of these leaders are true missionaries for their business philosophy. All have had years to fine-tune the philosophy, eliminating the impractical parts, identifying what kind of people perform best, and molding young recruits to their way of doing things. As the organization grew, the circle of influence could be expanded and disciples of the philosophy could be entrusted to continue putting the message out. For these leaders, creating a mission was not a difficult management task. It was something they did intuitively.

Because they were young organizations with few entrenched views and no established culture, the founders were able to mold the organization around their own personality and infuse it with their own integrity. Because they were individuals who had personal missions, they were able to transfer those missions to their organization. They didn't need to examine the mission intellectually or write it down. They lived it naturally and attracted others of like mind. People joining the organization could quickly recognize that they were joining a cause, not a bureaucracy. By joining, they were signing on. And after they had joined, the socialization process and the behavioral standards demanded of them reinforced the message. Individuals who felt uncomfortable would quickly realize that they needed to change their attitudes or follow a career elsewhere. In updating the mission, a successor could tap the respect for the founder and his or her ideals already embedded in the company culture.

For established companies without missions, the founder approach is obviously not possible. The leaders have to work within the constraints of an existing culture, management structure, and work force. For these companies the alternative to the intellectual approach is the operational approach. By recognizing the principles that make the founder approach successful, leaders using the operational approach can "found" a new mission, even one that involves radical change. In fact the operational approach is, in our view, the way to create a radically new mission in an established company with the greatest chance of success.

British Airways used this approach. Faced with the need to make a radical change in culture, strategy, and operating methods, the company did not start with the intellectual task of defining the mission. They started with the operational task. The initial focus was on getting aircraft off on time, improving the service given by front-line staff, and ensuring that British Airways flights offered competitive services. A new mission grew because the new operating behaviors became infused with values, but a formal mission statement was not developed until three or four years into the change program.

At British Airways the operating challenge of improving front-line service was linked with the slogan "Putting People First." The training carried out under this slogan communicated strong values about the importance of people. For most British Airways staff, these were attractive values. They gave a rationale for the changes in behavior that were being demanded, and for some they became an inspiration. The new mission grew because the new behavioral standards were underpinned by organizational values that were attractive to many of the service staff. Work became more fulfilling because it became a way of acting out some deeply held personal values. For some it was a longed-for release. The old British Airways values—associated with cost control, military lines of command, and engineering excellence—had acted as a straitjacket, causing the service-oriented staff to be disillusioned and demotivated.

Some companies have developed missions without ever having formal mission statements. One such case is Ind Coope Burton Brewery (ICBB), a brewing company located in Burton-on-Trent and a subsidiary of Allied-Lyons.[1] The company was faced with a declining market that demanded reduced costs, with outdated equipment, and with poor industrial relations that made change a potentially painful process. In 1982 David Cox was appointed managing director of ICBB; his mandate was to rebuild large sections of the brewery, restructure its management and work force, and introduce new working practices and payment systems, all within five years.

At ICBB, the values behind the management of the change project became the guiding values in the new organization. As with British Airways, the new behaviors Cox requested (teamwork, decentralized responsibility, multiskilling, and flexible working), were underpinned with values that were attractive to large sections of management and employees (such as long-term employment and free access to information). Those involved could see that the changes were going to make the brewery not only more competitive commercially but also a better place to work in. The values that emerged around the new operating procedures gave a rationale that people could relate to, something people could commit themselves to. Cox never had to write them down.

Our judgment is that companies facing a major change in mission will find it easier to follow the operational approach rather than the intellectual approach. There is no sound theoretical reason for this advice; it is based more on practical observation. The intellectual approach has more pitfalls. It is easier to copy the mistakes of Newman at the Metropolitan Police, and harder to stick to the principles of good mission management.

Principles of Good Mission Management

The management of mission is primarily about the management of culture and the management of change. These are subjects that have been extensively written about by other authors and we can draw on their wisdom to strengthen the messages we gained from our six case studies.

One of the first messages from the literature is that the chances of successful change are influenced by the context in which change is attempted. It is easiest when there is a strong leader, founder, or dominant group and if the organization is facing a crisis, an enemy or an external threat. If one of these conditions is absent, the other becomes even more important.

A second theme from the literature is that organizational culture is complex. It doesn't respond to simple programs or management initiatives. It needs to be manipulated with subtlety and won over to new values or new ways of thinking. The danger in defining some principles of good mission management is that we oversimplify.

One of the most authoritative authors on organizational behavior and change is Harold Leavitt, a professor at Stanford. In *Corporate Pathfinders: Building Vision and Values into Organizations*, he attempts to define what can be said about corporate culture that is relevant to management. He lists seven points:

1. We know that company founders have a very great impact on the cultures of their organizations, an impact that often lasts for generations.
2. The explicit and implicit messages recurrently transmitted by an organization's leaders become a major force in shaping the organization's culture. The stories that are passed on from generation to generation help to carry a company's culture along, just as they do in all other kinds of cultures.
3. Organizational cultures aren't shaped in a day. They take a long time to form.
4. Problems arise when an organization's culture differs sharply from that of the larger society around it, because members of the organization must also remain members of their larger societies. Great gaps between the two generate anger, suspicion, and rejection.
5. Organizational cultures are not necessarily internally rational and coherent. Subcultures, even countercultures, form and re-form within larger parent cultures, causing tensions that can result in revolution and collapse or in innovation and creation.
6. We know that outside enemies are powerful shapers of our cultures. The fact that there are bad guys out there helps us to know that we are the good guys.
7. And we know that while it's hard to confine and define a culture, it's even more difficult to change one.[2]

The other author we would like to quote in support of our principles is Michael Beer, a professor at Harvard who runs an executive program called "Managing Change." In one piece of research, he studied six companies attempting major change and tried to identify why some failed and others succeeded.[3] He concludes: "The lesson to be drawn is that successful transformations involve a reciprocal learning process between the top and bottom and between the periphery and the core. . . . There are no short cuts to this development process." It is, therefore, with a full recognition of the complexity of the task of managing change that we offer the following principles of good mission management.

1. Pick a Theme

Whether a fully formed mission exists or not, the starting point for managing mission is to pick a theme around which changes can be made or existing behavior can be reinforced. The themes of "quality" at Dist and "Putting People First" at British Airways gave the ideal focus to management efforts.

The successful theme will:

- be at the core of both the future strategy and the future value system
- be easy to translate into behavior standards
- have strong value associations that are attractive to large sections of management and employees
- be noncontroversial and enable all the power bases in the company to submerge their differences and give their support to it

Choosing a good theme is not an easy task. "Putting People First" at British Airways seemed to be an inspired choice. Service through people is at the core of both the British Airways strategy and the service culture Colin Marshall has been trying to create. "Putting People First" is an easy theme to translate into behavioral standards. In fact, it is itself a behavioral instruction. The values of people care underpinning the theme were attractive to most of the British Airways service staff, and the training they received helped to bring out these values. It was not just devoted to how employees could treat customers better; it addressed the whole of a person's life relationships and showed how "Putting People First" can help to improve all parts of an employee's life. For example, one of the sessions in the training was about how to greet your family when arriving home from work.

Lastly, "Putting People First" was a theme that it was hard for any power group to oppose. There were, we learned, some power groups in British Airways that did not believe that the service strategy would work. They felt that the attention given to supporting and training service staff was wasteful. For them, the key to a good airline was engineering quality and operating costs. Nevertheless, it was hard for them to undermine the "Putting People First" initiatives.

The "quality" theme at Dist has also proved to be a valuable focus for action. Interestingly, the first theme chosen by Dist management was shown to be less than ideal. In the early 1980s the central theme was "lifetime career." It was replaced by the "quality" theme when a downturn in the industrial control distribution business made it impossible to avoid compulsory layoffs.

"Quality" is a central thought for Dist's strategy and culture. It is reasonably easy to convert into behavioral standards. The values are similar to British Airways' "Putting People First" and, therefore, are equally attractive to the people that Dist employs. Lastly, the theme is noncontroversial, so long as Dist operates in businesses where there exists an opportunity for profitable differentiation based on quality. Therefore "quality" qualifies as a sound theme around which to start developing a mission.

"Quality" and "Putting People First" are interesting themes to compare because they are so similar and because they are both fundamentally trying to create the same behavioral standards in employees. It is our judgment that "Putting People First" has proved to be a more effective theme around which to build management action and employee enthusiasm. It has more of the qualities of a good theme. It is easier to translate into behavioral standards, it has more connection with employees' personal values, and it is less controversial. We believe that British Airways was unusually skillful or unusually lucky to pick the theme that it did.

Shell UK Refining also had a theme: "joint optimization." However, it failed to meet the criteria of a good theme, developed as it was by academic technicians rather than streetwise managers. It had few strategic or cultural links, was hard to convert into behavioral standards, had unclear value associations, and was too theoretical, promoting debate and controversy.

Picking a good theme is important because in any change effort management need to get started on a sound basis. Michael Beer also supports this view. He reached the conclusion that one of the four primary strategies for mobilizing energy for change was to find "a theme with which people can identify and derive meaning"(p. 29). "Quality" was a theme that served many companies well because it could appeal to all stakeholders, but he warns against themes such as "profitability." As an employee in one of the firms he studied said: "I can't get excited about 15 percent on equity" (p. 30). He also found that change programs that managers perceive as not addressing high-priority problems are likely to lead to cynicism and a loss of credibility and commitment.

Moreover, we noted that employees are quick to judge, as illustrated by the Metropolitan Police example, so management must gain some early success based on tackling important operating issues in a manner they intend to apply throughout the rest of the change program. If managers can show at the beginning that they intend to manage the changes around a few attractive principles, they can create supporters out of those who would be naturally hostile to change.

2. Actions Before Words

We have already emphasized in this chapter the importance of not focusing too much attention on words. The way to avoid this is to let actions communicate. Don't tell your organization what you plan to do—do it and then explain why afterward. Most employees have enough natural cynicism and practical experience to know that managers generally say more than they do. To gain the support of employees, leaders must try to select actions that are not only effective in their own right but carry with them clear messages about the new management philosophy.

Michael Beer's research also recognized the danger of relying on communication rather than action. He relates the story of a company in which task forces employing 100 managers spent a year developing a statement of mission and philosophy. The top management team signed on to the final product, but it met resistance further down the organization. By contrast, one of the most successful companies "*never* developed a mission statement, defined a philosophy, initiated a quality circle program, or tried to launch any other corporate program!" (p. 25). In fact, one of the reasons that this company had been successful was because it had managed to create tangible examples within the company of how it wanted to run its business. These examples helped managers and union leaders "visualize what the new ways will require of them or develop the confidence that they can actually be implemented" (p. 29).

We were particularly impressed by a manager in The Body Shop who explained that the company undersells its values to new recruits. "When they join us they are really surprised about how much we do on environmental issues and other things. After a few weeks they say, 'I know you said that you took these issues seriously, but I had no idea you actually did so much.'"

Of the case studies in which a change of mission was attempted, Shell UK Refining devoted the most management energy to documenting and communicating its philosophy; and it was probably the least successful in creating behavioral change or in converting managers to the new mission. British Airways, the most successful company, devoted little initial attention to statements and communication, focusing instead on making operational changes.

At British Airways one of the first actions was to reorganize the company's structure, creating new functions and new responsibilities for most senior managers. Another was providing training for all of the 35,000 staff. These two highly visible actions had a dramatic effect on the morale of the organization. They were reinforced by hundreds of detailed changes, ranging from a complete revamping of the corporate identity including items such as staff uniforms to a reduction in shift times on check-in desks and the introduction of hot meals on shuttle services. Some of these detailed actions captured the imagination of the organization and became as visible as the reorganization or the training. We were told one story about Colin Marshall helping at a check-in desk to reduce the line of people for the 7 a.m. Super Shuttle. Another involved senior managers helping the early morning cleaning crew to find the cause of toilet odors. The message was clear: Problems that affect customers must be resolved.

This action attitude was backed by a monthly executive committee that relentlessly followed up all these details. Through this committee, and with the help of consultants, Colin Marshall pushed through change after change. Communication was very important, but it was used, in the main, to explain why changes were being made, rather than to exhort people to change.

BA was facing a crisis at the beginning of the 1980s. It suffered enormous losses and faced the trauma of privatization. This crisis made the focus on action all the more appropriate. The organization needed the reassurance that firm action was being taken, and the crisis atmosphere may have made employees more willing to accept the action programs. Our judgment is that the element of crisis facilitates change, a conclusion that is supported by both Harold Leavitt and Michael Beer. Leavitt says:

> Crises—wars, revolutions, recessions—are great looseners of old cultures. They make it far easier for leaders to effect radical changes, even in stolid, traditional cultures. We have all seen that happen in great national crises—the American or the French or the Russian revolutions—but it also happens in organizations. Old roles and boundaries give way in crises. (p. 176)

Beer echoes the same theme in his analysis of six companies undergoing change: "Pressures, both external and internal, were the trigger for change in all six companies. In most cases, changes in the external environment were threatening the profitability and competitiveness of the company" (p. 27).

It is only when people can see that leaders really mean what they say that the supporters come out of the closet. Leadership action sets standards of behavior for the rest of the organization. Seeing a senior manager do something that perhaps has not previously been the norm says, "It's OK to do that sort of thing now." It enables people to change their behavior, without feeling that they are oddballs. The greater the visibility of the leadership style, the more rapidly people will adjust to the new order.

The Johnson & Johnson case seems to contradict our advice to focus on action, not words. James Burke's Credo challenge meetings and the subsequent redrafting of the Credo appear to be exactly the kind of management initiatives that we advise against. Yet Johnson & Johnson proved in the Tylenol affair to be a company that truly "walks its talk."

The message from Johnson & Johnson and other companies is that it is useful to focus on words and communication once the organization is highly supportive of the mission. British Airways, for example, devoted more management time to communication in the latter part of the 1980s. When the majority of people have bought into the company's culture change, it becomes appropriate to spend time enshrining the new mission in a statement. Periodically revised statements help to preserve and strengthen successful missions. But these writing exercises should not lose touch with reality. At Johnson & Johnson the Credo challenge involved testing whether the Credo matched reality. The most important of the three challenge questions was, "How should the Credo be implemented?"

It is interesting to note that, despite the huge amount of management time devoted to the Credo challenge meetings, the stories that Johnson & Johnson managers most frequently tell are about actions—the managers who were publicly fired for fudging their expenses; the Tylenol affair; and the reviews of customer complaints, safety, and other Credo priorities set by the Executive Committee. Actions are better communicators than words.

3. Focus on Behavior

Closely allied to the principles of "pick a theme" and "actions rather than words," is the need to focus on and subsequently enshrine a few key standards of behavior. A sense of mission comes from the link between behavior, organizational values, and personal values. If managers find that the way they are being asked to behave by the organization is based on some organizational values that are close to their personal values, they are likely to find work worthwhile and fulfilling—the starting point for generating a sense of mission. For example, employees asked to smile at and be attentive to airline customers because the company believes in "Putting People First" will find the work fulfilling if they personally believe that people are important.

Creating a sense of mission is about creating these behavior–values links. It is unrealistic to try to change many different behaviors at one time. Therefore focusing on a few key behavioral standards becomes essential. Creating behavioral standards is not just about promoting and encouraging the new behavior and skills, however. It is also about disciplining and removing those people who cannot or will not meet the new standards. One of the companies we talked to worked extensively with a corporate identity consultancy to define and develop its corporate image. The consultancy advised that one of the company's problems was the visual and human impression made by the front doors and reception areas of their hundred or more businesses around the country. A project was therefore launched to upgrade these areas and train receptionists to be welcoming and friendly. Large sums were invested in redesigning the head office reception in London as an example to the others. But the company kept on the same aging male porters to staff the new area. The greeting to visitors, whether from subsidiaries or outside the company, remained gruff and offhand. And within a few months these male porters had become a symbol throughout the company of the uselessness of the exercise. In no time the cynics had triumphed. I recall a finance director from one of the subsidiaries telling a story of spending ten days in London working at headquarters: "Every day I had to explain who I was at reception. Every day I got the same bored response from the porter, who then insisted that I spell my name out. And every time he wrote it down wrong." You need only a few stories like this circulating on the grapevine to undermine years of good intentions and hundreds of thousands of dollars of investment.

Michael Beer identifies the lack of a focus on behavior as a principal cause of failure in change programs. "Instead, they use words transmitted in classes, memoranda, speeches and glossy booklets. Employees have difficulty translating these words into behavioral changes" (p. 25). From his case studies he concludes:

> Those who implement successful transformations focus on behavior rather than simply talk about it. . . . Only a change in the context— structure, systems, staffing patterns, and management process—in which employees function can stimulate and sustain new management approaches. (p. 34–35)

Of the six case studies, British Airways devoted the most attention to shaping behavior and was rewarded with the most success. Possibly because the task at BA was so big a challenge, management realized that they needed to lead people by the hand to behave differently. Tremendous energy was devoted to setting a behavioral standard of helpfulness and courtesy among front-line service staff. And this was backed up by changes in the way these people were managed and supported.

A behavioral standard that is talked about less frequently at British Airways, but that was just as important to Colin Marshall, was a behavior that might be called "direct and swift management action." The problem that pervaded management ranks was symbolized by some company humor regarding telex messages. Before Marshall arrived it was not unusual for major problems to take months to sort out. The standard, almost certainly caricatured, response to anyone checking on progress was, "I sent a telex yesterday (or last week) and I am expecting a reply."

Marshall made it clear that this sort of behavior was unacceptable. The role of managers was to be at the place where action was most urgently needed, like a good football referee. If this meant flying halfway round the world to find out why spare parts were not getting to a service center, or getting up at 3 a.m. to find out why airplanes were not being cleaned in time for the early flights, then this was the duty of managers.

Marshall instilled this behavioral standard at the very highest levels of management through his executive group meetings. At these meetings he would relentlessly follow up on any and all of the problem areas that he had identified. Managers were not allowed excuses. If they did not have the answers at one meeting, they were asked to discuss it privately or to report fully at the next meeting. Because Marshall refused to drop items from the agenda until they were resolved, and because he was personally prepared to discuss each item at a detailed level, he insisted that his immediate subordinates did the same.

Focusing on behavior is not only about managing by example and training but also about people selection. In *Corporate Pathfinders*, Harold Leavitt addresses the particular problem of making change in old, well-established cultures. After discussing the role of crises and strong leaders he adds: "A third device for changing an old culture is so obvious that we might easily miss it. Change the people. Cultures are carried by people. One way to change a culture is to get rid of the old people and replace them with new ones." He further says: "Sometimes it doesn't work, usually because the surgery isn't radical enough."

British Airways was the company most committed to moving people who could not or would not change their behavior. Marshall launched his change program with the "night of the long knives." Managers remember vividly the telephone calls that they received on July 11, 1983, some in the middle of the night, asking them to come to a meeting early the next morning. Some had to leave home well before daylight to be there on time. In the reorganization, some 80 managers left, and most of the other top 100 or so found they had new jobs. The criteria for making these decisions was straightforward: Did the manager fit the new order of things Marshall wanted to create?

This determined approach to behavioral change was maintained over the next six years. One program particularly aimed at behavioral change was called "Managing People First." All managers attended it. Alongside this program the personnel function developed an appraisal form that listed the behaviors managers were expected to exhibit (see again Figure 3.1 on page 64, which illustrates a copy of the form). We were told one story of a French manager who was explaining to the personnel director, Nick Georgiades, that some of the behaviors listed were not appropriate in France. "You see, Nick, this is not the French way of doing things," he explained. The reply was, "You don't work for France, you work for British Airways, and this is the British Airways way of doing things. If you don't like it, go work somewhere else."

During Ind Coope Burton Brewery's rebuilding program, David Cox took on the challenge of creating a totally new, "greenfields" organization and plant without changing too many people or relocating from the existing site. One of many remarkable decisions he made was to create a new organization running parallel to the existing one. Cox was determined to have the right structure, and the right people in the right jobs. He also knew that he would need to reduce the number of managers by at least 10 percent. Rather than a "night of the long knives," however, he instituted a lengthy, highly open consultative process. It involved designing the new organization bottom–up around a team concept. The teams and jobs were identified, but no names were associated with the jobs.

The jobs were then filled in a cascade process from the top down. Only David Cox initially had a job in the new organization. All the senior managers went through an assessment process to see whether they had the appropriate skills, values, and personality. David then advertised internally the jobs directly reporting to him, interviewed the applicants, and made appointments. These managers then went through the same process to fill the jobs directly reporting to them, and so on down the hierarchy. Since there were fewer jobs in the new organization than in the old one, some 50 managers were left out.

It is interesting to compare the different approaches taken by Colin Marshall and David Cox. Their choice of mechanism for making people change matched well with the values and behaviors they were trying to instil in the organization. Marshall was seeking to promote a behavioral standard of "direct and swift management action." The "night of the long knives" was an outstanding example of how direct and how swift management action could be. Managers in British Airways were normally given months of notice of job changes to allow them time to wind down from one job and build up in the new one. On July 11, 1983, most managers' jobs were changed immediately. David Cox, on the other hand, was trying to promote teamwork and delegated responsibility. "Give a capable team of people a clear brief and they will do it" was his slogan. The process he used to form these capable teams was, therefore, fully in line with the values and behaviors he was trying to promote.

4. Expect It to Take Time

The fourth principle is to plan a process of mission development over years rather than months. While rapid progress can be made with changes to organizations or procedures, it takes much longer to change the way people behave and think. The simplistic view that senior management should develop a mission statement during a planning retreat and communicate it widely during the following three months is looking at the issue with the wrong time frame. Creating a new mission in an organization can take at least ten years and probably a generation. Almost every company would want the benefits Johnson & Johnson derives from its Credo, but one must remember that that statement has been in place for decades. Recognizing this time frame is important. It puts all of the other changes into perspective.

Harold Leavitt echoes our conclusion that creating a new mission takes time. He says: "Culture building . . . is a long ongoing process . . . they are shaped by . . . beliefs communicated again and again, day in day out" (p. 171).

The fact that the senior managers at Dist spent four years discussing *Our Principles* is not inappropriate if you view the whole process in a 10- or 20-year time frame. Also the long struggle Dist had during the 1980s to mold its industrial controls distribution business to the philosophy and vice versa might be seen by some as a failure—but not in the context of developing a sense of mission. The whole organization has learned a great deal from this experience and has had its values challenged at the roots. This has strengthened its understanding of the mission both from a commercial–strategic perspective and from a philosophical–moral one. The company should gain from the experience in the 1990s and thereafter.

The same is true for Borg-Warner. It took James Beré almost ten years before he felt that Borg-Warner management was ready for a statement of beliefs. Although he made a number of earlier attempts to develop a mission statement, he felt on each occasion that the organization was not ready and let the initiative drop.

If it is going to take 10 or 20 years to create a new mission in an organization, then consistency of top management is likely to be a critical ingredient. It is not surprising, therefore, that most of the organizations with missions shared by a high percentage of employees have had founders or founding families who have managed consistently, using the same values and behavioral standards over 20 years or more. The famous names such as Hewlett-Packard, IBM, Marks and Spencer, and Matsushita all benefited from continuity of leadership.

Among the six case studies, Jewel and Shell both suffered from management changes. At Shell the new philosophy was launched in 1967. It was designed to bring harmony of purpose between managers and employees, helping to reduce union militancy and overstaffing. At the beginning of the exercise, management worked hard at implementing and communicating the new philosophy. Although from our perspective they devoted too much attention to communication and not enough to creating behavioral standards, management did seek to ground the philosophy in action through demonstration projects. These projects were planned to demonstrate to managers and employees what the new order would be like. Initially, the efforts appeared to succeed in bringing management and the unions together. In 1971 the academics who had helped launch the initiative declared the exercise a success.

However, seven years later, and more than ten years after the new philosophy had been launched, different researchers came to a different conclusion. The successes achieved in the first three years seemed to have evaporated. Pressures to cut back production, a resurgence of union aggression, and setbacks in areas that had achieved the greatest success led to the new philosophy being discredited. Critically, the senior management changed during this period. The original missionaries of the new philosophy were not around to protect it when it came under fire or to stand up for the values when they appeared to be impractical. By 1978, the exercise had become widely referred to as the "be nice" philosophy that had failed. And by the late 1980s it had become an insignificant event only vaguely part of the organization's memory.

The fate of the Jewel Companies' "Jewel Concepts" shows how quickly missions can be left behind. When the company was taken over by American Stores, its chairman and the guardian of the Concepts, Wes Christopherson, departed. A new group of executives brought their own values and traditions. The Concepts are no longer circulated although they had been part of the company culture for 30 years. At stores that were part of the Jewel Companies the Concepts may be thought of as a quaint relic of past years.

That is not to say that missions do not survive the departure of the executive who instigates them. There is no doubt that Harry Smith's 15-year influence on Dist will have a lasting impact on the company's future mission; and that Colin Marshall's seven years with BA will leave a lasting impression.

Why does a mission take so long to get into the bloodstream of an organization? Why isn't it possible to define the mission in January and have your organization committed to it by December? Because it takes time to align the behaviors in the organization with the values, and it takes time to align the organization's values with the values of the employees. Converting a company to a new mission is like trying to convert a community to a new religion. If the conversion is forced, the new religion will be followed grudgingly, with people giving lip service and working to subvert the imposition. To get lasting change, the conversion has to be voluntary and as such it is a slow process.

Initially, there will be many people who instinctively support the new order. These individuals will be converted easily, probably by contact with the chief executive or leadership group. Just hearing the chief executive explain the philosophy may be enough. Seeing that person in action, changing things to support the new philosophy, will strengthen the bond. The commitment will come as much from the chief executive as from the mission itself.

After the natural disciples have been converted, individuals from the mass of the organization will gradually convert to the new order as it starts to affect their jobs and their behavior. If their values match the new values, they will gradually become committed as they find the work more fulfilling and more satisfying. If their values do not fit, they will become the organization cynics and, it is hoped, drift away over time.

But from the first there will be numbers of managers and employees who don't support the new mission and actively resist it. Many of these can be converted over time, but some will have to leave. Research into behavioral change has shown that people will accept new ways of behaving if they are gradually introduced to them. One famous experiment involved measuring how many householders would carry a large sign in their front garden supporting their political party. The researchers found that they had a higher success rate if they asked people first to put a political sticker in their window. Once the householders had taken even a small step in the right direction, it was much easier to get them to make the next step.

This process of conversion is slowed up by the inevitable ebb and flow of efforts to manage behavior. It is hard for managers to change behavior until the employees have converted to the new values implied by the behavior. And employees frequently won't commit to the new values until they see the new behaviors being acted out successfully (i.e., until they have a role model). It is a "catch-22." As a result, behavioral change and conversion of employees advance slowly and frequently face setbacks as a particular effort backfires or a new behavior pattern proves to be impractical.

5. Build and Sustain Trust

A final principle is to build openness and trust. This is partly about the way senior managers approach the changes needed, and partly about the visibility and accessibility of the leaders.

Building trust is seen by Michael Beer as one of the key means of mobilizing energy for change:

> Providing employees with information and thereby putting them in touch with the realities of the competitive environment was the basic strategy most widely utilized. In most cases this activity was preceded by trust building, although the process of information sharing itself built

> trust between management, workers and unions. Successful methods
> included sharing information about costs and quality in relation to
> competitors, employee trips to customers, and trips to Japan by union
> management teams. (p. 28)

Ind Coope Burton Brewery provides a particularly successful example of creating trust, which is all the more extraordinary because some managers in the old organization knew that they would not have jobs in the new one. David Cox achieved this trust by the open way in which he managed the rebuilding project and by the visibility and accessibility of the project team. Faced with the need to make appointments in the new organization as it developed and knowing that some of the managers could not have a place in the new structure, he chose a totally open selection process.

Most managers would have made the selection behind closed doors and waited until the last possible moment to announce the new appointment. They would have argued that the managers left out of the new organization would be disruptive and undermine the changes, and that it would be "kinder" to leave the announcements until the end of the change process.

Cox chose a process in which all jobs were advertised, individuals were assessed and interviewed, and the best candidates were appointed. He trusted people to behave responsibly; he gained their commitment to the principles and process for making the appointments; and he was rewarded for his openness with high levels of support, even from those left out. By choosing to manage an issue as sensitive as this in an open manner, Cox did much to build trust in the organization.

Another important part of David Cox's effort to create trust was the style in which the change project was managed. To symbolize this open style, the headquarters of the project team was located in prefabricated offices in the yard at the heart of the brewery. "It was designed to be the visible and focal point for the project which employees would be welcome to visit and to view progress," he explained. And this is how it turned out. The prefab offices were frequently visited by people seeking information or making complaints. They became a meeting place for people in the brewery involved in the change process. In time, as the project caught the imagination of managers, these temporary offices became a focus for their enthusiasm.

James Burke's Credo challenge meetings at Johnson & Johnson were designed to encourage openness and trust. He wanted to create an opportunity for managers to say what they really thought about the Credo and its relevance. In his opening talk he pointed out that if the Credo was just a pretense, "it should be ripped off the walls." Moreover, Burke insisted on these open discussions despite the resistance of his chairman, who was discouraged from attending the meetings because his presence would have reduced openness. Of all the managers in these cases, Burke most understood the importance of trust.

The process at Dist was less explicitly designed to build trust, but the result was similar. This was because the senior team approached the mission project with care and deliberation and because Harry Smith's style is to be highly visible, acting as advocate-in-chief for the mission.

After Dist's senior team had spent two years agreeing their *Our Principles* statement, they shared it with the next layer of management. Instead of creating enthusiasm, the statement caused consternation. The next layer of managers wanted to make major changes to the document. It would have been easy for Smith to have lost patience with the process and decided, however subtly, to push for a speedy conclusion. Instead, he sponsored a further two years of discussion before a new version was agreed upon. His motive was to build trust and consensus.

Lower down in the organization, trust was built by Harry Smith's visibility. A number of managers explained they had become committed to the *Our Principles* because they could see and sense the commitment of their leader. One manager (whose quote we have already used in the Foreword) described his conversion: "The integrity thing is very big for me. My father was a policeman, so I had already signed up for straight dealing and treating people well. I am a supporter of the philosophy because Harry obviously communicates it from the heart and his behavior supports it. It is really a commitment to Harry as much as anything else." *Our Principles* became a cause junior and middle managers could support because they knew the chief executive was committed, and they knew he would be in power for ten or more years.

As we pointed out in the previous section, the "night of the long knives" at British Airways was not a process likely to build trust.

Moreover, Colin Marshall's preference for one-to-one discussions as opposed to committee meetings was also unlikely to build trust. Working in his favor, however, was Colin Marshall's visibility and his unmistakable commitment and integrity. Everyone whom we spoke to who had a personal relationship with him commented on his commitment. Moreover, he made himself visible by visiting departments and by walking up to employees and talking to them. "When he talked to an employee you could tell that he was genuinely interested in the business and in how to make it work better," volunteered one manager.

In Shell UK Refining, the elaborate process for communicating and discussing the new philosophy was designed to build openness and trust. But the way it was handled, particularly by the consultants, left a bad taste in many people's mouths. They did not feel there had been a genuine attempt to listen to objections and disagreements. Unlike the process at Dist, managers felt that they had been sold the new philosophy without a chance to debate or consider it. This early disadvantage might have been overcome if senior management had been able to sustain the open, trusting style. But a breakdown in discussions with the unions and changes in the senior team resulted in confusing messages. As a result, the trust never fully developed.

One of the most difficult parts of creating and sustaining trust is to promise only what can be delivered. If senior management are seen to make promises that they cannot live up to subsequently, the spell is broken and all future promises are viewed with suspicion. This happened in the industrial controls subsidiary of Dist when promises of employment security could not be maintained in the face of an unexpectedly severe industry downturn.

Unrealistic promises were also perceived to have been made at Shell UK Refining. Union leaders complained that management had promised improvements in working conditions that did not occur. Whether this was a justifiable accusation or not is unimportant, because it inevitably reduced trust. In contrast, both Colin Marshall and David Cox promised very little and did not have to go back on their word.

The importance of keeping promises is another reason why publishing a mission statement at the start of a change program can prove dangerous.

Summary

Managing mission is about formulating the purpose, strategy, values, and behaviors that make up a mission. It is about disciplining the people in the organization to behave in accordance with the mission; it is about recruiting people who have a natural affinity to the mission; and it is about converting existing managers and employees to the mission in a way that engages their emotions. It has little to do with mission statements.

Mission statements are useful to those who have already been converted to the mission, as a checklist and reminder of what the mission is. They are also useful in communicating with outsiders and those who are not familiar with the company. But mission statements are not useful as a method of motivating employees or of changing behavior in employees who do not have a natural affinity to the new principles. Motivation and behavioral change are achieved only by face-to-face management and leadership, by training, and by example.

Most managers would expect to need to formulate a complete mission before they start managing the principles into the organization. Our observation is that this works well when the behaviors associated with the new mission are close to existing behaviors and values. When major change is needed, we have found that it is better to start making change based on one or two core principles and allow the mission to grow up around this core.

Whatever approach is taken, mission management takes time. A time horizon of five or ten years is realistic. Quick-fire projects don't work. Only persistence, consistency, and courageous leadership are likely to have a lasting effect.

NOTES

1. A longer version of this case study appears in the British edition of *A Sense of Mission* (London: Century Hutchinson, 1990), pp. 137–53.

2. Harold J. Leavitt, *Corporate Pathfinders: Building Vision and Values into Organizations* (Homewood, Ill.: Dow Jones–Irwin, 1986), p. 168–69.

3. Michael Beer, "The Critical Path for Change: Keys to Success and Failure in Six Companies," in *Corporate Transformation* (San Francisco: Jossey-Bass, 1988).

British Airways—
Putting the Customer First

. . . .

At the beginning of the 1980s, British Airways was in desperate trouble. As the then deputy chairman and chief executive, Roy Watts, said in a special bulletin to staff in September 1981: "British Airways is facing the worst crisis in its history. . . . We are heading for a loss of at least £100m in the current financial year. We face the prospect that by next April we shall have piled up losses of close to £250m in two years."

With hindsight it is easy to point to any number of factors that contributed to the crisis. The market had suffered a downturn, the merger of two former British airlines—the transatlantic carrier BOAC and the domestic and European carrier BEA—had left the airline overstaffed, management was bureaucratic, and industrial disputes were rife. Nor was service good. A high proportion of flights were late, the aircraft had a careworn, dated appearance, and the staff were described as being professional but aloof and impersonal.

The airline was in no state to be privatized, which was the intention of the recently elected Conservative government. The response at BA was swift and dramatic. Staff and overheads were cut radically and in the financial year 1982–83 profitability was reestablished. But while the numbers game was well on the way to being won, the underlying causes of British Airways's problems had not been tackled. The bureaucratic management was still there and staff attitudes to customer service still left a great deal to be desired. British Airways had to set about changing its corporate culture. How did it do this?

Making British Airways Profitable

British Airways was established in September 1972. Initially it was little more than a holding company for BOAC and BEA, which had previously been separate public corporations operating in separate markets. Full merger followed in April 1974 but it was not until 1977 that integration of the two management structures was finally achieved. Even so, the new company was still overstaffed.

The 1970s were difficult times for the new company. The decade started with the Middle East oil crisis, which brought higher operating costs and depressed economic activity. Competition was increasing. Another airline, British Caledonian, was competing directly with British Airways on scheduled routes and the British entrepreneur Freddie Laker had established his Skytrain transatlantic services offering low fares to a mass market.

Industrial relations at BA were a recurring problem. In the 1976–77 financial year, 87 disputes were reported, and in 1977–78 some 59,000 working days were lost. Productivity compared badly with other international airlines.

Financial performance was erratic. The decade had opened with both BOAC and BEA reporting substantial profits, but the mid-1970s saw losses at BA and a number of other airlines. In 1976–77 profitability was restored and BA continued to be profitable to the end of the decade. However, the level of profits was seriously affected by industrial disputes and low aircraft utilization. Undercapitalization and inadequate profitability had led to an increasing interest burden.

In the 1977–78 Annual Report Sir Frank McFadzean, the recently appointed chairman, said:

> Prerequisite for survival in a growing competitive market is a greater stability in industrial relations. Productivity must be improved to the level of our most efficient competitors by greater aircraft utilization and by restricting the increase in staff numbers, within a framework of corporate growth. Manpower control has never been easy, and implementation of the detailed strategy postulates considerable changes in attitude.

In 1978–79, under the management of Roy Watts, then director of finance and planning, British Airways formulated a plan for the 1980s. The key assumptions of the plan were:

- an expanding industry, with the highest growth in the leisure sector

- lower prices available from the leisure sector
- increasing deregulation, again bringing lower prices
- a need to replace a substantial part of BA's obsolete fleet to meet noise regulations
- an opportunity to reduce costs by the use of larger aircraft

The plan recognized that BA was overstaffed for its current level of activity, but it was felt that a program of layoffs would be long and costly. The strategy was to hold down staff levels and allow business to expand in line with market growth, the aim being to reduce unit costs sufficiently to meet the needs of the changing market.

In a letter to the staff, Roy Watts said: "The 1980s will not be for the faint-hearted, for the lazy, for the uncommitted, for the inflexible of mind, for those insensitive to the needs of customers and colleagues. If there are such people, they have no place in our airline. We have growth. We have a challenge. Let's get on with it. Now."

Unfortunately the key assumption of steady market growth in the 1978–79 plan proved badly chosen. The market began turning down in early 1980 and by September it was clearly in recession. The airline was £100 million below budget and was beginning to slim down its operations. By September 1981 the plan to maintain staffing levels could no longer be sustained and BA announced a survival plan. This entailed, amongst other measures, staff reductions of 9,000 by June 1982 and the suspension of 16 international passenger routes. Roy Watts described BA's situation as "the worst crisis in its history."

These cutbacks meant that by 1981–82 the airline was making a small operating surplus of £13 million compared with the substantial losses of the previous year. BA now began thinking in terms of recovery and it made reconstruction proposals to the government. The plan included a new management and organizational structure, and further staff reductions. These measures had a dramatic effect on the operating results, and in 1982–83 BA reported an operating surplus of £190 million.

King, Dunlop, and Marshall

In 1979 the Conservative government had come to power with intentions to privatize publicly owned corporations such as BA. In February 1981 Sir John King (later Lord King) succeeded Sir Ross Stainton as chairman of BA. King's long-term mandate from the government was to prepare the airline for privatization. He described his role in these terms:

> My endeavors will be concentrated on doing all I can to see that British Airways has all the resources it requires to maintain and improve its standing as one of the greatest carriers in the world.
>
> It is my intention that my principal contributions to British Airways shall be in planning, finance, and the maintenance of the well-being of the airline and its customers, all of which are vitally necessary in these days when even the strongest companies are suffering considerable change.

Two of King's early decisions were to appoint Gordon Dunlop as chief financial officer in the summer of 1982 and Colin Marshall as chief executive in January 1983 (in place of Roy Watts, who continued for a time as deputy chairman).

Dunlop had worked for DeHavilland and Hawker Siddeley Aviation. He had been chief executive with Commercial Union Insurance from 1972 to 1977 but had parted from them after a disagreement over policy. From 1979 he had spent two years with Inchcape, a shipping group in Singapore. His impact when he arrived at BA was to reverse the expansionist policies of the late 1970s and to institute rigorous controls on profitability. The volume-oriented growth policy had led to barely controlled discounting. With King behind him, Dunlop axed many of the unprofitable routes and sold off surplus TriStar aircraft to the government's Ministry of Defence. In 1981–82 the profit and loss account was showing an operating surplus, not entirely wiped out by interest charges. Dunlop decided to anticipate the costs of the intended layoffs and to write down the value of the fleet. These moves paved the way for a dramatic improvement in results in 1982–83.

Before Marshall arrived, there were the first signs of the clearing-out of managers that was to come in 1983. In the summer of 1982 Gerry Draper, the commercial director, and Stephen Wheatcroft, the director of economic development, both left the company. Draper had been closely associated with the commercial policies that Dunlop had just reversed.

Colin Marshall arrived in February 1983. At 49, he had had a distinguished career in travel and service industries. He had worked for Hertz and Avis, and had been deputy chief executive of Sears Holdings plc. At the time of his appointment he announced that his golden rule was "People Come First." Colin Marshall diagnosed the problems at British Airways in the following terms:

> What was clear was that we had an organization that didn't really understand the word profit, that was very fearful of moving into the private sector, that was quite demoralized, which was not surprising because of the 20-odd thousand employees who had been let go in the preceding couple of years. It was very demotivated indeed and therefore lacking in customer service. All that was quite obvious coming into the organization. Some of it was obvious even before I joined because I had been a very frequent commercial passenger over the years.
>
> It was also obvious to me that the organization was extremely introverted, had really no grasp of what the marketplace wanted, what the customer wanted—that the organization was almost totally lacking in marketing, certainly in marketing professionalism. There wasn't anybody in the company who had the word marketing in their title in any way at all. There had been a commercial director who had left a few months before I arrived on the scene, we had sales managers, we had advertising managers and that was about it.
>
> So it was perfectly obvious that there were an awful lot of things that had to be done. I believed that the most critical thing was for us to address the issue of customer service. In so doing we recognized the need to create some motivational vehicle with the employees so that we had a better prospect of raising their morale, and in turn seeing better customer service flow.

With hindsight it is possible to see a number of strands to the change in culture that BA experienced in the 1980s. The one with the most dramatic initial impact was the reorganization of 1983.

One of Marshall's first steps was to establish a small central group under Jim Harris, later to become marketing director, to reorganize the airline's diverse marketing operations. "One of the key groups right at the beginning, in 1983, was this ad-hoc marketing group that was put together by Jim Harris at my request. Four of the younger, brighter managers in the organization were asked to get something going. And after Jim had selected them, I interviewed them and agreed that they were the right guys."

This group was one of the main driving forces of a far-reaching reorganization of management, announced to the press on July 11, 1983. Seventy of the most senior managers were retired prematurely and the airline was reorganized under five main sections reporting to Colin Marshall: marketing (to be led by Jim Harris), operations (Howard Phelps), finance (Gordon Dunlop), engineering (John Garton), and marketplace performance (Peter Bateson). The total headquarters team would be only 100 strong.

The objectives were to anticipate rather than react to customer needs, reduce the layers of management, and enable problems and their answers to move up and down the chain a great deal faster. Marketplace performance, the department set up to ensure that the airline provided what it set out to provide, was a completely new creation and emphasized the importance of service in the new order. Colin Marshall described the new approach:

> We sought to avoid the traditional hierarchical approach to problem-solving in the airline, in which the task was handed down from A to B to C. This new approach meant injecting a commitment to personal accountability that in many departments had been lacking for too long.
>
> For instance, we gave one manager the specific task of getting the interiors of our aircraft clean. We also gave him the authority to cut across all the established lines of authority in order to get the job done. In fact he had to tread on very few toes, for once the senior line management knew what was expected of them, and understood that we wanted excellence, not excuses, remarkable things began to happen.[1]

The selection criteria for the managers of the new organization were based on "experience and intuition." As one manager explained: "In the end it came down to whether the guy could contribute to the vision of BA that we had, a BA with a marketplace focus and a responsiveness to the business needs."

The pace of the change was startling. Bob Nelson, one of the human resources managers caught up in the change, recounts:

> All appointments started immediately. It was done in a way totally different to BA's normal style where you had 28 days to move from your old job to your new job. Many managers were called up in the middle of the night and told to get on planes and come to London. It was very dramatic.
>
> I don't know if it was intentional to make it a shock event. It was probably the only way you could make the sort of changes they wanted to make.

This speed was quite intentional. To quote Colin Marshall: "It was done deliberately that way, rather than the Chinese torture dripping water method, in order to create the maximum impression on the organization, to give the message that things really were changing."

The new dynamism also showed itself in the way that Marshall managed. He was not a team man attempting to reach consensus; he managed one-to-one. His managers were given specific goals and were expected to get on with it. It was a style that emphasized individual responsibility. The approach was reflected in the board structure. Out of nine directors, only two were executive, Dunlop and Marshall. The company was run by a team of 19 executives, five of whom held the key positions.

Colin Marshall also broke down the tradition of committees, which had originated in the Civil Service and Royal Air Force connections:

> I said that the first thing that we have got to do is get rid of as many of these committees as possible without totally undermining the working of the business. So we certainly reduced an awful lot.
>
> You know the problem of committees. Nobody takes responsibility for a decision. You can never hang anybody with achievement or non-achievement. And all decisions were delayed until every member of the committee had his hand up.

The only time the executives met as a team was for monthly Executive Group meetings chaired by Marshall. He deliberately changed the emphasis away from group decision-making, allowing smaller, ad hoc groups to develop policy:

> Before I came it was recognized as the formal decision group in the company. There were 20-odd people in that group. From everything that I learned of it very quickly in talking to various people, it was a marvelous delaying tactic for decision taking, because there were 20-odd and they all wanted to express their view. So I said that it would be much more of an information gathering for the powers of the company rather than a decision-making group. We would take our decisions on an ad hoc basis in much smaller gatherings of people, tailoring each one of those gatherings to the specific issue that was at stake. So we didn't have other formal groups.

The focus in the Executive Group meetings was on issues to do with service rather than profitability or aircraft loading. Signposting, smells in 747 toilets, security gates on the flight to Belfast, the design of tickets, and how to get peanuts out of the back of seat cushions were all discussed. A manager recalls, for example: "On one Concorde flight the loo door came off on takeoff. He [Marshall] went on and on about the hinges to the engineers at every meeting."

The style of the reviews was quite hard-nosed. Notes were taken of the actions to be followed up and teams were expected to report back at the next meeting with progress. Marshall was prepared to force through his own judgments in the face of opposition. For example, when the domestic shuttle services were coming under attack from British Midland, Marshall insisted that hot breakfasts be introduced despite resistance on the grounds of cost and practicality (in the event his decision proved highly popular with hungry business travelers). The system was undoubtedly getting things done. It cut through the tradition of committees discussing things endlessly, and it overcame resistance to the concepts Marshall was trying to introduce.

Marshall was consistent about what he said and would back initiatives even in times of difficulty. As Bob Nelson said: "On every occasion I have heard him speak, whether to passengers on a flight, to graduate recruits, to managers or at a leaving party he said the same thing. He believed in it, he was committed to it and he consistently stuck with it."

Visible management was another Marshall characteristic, and one he wanted to foster in others. He went out and met the employees, and he rolled up his sleeves to help them if necessary. A senior manager tells the story of the first day of the new Super Shuttle service:

> We then had 96 people lined up in front of the BA desks. I was frantic. We were not clearing them fast enough. I tried to get some four-stripers [supervisors] to help but they said: "We are four-stripers, we can't do that." But then I happened to see out of the corner of my eye that one of the managers was helping. Guess who it was—Marshall. They were in horror, they were aghast.

Marshall himself saw part of his role as encouraging risk-taking and engendering a spirit of urgency:

> I think it was really encouraging people to get on and take decisions. I spent God knows how many hours with managers in those first years saying, "Look, you must take decisions. You have got to get your head above the parapet. If you are not taking risks you are not managing, you are not performing a management function." Everybody, or nearly everybody, was too keen on keeping their heads below the parapet. I said "I don't need managers like that."
>
> I forced a number of decisions in the early days which got some people coming to me saying that they had not had the opportunity to

give their views. I told them that that was all right. We had reached the stage that we had sufficient evidence to support taking the decision. Maybe we only had 50 percent of the evidence, but it was worth taking the risk to implement it now.

Putting the Customer First

Training had been one of the casualties in the cutbacks of the early 1980s. Marshall reversed this trend. In announcing a review of training to a press conference in March 1983, less than two months after taking charge, he said: "We may need to put people through refresher courses to really concentrate on teaching staff how to sell the airline and its services." The review led to a campaign, coordinated by BA's customer services manager Dennis Walker, which became known as "Putting the Customer First."

Passenger research showed that human relations were twice as important as operational factors in determining satisfaction or dissatisfaction. Passengers saw BA staff as being efficient but impersonal, cool, and aloof. Conversely, research into staff attitudes showed that they considered passengers in social terms, as being happy, pleasant, jovial, sour, or miserable. They saw their jobs in terms of being professional, efficient, and in control. They did not view passengers as individuals with different needs. A good passenger was one who was sociable and not "difficult." The management emphasis encouraged this view. It saw service in terms of the delivery of material products: food, drink, and duty-free items.

The first step towards creating new attitudes to customers was a training event called "Putting People First" (PPF), introduced in November 1983. The key message was "If you feel OK about yourself you are more likely to feel OK about dealing with other people." The scale was impressive. The aim was to put 12,000 customer-contact staff, in groups of 150 to 200, through a two-day course in the refurbished Concorde Centre by spring 1984. Michael Blunt, the editor of *BA News*, the airline's house newspaper, described the initial atmosphere:

> Quite frankly, the feelings among my colleagues at 9 a.m. last Thursday were anything but enthusiastic.
>
> We were a mixed bunch: 75 or so cabin crew, about half as many pilots, a score from Ground Operations London, a dozen from overseas,

about as many again from UK outstations, a couple of handfuls from Reservations, some cargo people, a telephonist or two. . . . Some had come with open minds, others keen or curious . . . the only things uniting many were the common source of pay packets and mutual bad vibes: skepticism, resignation, trepidation.

Over the two days, the participants were treated to a mixture of presentations, exercises, and group discussions.

Staff were invited to review their personal experience of dealing with other service organizations. The passenger research was discussed in detail. They were introduced to concepts of setting personal goals and of taking responsibility for getting what they wanted out of life. There were confidence-building exercises and an analysis of the power of expectation. The giving and receiving of attention was an important area of analysis . . . Simple techniques of behavioral modification were also taught to help staff to develop new approaches to dealing with upsets, coping with stress and developing a more positive attitude to themselves and others. A key theme of the course was the call to action, "What are you going to do about it?" . . . The proceedings were rounded off by a visit from Colin Marshall who gave visible support to the messages of the course and spoke of his hopes for the British Airways of the future.[2]

Reactions were mixed. Some people saw it as an attempt at brainwashing, and there were a proportion who dropped out at the earliest opportunity. Others were more enthusiastic: "I left my house thinking that I was going to be wasting two days, but I have found myself brimming with ideas. It's been very interesting," said a Senior First Officer. But perhaps the real significance of PPF was not the detailed content but what it said about British Airways' intentions. The investment of time and money, and the presence of the chief executive, emphasized the importance of service and gave people the courage to change. As a consultant employed at the time explained: "The problem is to create the emotional context in which it is all right for people to respond, it's all right to communicate with people on a nonrational basis. It made it all right for people to respond, all right to change."

PPF demonstrated that the highest levels of management recognized the importance of staff's contribution to the airline's performance. This had a strong effect, both on the level of cynicism and on the needs of the non–front-line staff to "belong" to what was going on. It was not long before staff who did not come into regular contact with customers were approaching Marshall to ask to be included:

> With the original Putting People First we started it with having only employees who were in customer interface jobs. We had a lot of cynics around in those first weeks. But after we had run the thing for something like eight weeks I had a deputation of employees from the non-customer interface jobs, the backroom staff, who said to me, "Do you realize that those people out there in the front line cannot possibly do their jobs unless we do ours well? And we see what you are doing for them, and the recognition that you are giving them, and we think that you should give us equal recognition." It was an absolute godsend having that coming from the behind-the-scenes employees. From then on we put them all together.
>
> The best thing about that was the clear indication that the cynicism had worn off and that people really had begun to believe that here was something new and perhaps this was something that was going to work.

PPF also raised other issues. Explained John Morris, a quality manager: "It was an act of faith. The message went down to the front line and it started to make them challenge what was being said by their managers. They began to say they didn't have the resources to do the job."

There were other elements to the "Putting the Customer First" program. "Customer First" teams applied techniques of quality circles to the problems of improving customer service in the employee's own workplace. This helped everyone to understand better how the organization worked. PPF was followed by "A Day in the Life," a training day involving a visit to another office or department, which gave individuals a brief introduction to staff and operational procedures in areas of the organization with which they might not normally come into contact.

Managing People First

So far, the various initiatives had been targeted at the staff level. There was an increasing recognition, however, that a change in management style was needed. The organizational changes of 1983 had begun to set the direction, a task force had been set up to examine the issue of management style, and the PPF participants were saying that their managers should be put through a similar course.

Under Nick Georgiades, the new human resources director appointed by Marshall in September 1984, a course was developed specifically for the 1,400 BA managers, "Managing People First" (MPF). Each day of the residential course had a specific theme, as an attendee described in *BA News* at the time:

> Day One was Urgency, which we were told "should come from the leader, not from events." Day Two looked at Vision—"having the image of the cathedral as we mix the cement"—creating a mental picture of what is required and what is possible. Day Three concerned Motivation, "management by expectation—expect the best, and catch them doing it right." Trust was considered on Day Four, "giving confidence to the individual to act alone and spirit to the group to act together," with Responsibility—"believing that I am in charge of my own behavior"— filling the final day.
>
> There were lectures where all 24 of us gathered together in the main room, activities for which we formed four separate groups, presentations by those groups to the rest of the team, individual work. . . . We simulated committee meetings, with video cameras trained unsympathetically on us, to show us where we had been going wrong.
>
> Half of us spent an evening blindfolded with the other half acting as guides, to show what it was like being totally dependent on, or responsible for, someone else.

The prevailing management style in British Airways was perceived as being dominated by roles and procedures:

> British Airways was a classical transport bureaucracy, somewhat analogous to the railways, whose primary agenda was to keep the aircraft flying safely. This culture had developed under government ownership in the postwar heavily regulated business environment that lasted till the early 1970s. As with all such cultures, performance was organized by roles and procedures. The underlying values were order, rationality, dependability, and system. The belief was that performance could be monitored by information systems rather than by face-to-face contact with people who do the work.[3]

MPF attempted to replace this style with something more open and dynamic. A post-course survey of MPF participants found the following results:

1. One quarter of all participants "are committed to MPF values as it is possible to measure and moreover they actively pursue its aims."
2. One third of all participants "are actively converting enthusiasm into highly committed action."
3. Twenty-eight percent had "taken virtually no action at all."
4. "Only 13 percent remained truly uncommitted to the idea."[4]

The messages of MPF were reinforced in a number of other ways. Colin Marshall and other directors attended the course to talk to the participants, and the six-person syndicate groups were transformed into personal support groups that maintained contact after the course.

A major component of the reinforcement package was the introduction of a pay-related performance appraisal system. The BA management appraisal form (see Figure 3.1 on page 64) is organized into 12 domains such as "strategic awareness," "judgment and decision making," "commitment," and "individual subordinate management." These domains are split down into 85 individual criteria against which managers are judged. Many of the criteria reflect the values being promoted in MPF, such as "Has a sense of urgency and energy to achieve results" or "Gives credit for achievements and successes of subordinates." Completed appraisal forms are then computer processed, with results being returned for discussion with the appraisee. The computer analysis monitors trends within the company, and allows a degree of checking for bias and other distortions. For the appraisee, the bottom line is that his or her level of pay is partly determined by the appraisal result, the aim being to motivate managers toward the pattern of thinking that underlies the MPF course.

Simultaneously with all these developments, the organization and the services being offered by the airline were being improved. Surveys of passengers and monitoring of complaints showed clearly that these improvements were having a positive effect on the customers, but it seems likely that they also had a positive effect on the staff. One stewardess described some of the improvements:

Crews have improved vastly. There are now much higher expectations from the top. Supervisors are now much more closely involved with the flight staff. The supervisors are now known as fleet directors and have desks in the same area as the pigeonholes used by cabin crew. This forces much greater contact. The staff didn't like the change to begin with because they felt they didn't need to be closely supervised, but it is an improvement.

Staff treat passengers better now. They are more efficient and have fewer sloppy habits. They tend to be more interested in the passengers.

Aircraft interiors, catering arrangements, and in-flight entertainment have been improved, and this was to some extent calculated to give the staff the tools for the job. Said one senior manager: "We wanted to get the cabin crews to smile, but that was pretty difficult to do when the coffee makers didn't work, the trolleys had wheels loose, and the loo doors jammed. We needed to fix the product line."

Since 1983, aging aircraft have been retired, new aircraft introduced, old interiors refurbished, and a new look given to the exteriors. The work schedules of check-in staff were also improved. It was difficult for them to maintain high standards of courtesy, friendliness, and concern when standing behind a counter for six hours on end, so they were assured breaks at regular intervals. Supervision in the passenger contact areas received particular attention. As a consultant retained at the time recounts:

> Before PPF I organized to take some supervisors to Bristol with Nick Georgiades and John Bray [another consultant]. It was part of a company-wide initiative to change the way the supervisors thought. The supervisors were always saying, "Thou shalt not," but it shouldn't all be issuing orders.
>
> We combined it with the creation of passenger service coordinators. We had been trying for ages to change the way the supervisors saw their duties. We created a new job, which was one grade up, and invited the old supervisors to apply. Linda Phillimore ran an assessment center to pick out the ones we wanted according to a new set of criteria. We were looking for candidates who were good at dealing with people.

Other improvements were less directly linked to employees but have no doubt contributed to the general air of professionalism at British Airways. The approach to quality management now in force is worth particular mention. Corporate quality standards are established centrally, with local variations being permitted if these can be justified. Responsibility for the preparation and execution of quality plans firmly rests with the local management, the central group providing support and counseling. The customer, however, remains the final arbiter, with consumer surveys and other reports providing feedback on performance. As John Morris, a quality manager, put it: "There is a much more positive attitude towards service nowadays and it produces results. In the old days, reporting used to be via locally produced returns and it was easy to pay lip service to the idea but not really do anything. Now we have a system of remote measures of performance, in addition to the local reports, which makes it quite clear what is going on."

BA's customer service handbook, *Quality in Customer Service*, classifies standards as being "soft" or "hard" according to whether they refer to the way that staff behave or to the performance of the airline systems. The soft standards place particular emphasis on the way that staff relate to passengers. For example, if you were a passenger, staff would be expected to:

- immediately acknowledge your presence in a warm and friendly way
- create an informal atmosphere to make you feel relaxed and able to approach BA staff
- have a positive approach and use your name
- give you factual explanations
- anticipate your needs
- tell you the genuine reason for your delay as early as possible and give you regular updates when promised
- realize that you may be upset and that you'll want to know what the staff will do about your problem
- not overreact and make promises that cannot be kept

The Development of a Mission and Goals

Since his appointment in 1983, Colin Marshall had spoken consistently about the need to make British Airways a service-oriented business. In fact, it was as early as April 1983 that the aim "To be the best" was set in a statement, which included the following objectives:

1. To provide the highest levels of service to all customers, passengers, shippers, travel agents, and freight agents.
2. To preserve high professional and technical standards in order to achieve the highest levels of safety.
3. To provide a uniform image worldwide and to maintain a specific set of standards for each clearly defined market segment.

4. To respond quickly and sensitively to the changing needs of present and potential customers.
5. To maintain and, where opportunity occurs, expand the present route structure.
6. To manage, operate, and market the airline in the most efficient manner.
7. To create a service and people-orientated work environment, assuring all employees of fair pay and working conditions and continuing concern for their careers.

The statement ended thus: "The achievement of all objectives will be managed so as to be consistent with, and contribute to, our earning a profit sufficient to provide an acceptable return on assets employed."

It was not until 1986 that this statement was developed into a formal mission statement. The pressure for a new mission statement emerged out of the "Managing People First" course, which had devoted some time to getting the attendees to develop their own vision of BA's future. It was natural for the attendees to ask how BA saw its corporate mission. To attempt to fill this gap, Nick Georgiades organized a conference for the BA executives at the Anugraha Centre in Egham, with a small team of consultants to act as advisers. Unfortunately, the executives could not reach a consensus, and no usable statement of BA's mission emerged.

Bob Nelson recounted how Georgiades got around this problem:

> So we got the course participants to do corporate mission statements. Each course produced four versions and these were presented to Marshall or Dunlop or whichever executive attended MPF. It became apparent that they were pretty good, and Marshall began saying, "Shouldn't we have one of these?"
>
> Nick and I wanted to make sure that Marshall and the board produced their own statement, so for a while nothing happened. After a year we had 240 different statements and Nick and I put together four composite versions.

Marshall used these drafts to produce a corporate statement of mission and goals, which he presented to the top 200 managers in a marquee in the still unfinished Terminal 4 at Heathrow. This was followed up with a center spread in *BA News* and the distribution of a plastic-covered pocket-sized memorandum (see Figure 5.1). As one manager explained:

> The choice of the venue for the presentation was creative and quite significant. He used an overhead projector and explained each statement step by step. It was obviously something he had thought a lot about and he used his own words to reinforce the messages.
>
> Now the MPF courses have a corporate mission they can start with. It hasn't changed the effectiveness of the sessions, but managers continue consistently to come up with better mission statements. And, of course, they get committed to their own statements.

With only minor adjustments to the wording, this statement was still in use at the end of 1988. The new statement still retained the original aim of being "the best and most successful airline in the world," but the rest of it was now couched in more high-minded terms. It talked about "corporate charisma," "a creative enterprise," "caring about its people," and being a "formidable contender." The whole tone had become more inspirational.

It is difficult to judge how useful this statement of mission and goals has been. Employees seem to remember the statement being publicized in 1986, but they tend to recall only the overall aim "to be the best" and a few of the phrases out of the rest. For example, Darren Briggs, former senior import assistant, now working in human resources, admits: "I couldn't recite it but I remember that it says something about being the best and most successful airline, and being the training ground for talented people. Being able to recite it would be complete brainwashing wouldn't it? I think most people are subconsciously aware of it."

Clearly, the statement was a useful device for the MPF course, concentrating the mind on where BA should be going, and at least one MPF attendee, Stan Mason, senior manager systems, has found it useful subsequently:

> Managers felt as though they had contributed to it. I can see some of the things that we said at the time [in MPF] as being in there.
>
> It helps individual managers to build up their own departmental objectives. Perhaps it is a bit over the top and verbose, but it is a good reference point. To be of value it needs to be used in a working environment, rather than just hanging it up on the wall.

Figure 5.1 **BA's 1986 Mission Statement**

BRITISH AIRWAYS

The Aim

To be the best and most successful airline in the world, earning good profits in whatever it does.

The Mission to 1990 and Beyond

British Airways will have a corporate charisma such that everyone working for it will take pride in the company and see themselves as representing a highly successful worldwide organization.

British Airways will be a creative enterprise, caring about its people and its customers.

We will develop the kind of business capability which will make British Airways the envy of its competitors, to the enhancement of its stakeholders.

British Airways will be a formidable contender in all the fields it enters, as well as demonstrating a resourceful and flexible ability to earn high profits wherever it chooses to focus.

We will be seen as THE training ground for talented people in the field of service industries.

Whether in transport or in any of the travel and tourism areas, the term "British Airways" will be the ultimate symbol of creativity, value, service, and quality.

The Goals Are to Be . . .

The best and most successful in the field of travel, tourism, and transport.

Known as the most efficient, the most customer-concerned as well as the safest at whatever it does.

Sure that the term "British Airways Manager" is synonymous with people-concern, high achievement, and general business capability.

continued

Figure 5.1 **(continued)**

Maintaining constantly improving targets as a good employer as well as manifesting concerns for social and community opportunities and environmental standards wherever the company operates.

Achieving a level of return on investment so that any shareholder will value his/her involvement with British Airways, and see it as an important and sound investment.

Source: British Airways News, Special Publication on Gatwick (Autumn 1988).

But another manager, Mike Bruce, senior development projects manager, had reservations about its effectiveness:

> It did reinforce the general thrust and direction. But the problem that managers have is that in business terms it's a cream puff. The statement of objectives that was subsequently produced gave a better insight into what the business is all about. But there is still an absence of linkage between the mission and goals, and the corporate objectives.

Has British Airways Been Successful?

From all the accounts given by employees, British Airways is now a radically different place to work when compared with the BA of 1980.

> "People develop a sense of self-preservation. Now things have got to get done. In the old days British Airways lacked the smack of firm government."—*Mike Bruce*
>
> "A manager I know who had gone to British Caledonian and who came back into British Airways said that the organization had been totally transformed. I have talked to one of the consultants who helped us with 'Putting People First' and who had also been into British Caledonian. I asked her how she would compare the two organizations. She said that British Airways was the most professional organization she had ever dealt with . . . but not the nicest. Caledonian are nicer people, but they are not professional."—*Mike Bruce*
>
> "Four years ago we conducted a massive research study. The average passenger saw us as cold, aloof, and distancing. This has all changed under Marshall."—*John Morris*

"Colin Marshall is unvarying in his message. It's always the same. I am not sure that there is the same sense of mission on the ramp and areas of similar culture, but certainly from the junior management upwards the message is crystal clear."—*John Morris*

"I feel proud to work for BA. People outside BA recognize the achievement, especially when they travel on the airline. They comment on the cabin service."—*Darren Briggs*

The view of a much improved business was confirmed by systematic interviews of BA managers conducted in the summer of 1988. They saw the airline as being more professional, customer-led, adapting, innovative, and full of purpose. British Airways is also producing better results. Since 1980, productivity has increased by over 50 percent, flight punctuality has improved, and profitability has been restored. The customers recognize the improvements in service as shown by BA's own statistics, which monitor passengers' response to cabin service. And the actual improvement in service is greater than these statistics imply. A survey in late 1986 showed that passengers' expectations had increased over the previous three years, reflecting the efforts of all airlines to improve service. BA has been improving in a market that is becoming more discerning.

The re-launch of the long-haul business service under the title "Club World" illustrates the impact that attention to service and staff can have. As Nick Cooper, Club World Brand Manager, explained:

Since its launch in January 1988, Club World has increased its share of the market by four or five percentage points.

On the human side we took the time to train cabin crews on Club World specifically. Up till then it had generally been only First Class that had a specific training program.

Club World actually came out of cabin crew feedback. The physical layout includes a lot of the features that they wanted. So they own it and believe in it. They are proud to present it.

The airline now regularly wins awards. Typical of these was the poll run by *Business Traveller* magazine, and reported in September 1988, in which BA was voted the world's best airline, beating Swissair, which had been winner for the previous four years. BA was cited for its "friendly attitude throughout the airline," "overall efficiency and excellent customer service." The airline won the award again in 1989, as well as a host of smaller, national awards.

But despite these improvements, the airline still has some way to go. The restoration of profitability and the improvement in punctuality came before the "Customer First" campaign was initiated, and the return on sales has actually declined somewhat since 1981–82. The cost base is still a cause for concern. Customer service also leaves room for improvement. While it wins awards on its overall service performance, it does not take all the laurels in specific sectors. In a recent *Business Traveller* poll, for example, Virgin Atlantic won the best long-haul business class category, with BA coming fourth. BA cannot yet claim "to be the best." A senior manager says: "There are still sections of the marshmallow to be tackled. Cabin crews, reservations, check in, and marketing have all changed, but there are other areas that have not."

If we accept that BA has established a new culture, and the evidence suggests that this is the case, what form does it take? At all levels it is clearly about "putting the customer first," the customer service focus established by Marshall back in 1983. At a management level, it appears to be about getting things done, responding to the business challenges, and not standing on ceremony in doing it. Other aspects of mission have been brought in, such as making sure that BA is synonymous with concern for people and making an adequate return on investment, but it is less clear whether these have been so widely taken on board either by the work force in general or by managers in particular.

Will British Airways Continue to be Successful?

The BA experience has not been without its problems. Some people saw an inherent conflict between the values being promulgated by MPF and the reality of the management style in the workplace. As one manager put it: "There's not a lot of point in taking water out of a muddy pool and purifying it, if all you are going to do is pour it back in the pool." And again from another manager: "There is still the underlying dilemma. Managers are being asked to care for their people, but they have difficulty in doing that if they don't feel cared for at a personal level themselves. Pressure on performance suggests to managers that this is more important than people." And yet again:

> The messages coming out of MPF conflicted with the style of the organizational changes that had taken place. MPF was about trust,

leadership, motivation, and visioning. In parallel with this, there was a machete environment of hacking out organizations. It produced a conflict in the minds of the managers and staff. I am not saying that the organizational changes were not necessary, but the way that they were made needed to be explained and reconciled with the values portrayed in MPF.

There are also some indications that the one-to-one management approach is not wholly appropriate to some aspects of what is undoubtedly a complex business. Explains senior development projects manager Mike Bruce:

> The problem is that there are many things in an organization, which is dealing with complex interactive systems, which cannot be fixed by one person because they transcend individual responsibilities. They have to be addressed on a team-working basis. One of Marshall's strengths has been to give people individual responsibility, but this has a downside. There are occasions where a team approach is more appropriate. Team-working is still a problem.

The recent appointment of new finance, marketing, and human resources directors has given Colin Marshall a team that is more of his own choosing. This may give him the opportunity to develop a stronger team approach.

British Airways sees itself as competing on a world scale, and of necessity this will be in an increasingly deregulated and competitive environment. Although BA has made major strides in the improvement of service and in cost reduction, it is a leader in neither field. As Marshall sees it:

> The big fields for us to conquer, to face up to in the future, I think are largely associated with liberalization of the air transport industry in Europe and seeing the opportunities and the threats that that brings along. And whichever way you finally elect to go will turn it either into a threat or an opportunity. That involves trying to imbue to the maximum extent possible the competitive atmosphere within one's employees, and particularly within one's managers—and the utmost in cost control, seeking to improve the unit cost factors.

As we have already seen, some managers register a conflict between the people-related values espoused by BA and the getting-it-done values dictated by the business environment. In the early 1980s generous severance payments and outplacement programs sustained the credibility of the caring values, but it is not clear that such an approach could be guaranteed at all times in the future. The increasing need to compete on a global basis will mean an increasing necessity to make the most cost-effective use of manpower. The challenge for British Airways is to manage these changes while still caring for its people and retaining their commitment.

Lessons from the British Airways Story

At this stage BA's efforts seem to have been successful. In fact, we would argue that BA has gone a long way toward creating a "sense of mission" among many people we spoke to. The keys to this success have included:

1. *The selection of simple and appropriate themes encouraging care for people and personal accountability.* Business success depends on good service and this means that staff have to care for customers. In turn, if managers care for their staff then staff will be more likely to respond to customers' needs. Success also depends on flexibility, professionalism, and the ability to seize opportunities in a dynamic marketplace. Encouraging personal accountability encourages these qualities. The choice of "Putting People First" as a theme for change was inspired and may have had more impact on the organization than insiders realize. It gave a moral rationale for changes that were initiated to meet a strategic need.

2. *Consistent, persistent, courageous, visible, and open leadership.* The symbolic acts of Marshall and some of the senior group reinforced the chosen themes and demonstrated determination. They created the trust and energy that was needed to bring about change.

3. *Focus on behavior.* From the first, management recognized the importance of changing people's behavior. This could be because British Airways is a service organization, where the behavior of front-line staff is an essential part of the product, or it could be because senior management recognized the importance of managing behavior. For whatever reason, the focus on behavior was one of the principles behind BA's success. It guided them into the "Putting People First" programs. It then guided them into the "Managing People First" theme

and the assessment forms based on behavior traits. The desire
to make sure behavior changed kept the efforts of management practical and to the point.

4. *A long-term view.* Marshall and others around him recognized
that the changes would take a long time. One of the striking
features of our interview with Marshall was his modesty
about what had been achieved and his focus on the work still
to be done. Also we were struck by the concern of other managers that the momentum for change should be kept up even
six years after Marshall had arrived. All seemed to be aware
that the organization could slump back into its old ways without constant stimulation.

As we go to press, BA has announced a new mission (see Figure
5.2). This has involved a major communication effort including a
corporate video and a cascade process for each department to
develop its own mission and goals in line with the corporate view.
It is being reinforced by a computer-based system for measuring
management's success in implementing the mission.

BA readily acknowledges that other than the overall "to be the
best" theme, the previous mission statement did not penetrate
deeply into the organization's consciousness. Few employees even
knew of the existence of the full, detailed statements. The new
mission has been simplified to make it more relevant, easier to
communicate and easier to remember. We feel, however, that it is
unlikely to make a more lasting mark than the previous statement
despite the effort to communicate it. This is because, like the previous statement, the new mission fails to communicate behavioral
standards and values that can touch the emotions of employees.
The statement does not pick up on the themes that we believe have
energized the organization, such as "Putting People First" and
Marshall's action orientation. In other words, we are not convinced
that the mission in the minds of employees is the same as either
version of mission statement.

We recognize that the new mission statement is an attempt by
Marshall to maintain momentum for change. Given his personal
energy and track record, we would expect him to be successful. But
we are concerned that BA has missed a chance to build into the
mission statement the themes that have energized the organization.
Time will tell.

Figure 5.2 **BA's 1990 Mission Statement**

MISSION AND GOALS

Mission

- To be the best and most successful company in the airline industry.

Goals

Safe and secure
- To be a safe and secure airline.

Financially strong
- To deliver a strong and consistent financial performance.

Global leader
- To secure a leading share of air travel business worldwide with a significant presence in all major geographical markets.

Service and value
- To provide overall superior service and good value for money in every market segment in which we compete.

Customer driven
- To excel in anticipating and quickly responding to customer needs and competitor activity.

Good employer
- To sustain a working environment that attracts, retains, and develops committed employees who share in the success of the company.

Good neighbor
- To be a good neighbor, concerned for the community and the environment.

To achieve these goals, we must:
- Deliver friendly, professional service consistently through well-trained and motivated employees.
- Search continuously for improvement through innovation and the use of technology.

continued

Figure 5.2 **(continued)**

- Employ planning and decision-making processes that provide clear direction and sense of purpose.
- Foster a leadership style throughout the organization which encourages respect for individuals, teamwork, and close identification with customers.
- Strive constantly to achieve agreed standards of quality at competitive cost levels.

In Chapter 11 we address the issue of mission statements and explain the basis on which we are able to judge statements such as BA's *Mission and Goals*.

NOTES

1. Sir Colin Marshall, "British Airways," in *Turnaround: How Twenty Well-Known Companies Came Back From the Brink*, ed. Rebecca Nelson (London: Mercury Books, 1988).

2. Mike Bruce, "Managing People First—Bringing the Service Concept to British Airways," *Industrial and Commercial Training* (March-April 1987).

3. Ibid.

4. Roger Poulet and Gerry Moult, "Putting Values into Evaluation," *Training and Development Journal* (July 1987).

Testing a Tradition at
Johnson & Johnson

· · · · · · · · · · · · ·

Johnson & Johnson is a widely diversified international health care corporation that has divided its operations into three major business segments: consumer, professional, and pharmaceutical. Founded in the late 1800s by three brothers, the company is still best known for its original business in baby products and sterile bandages. Today its products range from baby powder to toothbrushes, pain relievers to intraocular lenses. The company operates more than 170 businesses in more than 50 countries. Worldwide sales totaled over $12 billion in 1991.

Johnson & Johnson's corporate headquarters are located next to the original J&J site in New Brunswick, New Jersey. The rest of the organization is far-flung both geographically and managerially. Each company is headed by its own president (called a managing director in most locations outside the United States), and each has a board of senior managers to help set policy. The presidents report directly or through a Company Group Chairman to the powerful Executive Committee, all insiders with long-term operating experience at Johnson & Johnson. Company presidents, however, are usually left very much on their own in determining how they will manage their particular companies.

The company is almost fanatical in its emphasis on decentralization, a legacy of General Robert Wood Johnson, who became head of the corporation in 1932. J&J has resisted centralizing many familiar managerial functions, such as corporate strategic planning. It is nothing to hear that in entering a new market the corporation has directed a company president simply "to set up a new business." Attempts to centralize certain marketing areas in an effort to respond more efficiently to end-user needs have taken years to gain acceptance from company presidents.

Johnson & Johnson is widely celebrated for its corporate Credo. While the Credo is the "glue" that holds the company's values together, the ways in which it is made an effective element in managerial thinking are quite varied. There are many formal programs but also many informal and subtle reinforcements of those programs. This study of how J&J's Credo evolved and undergoes constant renewal is a vivid example of how a strong mission statement can have a profound impact on the way in which an entire company thinks about its managerial responsibilities.[1]

The Origins of the Credo

Johnson & Johnson's first businesses required a high emphasis on quality and brand reliability. Especially in wound dressings, the provision of a reliably sterile product established the company's reputation among medical workers. The health industry's trust in J&J products led to increasing business success.

General Robert Wood Johnson wrote down his general principles of success for the enlightenment of other business people in the trade. These included emphasis on product quality, decentralization, and many ethical principles concerning individual dignity. In 1945, after 35 years with the company, Johnson published these thoughts in a document entitled "An Industrial Credo." Richard B. Sellars, chairman of J&J in the 1970s, points out that although the General probably did not author the precise words of the Credo, the philosophy was his own, and that he was "really attempting to define for his associates and for the business community and for his peers some of the things he felt very seriously about."

Four central responsibilities were identified in the Credo. (A full text of the current Credo appears as Figure 6.1.) The statement is remarkably succinct, and surprising in comparison to most codes of ethics. Instead of stating a set of rules, "Our Credo" begins with a list of valued relationships:

- customers
- employees
- the communities in which these people live and work
- stockholders

Figure 6.1 **Johnson & Johnson Credo**

OUR CREDO

We believe our first responsibility is to the doctors, nurses and patients, to the mothers and fathers and all others who use our products and services. In meeting their needs everything we do must be of high quality. We must constantly strive to reduce our costs in order to maintain reasonable prices. Customers' orders must be serviced promptly and accurately. Our suppliers and distributors must have an opportunity to make a fair profit.

We are responsible to our employees, the men and women who work with us throughout the world. Everyone must be considered as an individual. We must respect their dignity and recognize their merit. They must have a sense of security in their jobs. Compensation must be fair and adequate, and working conditions clean, orderly and safe. We must be mindful of ways to help our employees fulfill their family responsibilities. Employees must feel free to make suggestions and complaints. There must be equal opportunity for employment, development and advancement for those qualified. We must provide competent management, and their actions must be just and ethical.

We are responsible to the communities in which we live and work and to the world community as well. We must be good citizens—support good works and charities and bear our fair share of taxes. We must encourage civic improvements and better health and education. We must maintain in good order the property we are privileged to use, protecting the environment and natural resources.

Our final responsibility is to our stockholders. Business must make a sound profit. We must experiment with new ideas. Research must be carried on, innovative programs developed and mistakes paid for. New equipment must be purchased, new facilities provided and new products launched. Reserves must be created to provide for adverse times. When we operate according to these principles, the stockholders should realize a fair return.

Long before the term "stakeholders" was created to encompass all people served by a corporation, J&J's Credo was directed to them. From the beginning, stockholders were listed last. John Heldrich, a former member of the Executive Committee, confirmed: "There's no separation of the responsibility we have to the four key components of the Credo. Our philosophy is that if we do them all well, the stockholders will benefit."

The Credo is, in former chairman and CEO James Burke's words, "the common denominator of what we can all believe in," yet it depends for its effectiveness on high individual commitment and autonomy. The concept of trust is essential. Top management trusts in an individual manager's ability to make the right decisions from both a business and a moral point of view. The business values that are stated in the first paragraph of the Credo and echo throughout the statement describe a set of conditions by which all of the company's constituencies may trust in Johnson & Johnson. At the same time, top management are ready to act as final arbiter and determine "the spirit of the Credo" on those occasions when there is disagreement and the company's franchise is in some way threatened.

Despite J&J's need for trust, the Credo does not include the word "honesty," and other ethical principles such as fairness and justice appear in only a few places. And yet the document's text is extremely important, for it manages to express in integrated terms sound ethical principles and the regular activities of business management: product choice, delivery times, costs, employee compensation, corporate taxes, maintenance of company property, new equipment, financial reserves. In short, the statement is succinct and relevant. It uses a vocabulary which is familiar to management but describes principles and relationships that extend beyond costs and earnings.

Though still true to the General's basic tenets, the Credo has not been an untouchable document. In 1948 the title was changed to simply "Our Credo," which it remains today. Later in the 1950s Jim Burke was among those who worked closely with the General to modernize and refine the statement's wording so that it was better adapted to in-house use. Among the changes made at the time was the substitution of the words "of highest quality" for the former "good quality." "Make them better at lower cost" was changed to "reduce the cost of these products." General Johnson remained active in the management of the company into the 1960s, and there were no distinct programs to reinforce the Credo during this period.

The Credo Challenge Effort

As the General's presence faded, more deliberate attempts to communicate the company's value system were instituted. In 1972 the Credo was the theme of the J&J annual report. During that same year, a series of ten Credo dinners, headed by then-chairman Philip B. Hoffmann, was conducted for more than 4,000 management employees to reinforce the Credo beliefs. The next major step in the Credo's evolving programs occurred in 1975 when then-president James Burke decided to hold a series of meetings with top management to test the validity of the statement. The Credo, now over 30 years old, was still significant to top management, but was it really as meaningful a statement of responsibility for all managers, as it had once been intended to be?

Several events led up to Burke's asking this question at this particular time. First of all, the American public was generally concerned about corporate misconduct. When an improper payments incident was discovered in one of the foreign operations, top management wondered whether a stronger statement of expected standards of conduct should be issued.

The Credo Challenge Meetings that resulted were not simply a quick housecleaning effort after the discovery of a few dust bunnies. They marked the beginning of a long-range program to challenge every manager to make an informed commitment to the Credo's way of doing business. This effort was in essence a series of "reality tests" to determine whether the Credo's principles were still relevant to the current business climate, whether the organizational realities reinforced or inhibited compliance, and whether the statement itself had a "real" presence in the company.

Burke's own belief in the statement was singularly strong, and he was personally bothered to think that it might be losing its meaning over time. His thoughts were strongly influenced by his own team. Ever since Burke had become president, one of the industrial relations executives had been arguing that although top management fervently believed in the Credo, little was being done to promote it within the company or even to communicate top management's commitment.

Burke resisted the idea of simply imposing a statement top-down, as so many mission statements and ethical codes are. When one manager suggested that the Credo be published once a week for a year in the company newsletter, Burke rejected the idea as "too pompous." When someone else suggested that each senior manager be allowed to sit in on one meeting of the Executive Committee in order to get a feel for the values which drove their decision-making, Burke felt it would be "too confusing." The extreme emphasis on give and take, the evolution of policy over time, and the lack of rigid territorial boundaries in the Executive Committee's comments would fail to provide any meaningful leadership to the operating managers.

Burke decided instead to hold a series of "discussions" with top managers about the validity of the Credo in their own business climate. This idea was in true J&J style. They would start with the one unifying standard the company had—the Credo—and then turn over to the operating managers the responsibility for evaluating how relevant its statements still were. Out of this notion developed the Credo Challenge Meetings.

The suggestion to hold such meetings had met with resistance. Burke especially recalls the strong reservations of Richard Sellars, then the chairman and CEO. Sellars felt that neither Burke nor any other manager had the right to challenge the Credo. Its authority superseded any individual in the organization. Moreover, what if the company presidents rejected the document? This was the only serious disagreement Sellars and Burke ever had. Burke continued to press for the meetings, arguing that the Credo could never be dictated and needed more visibility. If it wasn't meaningful to the thousand-plus managers in top positions around the world, he argued, the statement was a farce.

The Credo Challenge Meetings took place over more than three years, beginning in 1975, with a total of 1,200 managers attending. Company group chairmen, company presidents, managing directors, and other executives gathered together in groups of 25 or fewer to discuss the Credo over a two-day period. Either James Burke or corporation president David Clare presided.

The meeting leader began by asserting his own belief in the Credo, and his insistence that the company have a basic philosophy

that reflected the real beliefs and needs of the corporation. He read
through the statement, discussing his own interpretation of individual points in it either by telling war stories or by simply explaining
the words in more detail. Then he turned the discussion over to the
other managers.

Three challenges were issued:

1. Is the Credo still applicable in whole or in part?
2. Are there any changes which should be made?
3. Most importantly, how should the Credo be implemented in
   the management of Johnson & Johnson companies?

Burke and Clare continually emphasized their determination to
take a hard look at the Credo. The mere fact that they were holding
these meetings indicated their seriousness—very few centralized
meetings are held at J&J. Equally important to the final impact of
the process, they encouraged an open discussion. This may have
been easier to achieve in the J&J culture, but the emphasis on openness cannot be taken for granted. Richard Sellars, for instance, had
to remove himself from these meetings. In his words, he "breathed
too heavily on the process." Burke confirmed: "Dick was not autocratic about many things, but he was on this one thing."

Burke helped encourage open discussion by observing at the
outset of the meeting that the Credo was hanging in J&J offices
around the world, but if people were not committed to it, it was "an
act of pretension and should be ripped off the walls."

What resulted was, in Burke's words, "A turn-on. A genuine
happening." As managers struggled with the issues of the Credo,
two things became clear: balancing all the responsibilities outlined
in the Credo was very difficult and required discussion, and most
managers had an intensely personal commitment to seeing that the
Credo was preserved. No one was trying to "teach" ethics or proclaim a mission. Managers came into the meetings with their own
beliefs and did not leave with a totally new set of beliefs. Rather, the
discussions were effective at sparking a greater intensity of
commitment and a deeper understanding of what a Credo business
philosophy involved.

One of the most effective aspects of the Credo Challenge Meetings, according to Corporate Vice President James Utaski, was the
voice of collective experience. When, for example, some managers
questioned whether it was really the case that top management

would not allow stock price to override other considerations of the Credo, many others told of specific experiences where this was clearly the case. The general consensus was that though the values were "somewhat idealistic," they were not far off from reality.

Another company president confirmed this opinion:

> At the Credo Challenge Meetings you discover, listening to your peers, that it [the Credo] has crept into everyone's value system. Finding that out is really beneficial. You come away with a healthy respect for the document and what it says, and you pass that on in your own companies.

Furthermore, interviews repeatedly revealed that the meetings brought the Credo principles out of the closet, as it were, so that managers further down in the organization felt as comfortable about referring to the Credo or its principles as did those at the top of the organization. Most managers emphasized that the Credo has an indirect but nevertheless powerful influence on their decision making and behavior. It is not that they constantly refer to it by pulling out the document whenever they have an important decision to make. Rather, it stands for values that are expected every day and that are important to maintain in the future.

Credo Challenge Meetings are still held for new top managers. In addition, these two major follow-ups extend throughout Johnson & Johnson.

1. Company Challenge Meetings

Company presidents are encouraged to hold their own Credo Challenge Meetings with their own top management groups. A kit has been provided for this purpose, which includes very general guidelines for the discussion (including the three original challenge questions). This program is not without its own challenges. As one company president remarked:

> You feel pretty awkward getting up in front of your people and saying, "Now I'm going to read through the Credo." But when you've seen Jim Burke do it and how it inspires you, well you just go ahead.

2. Revision of the Credo

The second major development of the Credo discussions was the 1979 revision of the Credo itself. This process involved top discussion in the Executive Committee and much personal commitment from the top two officers of the company. Jim Burke estimates that he spent at least 50 to 60 hours on the wording of the revisions, some of which are major changes in format, while others are simply a matter of fine-tuning the statement to the current business environment. The most controversial deletion was the phrase, "with God's grace." Among additions, responsibility for a working environment that is healthy and safe as well as clean was spelled out, while responsibility to the environment and natural resources was added to the definition of good community citizenship.[2]

Most of these changes could be said to reflect major social issues in American society as a whole during the late 1970s, but two were purely a result of the corporate world view: The word "products" was changed to "products and services," and the phrase "our dealers must make a profit" was altered to read "our suppliers and distributors must have an opportunity to make a fair profit." The last change seemed to be a more accurate reflection of the responsibility of the company toward suppliers, and the fact that so minor a difference in wording was incorporated is one indication of how important it was to top management for the contents of the Credo to be realistic.

James Burke introduced the new document before 150 managers at the Worldwide Managers Meeting, which is one of the most significant meetings at J&J. He called it a "revitalized Credo—a statement of purpose that everyone now not only understands but has had the chance to contribute to." Typical of J&J's culture, everyone was said to own a piece of the Credo, and the tenets have remained generalized so that each individual has the discretion to apply it most appropriately to his or her business.

Communicating the Credo

The Credo is very much a living document at J&J. It is given high visibility through a variety of communication channels. Copies are everywhere, from the employee entrance at headquarters to brochures produced by various departments. The Statement of Strategic Direction refers to the Credo in its first line. Annual reports frequently mention it. The company recruiting brochure for college graduates and MBAs, entitled "The Johnson & Johnson

Way," begins: "The Johnson & Johnson Credo—a statement of corporate responsibility—spells it out. . . . Everything we do must be of high quality. And whether it is in manufacturing a product or in developing human resources, quality is the Johnson & Johnson way." The Credo is printed in toto on the back cover.

Obviously, it takes more than PR and discussion groups—however good—to make a statement like the Credo meaningful in a company as large and diverse as J&J. One cannot understand how the tenets of the Credo are given credibility at the company without looking at the role that the office of the chairman plays in the process. There is no doubt that the impact of the J&J Credo depends heavily on the top officers of the company. Even though the culture itself has been shaped by the General's tenets for more than 40 years and the top officers are a product of that culture, it is Burke and Clare's visible commitment to the Credo that managers mentioned most frequently in interviews.

The real issue, Burke makes clear, is not ethics; it is trust. David Clare agrees:

> When a consumer buys a box of Band-Aid brand adhesive bandages, he or she trusts that it will be the same quality as the last box, and the box before that. Our employees should be able to trust that we will provide safe working conditions and fair treatment. Without trust, we can't be a good business.

Trust was at the heart of Burke's and Clare's management styles and how they promulgated the Credo. In most instances managers are trusted—and expected—to figure out for themselves what is the right way of doing business.

In Burke's opinion, everyone has to live and work from his or her own values. He feels that a highly detailed set of rules would not be as effective as the General's tenets in ensuring commitment to basic company responsibilities.

> The law libraries are full of texts about the codification of laws. As soon as you make a rule, people argue about it. What is so powerful about the Credo is that the document is so simple. You have to decide what is the right course in a specific instance.

Fortunately, the Credo provides a shared sense of reference, a common company language. It is easy for a manager to think or ask, as J&J managers do, "Is this really what the Credo would say to do?" Eventually discussions based on the Credo become habitual.[3]

It sometimes even happens that top management will be challenged by their own team on a Credo issue. One manager, for example, told of the time he approached Clare on a promotion case. He felt that to promote someone above someone else in line was against the Credo. Clare considered the point and agreed.

In most cases, however, there is more information sharing and give-and-take than there is autocratic control. As one manager commented, top managers are pivotal in making the Credo meaningful in the company, but they do not give the Credo its high impact in a commanding way. Rather, they take a rational approach. They'll review its history; they'll discuss what it actually means. In this manager's words, "They're not just doing a sell job."

Take, for example, product quality. The company believes in high quality and this is explicitly stated in the Credo. In Burke's words, if there are 2 percent defects in a given company, the Executive Committee will ask the product manager what is going wrong. They will give the product manager a chance to explain; they will also summarize their own position. In most cases the manager will initiate the corrections—he or she will spend more money than was allocated in the plan or contact the quality assurance department for help. "But the overriding value," according to Burke, "is that we all make sure that you [the customer] can trust that we are going to deliver on what we say, package by package."

This is not to imply, however, that there is no monitoring of Credo performance. For example, twice a year every member of the Executive Committee receives a report on consumer/customer complaints from all the J&J companies. These are reviewed very carefully, as are employee safety reports. In the latter case there are very strict procedures for cited managers to account for safety lapses. Company presidents are in attendance when such reports are reviewed, and they must be prepared to talk about the results. According to one company president, such meetings "can't be faked. Because it's on the mind of our leaders, it [the Credo] is made important."

What about the manager who really does not share the world view of the Credo, whose personal business values are at odds with the statement's tenets? In few cases will there be a direct firing on this basis. First, there will be the informal feedback and education mentioned before. The first assumption is that he or she needs help in understanding the principles. As Jim Burke commented, it is a matter of education and exposure to the J&J way of doing things, and to how top management expects things to be done. This includes not only a negative response to avoiding the responsibilities of the Credo, but also a working knowledge of what management will not punish you for (as in, say, the recall of a questionable but profitable product if there are doubts as to its safety). In such matters the Credo is not always mentioned but frequently does enter the discussion. If, for example, a company manager is reluctant to reserve funds for purchasing equipment that would significantly improve product quality or the safety of the operation, it will be pointed out that this is not really in the spirit of the Credo. These observations usually have a significant impact over time.

Employees who continue to be at odds with the Credo will be counseled more formally about their performance on these issues. If it appears over time that a manager simply cannot operate in accordance with the principles of the Credo, there will be a move to separate.

Internal Auditing

Decentralization could in theory present tremendous obstacles to monitoring Credo compliance if the Executive Committee relied only on self-reported violations from the company managers. This is not in fact the case. There are several important company monitoring functions. Safety and quality auditing have been mentioned. One of the most important mechanisms is the internal financial auditing. J&J makes every attempt to ensure that records are kept as accurately as possible. So dedicated is it to this task that unlike most public corporations, the company had an internal auditing department long before it had outside auditors. It has been called "the eyes of the company."

According to Jack Begley, who headed J&J's auditing division, his job was made very easy because of the total commitment to accurate reporting and management integrity at the top. "There is no guessing," says Begley. "I don't have to play a double standard. . . . We're puritanical in this respect."

When some expense account improprieties were uncovered among very senior executives in the recent past, their position and the fact that the dollar amounts were not very big had no influence on Burke and Clare's decision: The executives were immediately fired. Clare then circulated what was in Begley's mind "a very clear letter on the subject of management impropriety." Not only did this letter specify that senior management had committed "serious improprieties," but it listed the specific incidents to which "all of our management should be sensitive," including frequent flyer coupons, changing one's own approved benefits, and charging expenses of an outside business venture to the company. To Begley, the letter was important in that it set the record straight and discussed the precise policies that had been broken. "It sent the message that management is just."

In some ways J&J's internal auditors are the company's messengers about its commitment to the Credo. Auditors display foreign-language copies of the Credo on their office walls as a symbol of where they've worked for the company. The internal auditing program for monitoring compliance with the corporate code of conduct is seen as an additional program, not a threat, to the Credo.

The Ultimate Challenge

Every war has its significant battles, and every policy has its significant test before it becomes ingrained in the company's way of doing business. No one would welcome the crisis that hit Johnson & Johnson in the form of deadly product-tampering, but once it occurred, James Burke recognized that all the good intentions and learning from the Credo Challenge Meetings and recent Credo revisions were up against a crucial reality test. The public was watching the company not only out of concern for public safety, but also to see if a large American corporation "really cared."

In 1982 Tylenol was the leading nonprescription painkiller in the United States, with 37 percent of the market by volume. This was remarkable growth in the seven years since J&J's McNeil Consumer Products company began marketing the drug to consumers as well as physicians. Tylenol had further shaken up the market by introducing Extra-Strength Tylenol, an "extra-strength" formula that accounted for 70 percent of the brand's sales.

On September 30, 1982, the Cook County medical examiner reported that seven people in Chicago had died suddenly after taking Extra-Strength Tylenol Capsules tainted with cyanide. (The report also stated that the poisoning probably occurred after the

bottle left the factory.) Shortly after the news reached Johnson &
Johnson, the company recalled all Tylenol capsules from the batch
that had been poisoned—93,000 bottles in all. By midafternoon,
McNeil had sent 450,000 messages to doctors, hospitals, and
retailers, warning them of the threat.

Johnson & Johnson tended to conduct business privately, and
most of the company's executives were unaccustomed to speaking
to the press. This situation demanded a pledge of safety, however,
both for the public good and for any possible survival of the
Tylenol brand. Still hoarse from a full night of dealing with the
crisis, James Burke met with reporters on October 1 and described
the events as "an absolute nightmare." He impressed the press and
the public with the sincerity of the company's concern. Eventually
Burke appeared on *60 Minutes, Donahue,* and other national tele-
vision shows, speaking up for J&J's traditions.

It was clear that the company's proud reputation for safety,
embodied in its Credo, was on the line. A front-page story on J&J's
handling of the crisis in the *Wall Street Journal* started by quoting
from the Credo on the wall of the old headquarters. If the Credo was
to work, the Tylenol incident had to be a living demonstration of its
effectiveness and relevance to business decisions. J&J's response was
unified by its mission; in company discussions Burke tempered
McNeil marketing executives' aggressiveness with a voice of caution
and safety. The crisis also demonstrated how important it is to have
90 years of public good will in the bank. On the day after the poisoning, the corporation canceled all its Tylenol advertising except for
one commercial asking the public to maintain its trust in Johnson &
Johnson.

In the week after the deaths from Chicago, J&J took the following
costly steps to resolve the crisis and to reestablish trust:

- *Recall*—On October 5, McNeil telexed 15,000 retailers and
  distributors, asking them to remove all Tylenol capsules on
  their shelves. Two days later, J&J invited consumers to mail in
  capsule bottles, to be replaced with tablets that were secure
  from poisoning. The company estimated the recall covered 11
  million capsules on the market and 11 million more in people's
  homes.

- *Consumer refunds*—A toll-free number, staffed by volunteers
  from within J&J, was installed to enable customers to get

refunds without submitting proof of purchase. More than a million calls were handled in one weekend; many were not requests for refunds but good wishes from the public.

- *Reward*—McNeil offered $100,000 for information about any product tampering.
- *Cooperation with government*—J&J agreed to underwrite the FDA's analysis of thousands of Tylenol capsules. It also offered its testing labs to the investigating task force. (This offer was refused, causing some friction, because it implied J&J might have control over the investigation.)

Just as consumers watched J&J's behavior, J&J employees around the world were watching to see what their company would stand for. At least one manager thought the Credo was no more than public relations cheesecake, but J&J's response to the Tylenol crisis, well publicized throughout the organization, changed his mind. Another employee stated:

> Tylenol was the tangible proof of what they said at the Credo Challenge Meetings. You came away saying, "My God! You're right: we really do believe this. It's for real. And we did what was right."

Years afterward, employees still cite the original Tylenol poisoning as evidence of the company's commitment to the Credo.

The person responsible for the Tylenol poisonings has never been found, but Johnson & Johnson's handling of the crisis points to some definite conclusions. The lesson for any mission based on ethics is that a crisis can be the best opportunity to take a strong stand on living out that ideal philosophy. Not only will this be the best proof of commitment at the top, it will also help managers learn how difficult moments ought to be handled. It demonstrated that a strong commitment to ethics and quality could be communicated widely. Most of all J&J's response demonstrated the strength of trust. Top management asked employees and the public to trust its judgment, and they responded.

The recovery of Tylenol as a consumer brand was remarkable. Industry experts wrote off the painkiller because its name had been indelibly linked with product-tampering, but McNeil insisted it could reintroduce the brand with a marketing strategy based on trust. Employees made buttons that said, "We're coming back." By December, Tylenol had come back. Buoyed by a massive mailing of discount coupons, improved tamper-resistant packaging, and trust in J&J, Tylenol had regained 95 percent of its previous market share, once again leading the pain-relief field.

In February 1986, the nightmare returned with the discovery of new cyanide-laced Tylenol capsules in New York. Eventually three tainted bottles were found. Again the company offered consumers a free exchange of capsules for tablets or "caplets." Nine days after the discovery, J&J announced that it would stop manufacturing all over-the-counter medicines in capsule form. This was James Burke's decision. Other drug companies retained capsules in tamper-resistant bottles, but Burke felt these measures could not ensure Johnson & Johnson's responsibility for the safety of its customers.

The Credo Survey

Since the the original Tylenol scare, J&J has continued to work on revitalizing the Credo throughout its businesses. One of the most formal programs has been the Credo survey, started in 1986 and continuing today. According to Peter Dinella, who first headed the survey, it was only a matter of time after the challenge meetings before someone at the top would ask, "How are we doing?" As Oscar Wilde once said, "Only the shallow know themselves." The survey provides some specific answers and also is designed to encourage change where needed.

The survey is a 240-item confidential questionnaire about the company's Credo performance. It is organized around the four principal responsibilities defined in the Credo, and asks employees to rate how well their company, their company's management, and their immediate supervisor are meeting specific aspects of the Credo. Like other parts of the Credo program, the survey places a strong emphasis on learning and results. It has been designed in the spirit of the Credo and the J&J culture. It is deliberately intended to encourage participation at the company management and employee level, and there is even a training video developed by the Credo survey program to help managers in this task.

All J&J employees, from Chairman Ralph Larsen to the floor sweeper at the smallest plant, are sent a questionnaire. The results are tabulated in the Credo Challenge manager's office and kept strictly confidential. Each company president or corporate department head receives the results for his or her company only, along with the figures for the corporation as a whole. It is then the responsibility of these managers to present the results to their own management board and develop an appropriate response to the information. According to one manager, the feedback meetings have had more interaction than most company discussions, and the people are taking the survey results quite seriously.

A second round of questionnaires must be distributed no sooner than 12 and no later than 24 months after the first survey has been conducted. While the company results will eventually be reviewed once a year by the Executive Committee (and thus by a company president's direct boss), in the short term only the company president and the tabulator know the results. According to Peter Dinella, if a group chairperson calls and asks him for a specific company's results, he tells that chairperson to call the company president directly for the information. Reports Dinella, "I haven't received many calls recently after the first refusals."

The extremely decentralized execution of the survey mirrors its purpose, which is not to punish managers with relatively poor Credo performance but rather to serve as a resource for the managers themselves to align various aspects of their company more closely with the Credo. The questions are highly specific and range from how much management strives to reduce costs to one's personal sense of job satisfaction. The questionnaire is heavily weighted toward the second responsibility in the Credo, which is toward employees. This is partly due to its being an employee (as opposed to a customer) survey, and partly due to that fact that for a long time Jim Burke had the sense that employee responsibility was probably the weakest area of Credo performance in the company. This orientation also reflects the history of the company culture, and the General's pioneering policies on employee welfare. In fact, when Dinella held initial meetings with various managers to discuss the potential design of the survey, there was great unanimity to weight the questions toward the second paragraph of the Credo, which discusses employees.

The overall results of the survey of domestic companies confirmed this suspicion. In the areas of customer, community, and stockholder responsibilities the companies received on average a "very good or good" from between 72 and 82 percent of the employees. Employee responsibility was assumed to be good or very good by about 60 percent.

The results of the survey within the domestic companies have been very interesting. According to Dinella, at the very least no one has complained that the profile of a particular company has been inaccurate. In many cases the feedback has been that the survey proved to be a tremendous source of information. Not only does the survey provide feedback on performance, perhaps more importantly, it has offered a way of encouraging further questioning and understanding of the Credo throughout the organization.

The survey program has sparked an overt discussion between management and employees on topics that are often taboo in the day-to-day operations of a large organization. At one company, for instance, there was some problem with the ratings on management trust. The president wanted to pursue this, so he ran a small blurb at the back of the company newsletter soliciting anonymous comments about what trust means at J&J. The response was enormous and has already led to several changes in employee communications. For example, the company goals are now communicated more frequently and further down the line than before.

At another company where management received unsatisfactory ratings on open communications and several other aspects of employee relations, the president decided that the next time a problem came up for management, the very first discussion of it would occur in front of the line supervisors and some employees. This was a dramatic shift toward participatory decision making without any directive from on high. This same company recently ran its second round of the survey and showed significant improvement in the areas which had been of concern.

Another extremely important by-product of the survey is its ability to strengthen managers' awareness of the commitment of their own employees to a Credo way of doing business. One U.K. president, for example, had initially been quite negative at the start of the survey process. He later called Dinella to report that the questionnaire process was nearly completed and that he had been surprised to discover that his employees were intensely committed to filling out the questionnaire, that they had done so with "purpose, intent, and good will."

Lessons from Johnson & Johnson's Tradition

In trying to assess the individual effectiveness of each part of the Credo program, it is very difficult to distinguish cause and effect. The Credo is so ingrained in the company culture that it can seem on the surface to be absorbed by osmosis. If one asks top management, "How do you develop a mature Credo?" most often the answer will be, "Well, first you have to have it in place for forty years. . ." Yet Jim Burke also says, "If we hadn't had a Credo, we would have had to invent one."

These points are well taken. The venerability of the Credo and the formal processes that surround it are important in establishing its power, but the subtle, sustained process of managerial commitment is equally vital. Perhaps the most important lesson of the Credo at J&J is that it needs constant reinforcement. No one-stop ethics program is very effective.

At the same time, the ways in which a Credo is established, tested, and communicated are extremely effective. At the risk of grossly simplifying the many complex processes that contribute to the Credo's impact at J&J, we will list the program's critical factors:

1. The statement is succinct, clear, and easily made visible.
2. The statement closely integrates ethical tenets and practical business concerns. It also presents the company's four responsibilities in a balanced way; none has priority over the others.
3. There is a close relationship between idealistic words and reality as seen in the history of the company and its culture. The statement is not anonymous, meant for any corporation; rather, it gives an idealized portrait of Johnson & Johnson.
4. The statement and the organization share a high value in trust—having it and earning it.
5. The company communicates the Credo in many ways. It has strong educational programs, teaching both through examples (starting at the top) and through discussion of the statement.
6. Though committed to the Credo, J&J is willing to let its tenets evolve when needed. There has been sustained

attention to the statement over time, to allow for appropriate updates on its relevance and meaning.

7. The company seeks out and provides many indirect checks and balances on how employees comply with the Credo: safety policies, financial accounting system, consumer complaint reviews, employee recruitment, etc. Compliance with the Credo is also considered informally as part of management performance.

8. J&J maintains a constant tension between the absolute authority of the statement and great personal discretion on how it can be applied.

9. Top management is personally committed to the statement. J&J's Executive Committee is not shy about explicitly referring to the statement and taking a stand on its principles, and that behavior is reflected in lower echelons. Top management is also ready to act as a final arbiter on the really hard calls.

10. The Credo program has consistency. The mission statement describes every major aspect of the business and every major aspect of the business is expected to be consistent with the statement.

NOTES

1. This study of Johnson & Johnson is based on *Corporate Ethics: A Prime Business Asset*, a report on policy and practice in company conduct (New York: The Business Roundtable, February 1988). Quotations from company managers were compiled in that report.

2. In 1989 Johnson & Johnson altered its Credo again to include fathers as well as mothers among the people who use company products, and to state, "We must be mindful of ways to help our employees fulfill their family responsibilities." As Vice President for External Communications F. Robert Kniffin explained, "Both [changes] reflected the changing customer and employee environments."

3. On hearing how J&J managers discussed whether drug-labeling policies continued to conform to the Credo as government regulations changed, a manager from a securities firm demanded, "You mean to tell me they really do that?" This reaction is typical of someone in a non-Credo environment.

The Beliefs of Borg-Warner

. . . .

The following account, prepared by Harvard Business School, gives an insight into how the various components of mission—purpose, strategy, values, and behavioral standards—gradually become entwined with each other to form a strong mission.

For Borg-Warner, a sense of purpose and a corresponding clear strategy evolved over a period of decades. Each successive chief executive further refined and honed these two aspects of mission. However, the evolution of clear values and behaviors was a more lengthy and difficult process and required the company to go through major structural and cultural changes.

The vision and personality of the company's successive chief executives had a crucial influence on this process of change. For example, Robert Ingersoll, Borg-Warner's CEO from 1961 to 1972, pushed for the company to reexamine its attitudes toward the role of the corporation in the life of the community; the need for values in business; and the importance of recognizing and respecting the rights and individuality of employees. Ingersoll's successor, James Beré, continued this cultural change by emphasizing the link between values and commercial success and the ensuing need for Borg-Warner to articulate all that it stood for. Beré, too, saw clearly the link between corporate values and day-to-day business behavior and management style.

Most importantly, the following account illustrates how it is sometimes necessary to allow values and behaviors to evolve over time in order to ensure that all employees, not just senior managers, have a sense of ownership and commitment. Clearly, this was a lesson that Beré learned. It took around 12 years before Borg-Warner

achieved enough agreement about its beliefs to express them in a
written statement. Beré made no fewer than three attempts to reach
this point but was prevented each time by a lack of commitment
among employees. In the end, he simply progressed at the pace
required by the organization and was finally rewarded by seeing a
cohesive framework of beliefs emerge in 1982.

CASE STUDY[1]

THE BELIEFS OF BORG-WARNER:
TO REACH BEYOND THE MINIMAL

Any business is a member of a social system, entitled to the
rights and bound by the responsibilities of that membership. Its
freedom to pursue economic goals is constrained by law and
channeled by the forces of a free market. But these demands are
minimal, requiring only that a business provide wanted goods
and services, compete fairly, and cause no obvious harm. For
some companies, that is enough. It is not enough for Borg-
Warner. We impose upon ourselves an obligation to reach
beyond the minimal. We do so convinced that by making a
larger contribution to the society that sustains us, we best assure
not only its future vitality, but our own.

This is what we believe.

We believe in the dignity of the individual.
However large and complex a business may be, its work is still
done by people dealing with people. Each person involved is a
unique human being, with pride, needs, values, and innate
personal worth. For Borg-Warner to succeed, we must operate
in a climate of openness and trust, in which each of us freely
grants others the same respect, cooperation, and decency we
seek for ourselves.

We believe in our responsibility to the common good.
Because Borg-Warner is both an economic and social force, our
responsibilities to the public are large. The spur of competition
and the sanctions of the law give strong guidance to our behavior, but alone do not inspire our best. For that we must heed the

continued

voice of our natural concern for others. Our challenge is to supply goods and services that are of superior value to those who use them; to create jobs that provide meaning for those who do them; to honor and enhance human life; and to offer our talents and our wealth to help improve the world we share.

We believe in the endless quest for excellence.
Though we may be better today than we were yesterday, we are not as good as we must become. Borg-Warner chooses to be a leader—in serving our customers, advancing our technologies, and rewarding all who invest in us their time, money, and trust. None of us can settle for doing less than our best, and we can never stop trying to surpass what already has been achieved.

We believe in continuous renewal.
A corporation endures and prospers only by moving forward. The past has given us the present to build on. But to follow our visions to the future, we must see the difference between traditions that give us continuity and strength, and conventions that no longer serve us—and have the courage to act on that knowledge. Most can adapt after change has occurred; we must be among the few who anticipate change, shape it to our purpose, and act as its agents.

We believe in the commonwealth of
Borg-Warner and its people.
Borg-Warner is both a federation of businesses and a community of people. Our goal is to preserve the freedom each of us needs to find personal satisfaction while building the strength that comes from unity. True unity is more than a melding of self-interests; it results when values and ideals also are shared. Some of ours are spelled out in these statements of belief. Others include faith in our political, economic, and spiritual heritage; pride in our work and our company; the knowledge that loyalty must flow in many directions, and a conviction that power is strongest when shared. We look to the unifying force of these beliefs as a source of energy to brighten the future of our company and all who depend upon it.

Stating the Beliefs of Borg-Warner[2]

It was May 19, 1982, the last day of Borg-Warner's 1982 chairman's meeting, and CEO James Beré closed the final session of the meeting by speaking about the development of "The Beliefs of Borg-Warner":[3]

> For some time, Borg-Warner has been a company in search of an identity. I am not sure that during most of the half-century of our history we ever really ourselves questioned what we stood for, what needs we fulfill, or where we were going. But before we can know surely where we are going, we must first know *what* we are. So we are beginning a long re-examination. Why now? Because right now we are at a turning point in a long and massive transition in the company . . . because in a sea of violent change, guidelines are vital to avoid being swamped . . . because values and profits are inseparable.

He also talked about what the "Beliefs" meant and how they would affect the company:

> With this formal document, we are saying, both as a corporation and as individuals, that we believe that inherent values are as applicable in our work as in our personal lives. In fact, these values may be even more important on the job, since our business actions affect far more people than do our personal affairs.
>
> So if it sounds familiar, please do not dismiss it. These are not one-day-a-week precepts—they are basic guidelines to the day-to-day running of a business.
>
> We know we are not going to change our activities and our personality overnight. It has taken us a full decade to shift from a stodgy manufacturing company dominated by the auto industry to the degree of balance that we have now. Events move faster today—but it would still be a mistake to expect us to become something radically different very quickly.
>
> But we know we *will* change. We have a very strong base of people, and operations, and financial structure to build upon. With an equally strong framework of shared values to guide and strengthen us, I believe we can become *anything* we want to.

Beré ended his speech by asking the company's managers to commit themselves to the "Beliefs" and to make them meaningful through their own words and actions: "One of the noble houses of England has as its motto a Latin phrase that translates essentially as, 'What I promise, I will do.' This statement today is our promise to the future. Please join me in that promise."

The Chairman's Meeting

Once every two years the 100 senior managers of Borg-Warner, along with spouses, would gather at the chairman's meeting to discuss important long-range issues. Whereas the annual president's meeting afforded a regular opportunity to discuss operating business issues, the chairman's meeting was viewed as a special session that allowed a retreat from the daily pressures of management so that participants could reflect on the company's health and direction. With a theme of shared values, the 1982 chairman's meeting had concluded with the release of "The Beliefs of Borg-Warner."

The development of this statement of beliefs had begun long before the 1982 chairman's meeting was even scheduled. While the "Beliefs" had only come to fruition after ten months of intensive work, they were also the product of the company's long history, its culture, and the ideals of its chief executive officer.

Company History

Borg-Warner Corporation was born at a time when America's love affair with the automobile was in full bloom. A whole new social, economic, and transportation pattern had developed around the motorized wheels. Yet, despite the big annual increases in car production during the 1920s, the industry was going through a stage of consolidation.

Early Acquisitions.   On June 5, 1928, Borg-Warner was created when four established auto parts manufacturers agreed to consolidate their assets in a holding company. "What we want," said George Borg, first president of Borg-Warner, "is a corporation which cannot be made or broken by the fortunes of any single division, or the market for any one product." Each of the participants maintained its identity and operating methods while the corporation supplied the "fiscal glue."

In just over a year Borg-Warner added five more operations, thus establishing itself as a major force in the automotive industry. A published company history explained developments:

> These nine tribal fiefdoms were to remain the heart of Borg-Warner for almost 25 years . . . The nine companies had the same customers and parallel technology in common—but little else. Each considered itself as still independent . . . Borg-Warner was not considered as a parent—it was known as the "central office." The charter of the corporation stated

that "individual divisions retain all powers not expressly limited to the central corporation."

The philosophies that were to guide, or to dominate the operations of Borg-Warner through much of its history, and to be the roots of both its strengths and its weaknesses were really established from the day the merger began.

Charles S. Davis, Borg-Warner's chairman, served as a referee who helped maintain the growth of the independent divisions. In an effort to lessen Borg-Warner's dependence on the automotive industry, Davis helped acquire an electric refrigeration business, a small chemical operation, and an aviation supply firm.

In 1950 Roy C. Ingersoll, an entrepreneurial division executive, became CEO. Whereas Davis had been content in his role as central banker, Ingersoll wanted to *run* the corporation. He was frustrated, however, as were his successors, by the organization of the company: 44 people reported directly to him—35 division heads and an assortment of staff people—representing a wide spectrum of activities and policies and a wider range of operations. There was little time for communication, and, given the tradition of decentralization and divisional autonomy, there seemed little that Ingersoll could do about the organization. A company document stated that "the central office had only two real controls over a division: It could refuse to allocate further capital funds, or it could fire the division president." Ingersoll eventually presided over the first restructuring in the company's history, thus improving communication within the organization.

Period of Redevelopment. Once a consensus developed that Borg-Warner needed to reduce its dependence on Detroit (a full two-thirds of the company's business was going to the automotive industry), Roy Ingersoll set the transition in motion. Existing operations—the electric refrigeration and chemical businesses— were rebuilt and expanded. New operations—oilfield supply-service and air conditioning businesses—were acquired.

In 1961 Robert Ingersoll became CEO only after his father reluctantly agreed to step aside at age 73. While Roy Ingersoll had instinctively been a dynasty builder, his son offered a different style of leadership. "Bob Ingersoll was a new type at Borg-Warner. Neither a driver like his father, nor a negotiator like Davis, he was probably a better manager than either one."

Robert Ingersoll succeeded in grouping the divisions more along business lines, and set up group administrations through vice presidents who would have responsibility for compatible industries—such as automotive, chemical, construction, industrial, and so forth. By 1964 his new group organization was in place and attitudes slowly started to change. Communication between divisions and the corporate office improved and it became possible to find out what the divisions were doing ahead of time, rather than after the fact. The corporate office knew how earnings projections were arrived at and which "losers" among division products had been maintained and protected. The central office was referred to as a central bank and sometimes as a management consultant.

Robert Ingersoll introduced a new policy by ending the tradition that the company acquired operations but never got rid of them. Long-term commitment to an operation was a great ideal—but he insisted on justification for that commitment. Although a large number of persons objected to any divestiture, Robert Ingersoll sold the electric refrigeration business—it was the first real divestiture the company had ever had in its 40-year history. Other smaller divestitures followed and included companies that had been acquired under his father's direction. He oversaw other fundamental changes in the character of the company. International operations accelerated and the chemical operation spawned a highly successful plastics business that held great promise.

The Beré Years

In 1972 Robert Ingersoll left the company when President Richard Nixon appointed him U.S. ambassador to Japan. James F. Beré was chosen to be the next CEO, representing yet another style of leadership. As a company observer noted: "Beré was the company's first professional manager, one with strong humanistic overtones, as keenly aware of a big company's obligations to society in general as to its stockholders. He was also the first chief executive with no personal connection to the 'early days'—and probably the first one to make decisions on a basis of company needs rather than company traditions." Beré joined Borg-Warner in 1961 as a seasoned business executive, and in an unusual move he was immediately named president of an automotive parts division. Subsequently, he occupied the group vice president's chair, acting as an ombudsman between the divisions and corporate staff. He established his reputation as an operating manager even though it was not his strong point. This reputation did, however, help him win the confidence of

Robert Ingersoll and eventually gain the position as Borg-Warner's president. He had only been with Borg-Warner for seven years, but his lack of experience with the company was viewed as one of his assets in getting the job. Beré preferred to involve himself in long-term policy and strategic matters, while Chairman Ingersoll consistently involved himself in the day-to-day division affairs. Even though Ingersoll remained the boss until he left, the two men had apparently worked out an unconscious role reversal, one which made their working relationship strong. When Ingersoll stepped down, Beré was ready to assume the formal title of CEO.

After the shock of the 1974–1975 economic downturn, Beré realized that he had to improve communications between corporate staff and division management. In late 1975 Borg-Warner introduced a strategic planning system that involved many more people than previously, including division-level people all the way down to individual product areas. The operating manager now had to ask hard questions: What business am I really in? What future does the business have? Should we be in it at all? The discipline of such self-examination forced groups and divisions to make their own hard decisions about how to allocate their resources to the areas providing or promoting the best return. For the first time, the operating people aimed for clearer goals other than just next week, next month, or at most, next year.

By 1976 Borg-Warner's nonproductive activities had been shed and modern management systems installed. The transportation equipment business remained the largest segment of the company, accounting for one-third of total earnings. The air conditioning, chemical and plastics, and finance operations had helped to diversify the corporation's earnings base. Beré continued to believe the company needed some new directions.

Recognizing that consumption of services was beginning to exceed consumption of manufactured products in the economy at large, Borg-Warner's management began to think about adding a service business. In 1977 the company acquired Baker Industries and gained a substantial foothold in the protective services industry. During late 1978, Borg-Warner and Firestone Tire and Rubber Company, with annual sales twice those of Borg-Warner, mutually agreed to consider a merger of their companies. After serious negotiations, each company decided to retain its independence and the merger talks ended. In mid-1982 Borg-Warner acquired Burns

International Security Services and thereby became the largest protective services operation in the world.

In 1982 Borg-Warner Corporation was a diverse, multinational corporation that was listed among the 500 largest industrial corporations in the United States. According to *Fortune*, it ranked 154 with sales of $2,761.2 million, 117 with net earnings of $172.1 million, and 71 with 55,700 employees. (Exhibit 1 presents a corporate profile). Table A (on page 170) illustrates the change in the character of the company over the 1970–1980 decade.

Early Attempts at Developing a Corporate Creed

Borg-Warner's first attempt to formally articulate a statement of beliefs occurred in 1970. During Robert Ingersoll's administration, the public relations department drafted a "Borg-Warner Creed" that mentioned the company's obligations to shareholders, employees, customers, suppliers—and society (see Exhibit 2 on page 170). While many U.S. companies publicly adopted similar codes of ethics around this time, Borg-Warner was unable to achieve a consensus on any such statement. Initial efforts fizzled in the company's policy committee.

Ingersoll had frequently urged company management to reexamine attitudes and beliefs about work and the role of the corporation in modern society. As a company document explained:

> He was the bridge between the old attitude that an employee was literally nothing but a cents-per-hour cost, and the current belief that the employee, at all levels, has an individual personality and individual rights.
>
> When he interviewed someone for an upper level job—he often started the interview with a thoroughly unexpected question: "What is your philosophy of life?" He was looking for honesty and a sense of dedication to company and customer, rather than followers of the old tradition of "make a buck any way you can."

While Ingersoll's beliefs were well known, his successor had to formalize a corporate statement of ethics. During a visit to a Texas Instruments' facility in early 1974, Beré had been handed a copy of its code of ethics and was impressed. He decided the time had come for Borg-Warner to articulate a statement of values and beliefs.

Borg-Warner's Ethics. After several drafts, "Borg-Warner's Ethics" was published as a booklet for senior management review. As its

Exhibit 1 **Corporate Profile**

In 1982 Borg-Warner was a $2.7 billion diversified manufacturing and services company involved in eight markets basic to the world's economy: transportation, construction, consumer products, machinery, agribusiness, energy, financial, and protective services. Borg-Warner had operations in 20 countries on six continents. Its more than 100 operating units were organized into six product and service groups, described below.

Air Conditioning

This group manufactured a broad range of air conditioning, refrigeration, and heating equipment under the York, Fraser-Johnston, Luxaire, and Moncrief brand names. These included engineered systems for large buildings; industrial refrigeration equipment for the petrochemicals, food and other process industries; commercial air conditioning equipment for small buildings, schools, factories, and apartment buildings; and residential air conditioning systems, heat pumps, and furnaces. In 1981 sales for the group were $571 million and operating profit was $30 million.

Chemicals and Plastics

Borg-Warner Chemicals was the largest producer of ABS—a family of engineering thermoplastics used in a growing variety of applications around the world. Borg-Warner Chemicals also was in the specialty chemicals business with a growing line of intermediates, additives, and alkylphenols. The group produced styrene monomer for Cycolac ABS and for sale on the open market. Group sales in 1981 were $664 million; operating profit was $61 million.

Energy and Industrial Equipment

Major products in this group included centrifugal pumps (for power plants; petroleum production, processing, and pipelines; agriculture; and general industrial applications); precision seals for pumps and compressors; valves; chains; bearings; and other power transmission products for general industrial applications.

continued

The group also made audiovisual educational systems. In 1981 sales were $480 million and operating profit was $36 million.

Financial Services

Borg-Warner Acceptance Corporation (BWAC), the twelfth largest independent U.S. finance company in 1981, was the group's major unit. With more than 330 branches throughout the world, BWAC was the largest consumer durables floor-planning organization in the country, excluding captive automobile finance companies. BWAC also provided commercial, industrial, and leveraged lease financing; insurance premium financing and other insurance-related services to businesses; it also provided marine, agribusiness, and automotive financing. The unconsolidated units that made up the financial services group contributed $32 million of net earnings in 1981.

Protective Services

Acquired in 1977, Baker Industries offered the broadest range of protective services in the security field. It provided Wells Fargo alarm, guard, and armored services; Pony Express courier service; and Pyrotronics fire and smoke detection and extinguishing systems. In mid-1982, Borg-Warner also acquired Burns International Security Services. The combined Burns and Baker operations made Borg-Warner the largest protective services entity in the world, with the world's largest security guard service operation. On an annual basis, the group's revenue approached $700 million. In 1981, before the Burns acquisition, revenues were $364 million (not included in the consolidated financial data) and operating profit was $33 million.

Transportation Equipment

This group supplied component products to the manufacturers of automobiles, trucks, and off-highway vehicles and to replacement part distributors. Included were transmissions and transmission parts, clutches, axles, four-wheel-drive units, electronic sensors, control devices, and engine-timing components. Sales for the group in 1981 were $1.02 billion and operating profit was $78 million.

Table A Changing Corporate Business Mix

	Early 1970s	Early 1990s
Net earnings	$50 million	$170 million
of which:		
Manufacturing: air conditioning group, chemicals and plastics group, energy and industrial equipment group, and transportation equipment group	88%	40%
Services: Financial services group, and protective services group	10%	27%
Affiliates: Major equity investments including a 19% interest in Hughes Tool Company, a 22% interest in Echlin, and a 24% interest in Amedco	2%	33%

Source: Borg-Warner's Investor Facts, 1982.

Exhibit 2 Proposed Borg-Warner Creed, 1970

Borg-Warner Corporation is owned by the shareholders who supply its capital funds, but is responsible also to employees, customers, suppliers, and to society. Operating within a free enterprise economy, the corporation acknowledges its obligations to the following groups:

Obligations to Shareholders
To earn a return on their investment that compares favorably with other leading companies in our industries, enhancing over the long term the value of that investment. To pay out a fair proportion of income in dividends, consistent with the corporation's continuing need for capital for growth.

Obligations to Employees
To pay an adequate wage to each employee commensurate with his individual contribution to the corporation's work, and at least at the average level of the community where he is employed. To provide the best and safest possible working conditions. To give each Borg-Warner employee equal opportunity
continued

for personal achievement and recognition for such achievement. To provide a work environment in which initiative and creativity are recognized and rewarded.

Obligations to Customers
To develop, through skill, innovation, and enterprise, products and services of the highest quality for the purpose intended, and sell them at a price competitive with other producers. To be guided in developing products by the needs of present and prospective customers. To strive always to be a reliable supplier, justifying a reputation for dependability and good service.

Obligations to Suppliers
To be a reliable customer, working with suppliers as business partners to ensure mutually satisfactory standards of quality and schedules for delivery. To follow business practices that are fair and responsible.

Obligations to Society
Shareholders, employees, customers, and suppliers all are people who live within a society. To provide for the interests of all these groups, Borg-Warner is obligated to preserve that which it considers good for society, and to take the necessary steps, including the commitment of corporate resources, to improve it when practical.

Source: Draft company proposal, September 16, 1970.

foreword suggested, this was food for larger thought. It asked such questions as: "What ultimate standards do we cling to at Borg-Warner?" "In conflicts of purpose, how do we expect you to choose [what is best]?" The booklet was meant to offer guidance to managers wrestling with ethical dilemmas. The seven parts dealt with the law, company policy, affirmations of ethics, employee relations, consumer affairs, community relations, and corporate "sociology."

Although a senior management committee recommended that "Borg-Warner's Ethics" should eventually be published in a book, it suggested that management first establish a foothold for such a standard of ethical conduct. The committee thought the company had not yet attained the standards set forth in the drafted statements. Like the earlier effort, therefore, this attempt also sputtered.

Beré's Concerns About Corporate Ethics. Following widespread
reports of illegal and improper conduct during the first half of the
1970s by employees of public companies, Beré rekindled the discussion about corporate ethics in mid-1976. In a letter to all company
employees, Beré stated that "Borg-Warner does not want you to act
in any way contrary to your ethical principles." He urged employees
to seek guidance from their supervisors or coworkers if in doubt
about the morality of a certain action (see Exhibit 3 on pages 173–4).

The 1976 annual report included a discussion about the social
responsibility of business, along with the usual reporting of sales
and earnings results. Beré began to speak more frequently about
"building the character of our company," and he argued that Borg-
Warner had to manage its business so as to create public confidence
by considering the "*economic* and *social* needs of its constituents."

At the 1977 annual shareholders' meeting, Beré delivered a
special "Report on the Non-economic Side of the Business," addressing the public's dissatisfaction with big business:

> Americans are dissatisfied with business, not because of complaints
> about its economic performance, but because they see corporations and
> their managers as too self-serving, too remote, too purely economic in
> our approach to human needs.
>
> The public today judges corporations more by our social perfor-
> mance—that is, by the effect of our routine conduct of business on the
> quality of life of people we touch: our employees, the people in our
> plant communities, our customers and the ultimate users of our prod-
> ucts or services."

In the future, managers of Borg-Warner's businesses would be
required to assess and respond to the needs of their customers,
general public, and civic officials as part of the strategic planning
process. At a senior management conference in late 1977, Beré
declared that managers would be judged on their ability to meet
social performance goals. As he put it, "Our objective will be to
generate public approval based upon a sense of commitment to the
company, employees, and society."

According to one corporate officer, "Beré had the right idea
[about a code of ethics] but the timing was wrong. There were
powerful people around Borg-Warner who still gave only lip service
to the concept. The 'snicker index' was simply too high." Since
Beré's own thoughts had solidified, he believed that some progress

Exhibit 3 **Beré's Letter to Employees**

Borg-Warner Corporation   June 23, 1976
200 South Michigan Avenue
Chicago, Illinois 60604
Telephone: (312) 663-2060

To: Borg-Warner Employees

In view of widespread reports of illegal or improper conduct by employees of public companies, you may have asked yourself: What standard of conduct does Borg-Warner expect of me as its representative?

In the past we have stated that our policy is to comply with the letter and spirit of all laws, wherever we operate. In addition, we will soon issue an expanded statement that reaffirms this policy and deals with political contributions and improper payments.

Such policies are concerned with laws and regulations, and therefore are relatively specific. However, the question itself is broader, relating to the ethical aspects of actions we take on Borg-Warner's behalf that might violate no law, but could violate our personal codes and consciences.

Borg-Warner's philosophy of management puts a premium on individual judgment. We believe most decisions should be made by managers close to the action—not by corporate decree. However, you should know what we expect of you in dealing with the moral and ethical content of decisions.

Briefly stated, it is this: *In Carrying Out Your Duties, Borg-Warner Does Not Want You To Act In Any Way Contrary To Your Ethical Principles.*

I realize that business is conducted by people whose personal standards vary widely. However, at Borg-Warner, we traditionally seek to hire only people of high moral standards and, believing we have done so, we trust you to maintain those standards in your service with us.

continued

Exhibit 3 (continued)

Should there be any doubt about the morality of any action you are considering on Borg-Warner's behalf, ask yourself these questions:

Would I be willing to tell my family about these actions I am contemplating?

Would I be willing to go before a community meeting, a congressional hearing, or any public forum, to describe the action?

In any case, if you would not be willing to do so, Borg-Warner would not want you to go ahead with the action on the assumption it would help the company.

I might make a final suggestion, based on the variations in interpreting ethical conduct, even among well-meaning people.

If you apply the above test and still have doubt about what to do, discuss it with others in the company for whom you have respect—whether peers, subordinates, or superiors. I am sure this will help to guide you.

In summary: Your actions in representing Borg-Warner should be always lawful and proper, always capable of withstanding public disclosure, and always guided by your personal code of conduct.

I am confident each of you will abide by that standard.

Very truly yours,

James F. Beré
Chairman and Chief Executive Officer

could finally be made to articulate a corporate statement of ethics. One senior manager noted that Beré was still quite vague about what such a statement would actually say. "But," he said, "Beré was determined to develop one—soon." Beré was often heard to say that "when we have a code of beliefs it should include. . . ."

Developing a Statement of Beliefs. In summer 1981 Beré made another attempt to develop a corporate statement of beliefs. During an officers' meeting, he reviewed his own initial attempts to develop a corporate statement:

> I did not have the nerve to issue a statement of beliefs in the mid-1970s. I had gone to some of our senior managers with the concept and they told me it was a stupid idea because, as they said, "we have actions in our company that cannot measure up to a standard of ethics." I finally became mature enough to realize, that regardless of any past mistakes, a norm was essential to this company. Others, like our public relations people, believed it was a good idea, but were dubious that we could live up to it. Some also felt it would detract from the business of running the company.

When asked why such a project should be attempted under such difficult economic conditions, Beré talked about the things that had prompted him to proceed:

> Why do it in 1981? There is a mosaic of factors that has triggered my actions.
>
> First, I attended a seminar sponsored by the American Enterprise Institute and was moved by the words of one of the speakers, Michael Novak. Novak was convinced that we had a leadership dilemma in our society. Political leaders, he felt, would not speak from an ethical point of view—because it was not in their self-interest. The church, he argued, was divided and had lost its way—it was not providing people with needed guidance. Schools had lost their capability of providing an ethical norm for society. The family structure was in a state of decay. Novak made a strong plea: "If we are going to have true beliefs in the business sector, you, as business leaders, better stand up and realize that it is time to decide what your culture is—and give it some beliefs." I was convinced he was right! There had been a deterioration of ethics in our society. The norm was gone, and people were looking for leadership—but they wanted *quality* leadership.
>
> Secondly, I have been CEO long enough so there is no way people are going to detach my actions from what I plan to publish.
>
> Thirdly, I have confidence in our corporate communications department. They are the professional communicators and I know they will have to play a major role in shaping this document. When they appeared receptive to the idea, I felt confident we could proceed.
>
> Lastly, when I visited our management training sessions, I heard a lot of our managers, particularly the younger ones, say they wanted to identify with a company that stands for something, that has a vision about what it is doing. For many of them, something was missing.

Beré was convinced that business could provide quality leadership by developing norms and went on to talk about the duties and rights of the modern corporation:

> I think I have an obligation as a corporate leader to establish standards. I do *not* think I have a right to be so exclusive that I become a bigot. But I do think I have a right to not deal with the extreme 10 percent in society. My job is to cater to the middle 80 percent in society—any person with qualifications, regardless of background, is permitted to come. But we are not going to take the whole range of society. What I am saying is . . . we have a right to have beliefs in a company, to tell you what they are, before you join us.
>
> A corporate statement of beliefs can give people a norm . . . it is similar to athletics. The best athletic events all have rules. You do not play basketball without a set of rules. I happen to think that people in business, which is also highly competitive, really admire a person who has made it big . . . as long as they have played by the rules. They absolutely despise a person who has cheated.
>
> While we have an obligation as leaders to establish that norm, we must remain humble enough to realize that the norm may be wrong. It is not something that is fixed in concrete.

By mid-1981 a great deal of spadework had already been done to develop a corporate statement of beliefs. Yet, as one company officer put it, "We are shooting arrows and drawing the target around the points where they landed." Few understood what a corporate statement of beliefs was going to say and do.

Developing Shared Values

In September 1981, Beré put the task of developing a set of corporate beliefs before the company's senior managers. Speaking at the annual president's meeting, he talked about the company's strategy and performance:

> In the business world, there is a tendency to think of strategy as some cosmic approach that somehow takes place on the top floor of a corporate headquarters. We've had a certain amount of confusion about it in this company, too. For instance, we've said we wanted to reduce our dependence on the highly cyclical automotive market. We've said that with the country swinging steadily toward a service economy, we had to direct more interest to the service sector ourselves. Well, we've done both of these things.

He believed the company's view of strategic planning had to be enlarged:

Now I think it may be time to redefine our understanding of what strategy should mean to Borg-Warner. Part of that goes back to the original meaning of the word *company*. [It is] a group of persons with common interests banded together to achieve a common goal. Common interests. Common goals . . . I am not sure we ever really had enough of them.

To my mind, shared values—a company-wide set of principles against which all business decisions can be measured and tested—must be the base upon which concrete long-term objectives are built.

The Japanese, he argued, offered a model worthy of emulation but not outright imitation:

In large Japanese companies, for instance, there is an understanding, often unspoken but spread through the ranks, of where the company wants to go, what it wants to be, and what it will do, and how to gain those results. That really is possible here, too.

I do not believe that the Japanese style of management by consensus really holds promise for close imitation in the United States. There is a homogeneity of approach and tradition in Japan that carries over from the culture to the workplace. I hope Americans never lose the sense of drive, of individual achievement, that made this country great in the first place.

But I do believe that in the American system, there is a great deal of room and flexibility for individual achievement within the larger framework of group achievement—room for both independence and interdependence.

As he finished his speech, Beré started the clock ticking toward the next gathering of Borg-Warner's senior management: "We are going to raise our strategic sights now . . . we are going to try to codify and publish the values that will guide us . . . all of you must be involved . . . The theme of our chairman's meeting next May is going to be where we stand, what we believe, what our shared values really are. We would like to have our compendium [of beliefs] ready by then if we can."

Management's Response

Only seven months remained to discuss, develop, and publish the actual words for a company statement of beliefs. Beré asked each manager to think about the actual contents of such a corporate statement and to write to him with suggestions. (Exhibit 4 presents excerpts from some of the 40 responses out of about 90 managers who attended the meeting.) It was critical for Beré and the company to achieve wide participation. Otherwise, he felt the beliefs would

Exhibit 4 Excerpts from Management Letters

There are several areas that I feel should be addressed in this policy statement:

1. The philosophy should be customer oriented so that the policy will clearly support our new "marketing" orientation and can serve as a sales tool.

2. The philosophy should as clearly as possible describe the kinds of businesses and products we wish to have in our corporate lineup.

3. Clearly define the financial objectives of the corporation.

4. Describe the interaction between the employee and the corporation. What is expected of the employee and what the employee can expect should be described at least in general terms.

I have purposely excluded a discussion of business ethics since our current policy seems completely clear on the subject.

—*A manager, Transportation Equipment Group*

In response to this request, I submit the following: To create an environment which will assure the *long-term viability* of Borg-Warner or its successors by supplying *quality goods* and *services* in world markets that generate adequate capital to finance *growth* in *new, existing, and emerging markets.*

—*A manager, Transportation Equipment Group*

Bill Kieschnick, Atlantic Richfield's new president, made the following value statements during a recent speech: "Atlantic Richfield Company believes that to serve its owners, employees, and society well, it must have a consistent and coherent set of values on which it premises all of its policies and actions."

—*A manager, Energy Equipment Group*

As management's relationship with employees is such an important ingredient in any formula for success, I propose to limit my further comments to one particular aspect that worries me—the apparent conflict between the company's support for QWL [quality of worklife] programs and its policy of divest-

continued

ment where a business unit is not considered to fit into its long-term business strategy.

The fact is that, especially in Europe, there are large numbers of employees very worried and insecure about their future because they surmise that their units are up for sale or may be closed. The attitude of these employees is not unnaturally tempered by the circumstances, but would, I'm sure, be greatly improved if they could be assured that divestment is always the action of last resort.

Although probably a question of policy rather than philosophy, I do feel that a code of divestment practice is needed that employees will accept as fair and reasonable. As mentioned earlier, I also feel that an essential element of such a code would be that divestiture or closure will be an act of last resort, authorized only when every possible effort has been made to effect a "cure" by some other means.

—A manager, overseas corporate office

In response to your request at the president's meeting that we set down some suggestions for "Principles of Borg-Warner," I have distilled my thoughts to the following:

Philosophy: Borg-Warner wants to be the *best company* in any area in which it operates. It wants to be *flexible* in attainment of its strategies. *Decisions* are to be made at the *lowest level* (i.e., nearest to the facts) with an *acceptance* of the fact that taking risks sometimes entails making errors.

The company's people will have a *trust* in each other and *share* in its successes and failures. *The company, through its people, will be dedicated to balanced service to its several constituencies,* i.e., stockholders, customers, suppliers, community, and employees. Its people will *contribute* as they are able and be *credited* according to their contributions.

Goals: The company shall have goals of *profitable growth* in the value of its stockholders' investment, *personal development* of its people and a strong orientation to *improving service to its customers.*

—A manager, Transportation Equipment Group
continued

Obviously, as an outside director, the potential for a meaningful contribution is limited, so I hope you will not be disappointed by my thin offering.

You have sponsored a high regard for the individual and good participation by all parties—as evidenced by the procedures in this program. There seems ample evidence of decentralization and participation, and perhaps more importantly, of a human face to the entire organization.

There is one area where I believe focus and consistency could be greater. As a descendant of a parts manufacturing operation, it is not surprising that Borg-Warner does not appear to demonstrate a high degree of marketing sensitivity. What seems to happen is that you at the center supply the strategic insights on market potential, which leads to acquisitions and divestitures. But in a way, these rather severe approaches are a substitution for marketing sensitivity and responsiveness in the traditional units. Perhaps organizational evolution and modernization would be a smoother process if it were more organic.

Accordingly, I suggest that somewhere in the beliefs and practices you have a fundamental statement of purpose that you succeed by finding customer needs and by responding to them with unique quality, service, and price.

—*An outside director*

mean very little to the company's employees. To do this, Beré looked to Robert Morris, vice president of communications, for assistance.

Morris was familiar with the work of other companies that had undertaken similar efforts—notably his previous employer, IBM. He began by spending a great deal of time talking with Beré to flesh out what he was asking for. Although the quantity of responses from management had been fairly good, the content of the letters indicated that there was considerable confusion about Beré's request for help in drafting a statement of beliefs.

Morris advocated more discussion with the company's management. He solicited more letters from division management; he also considered setting up field interviews and roundtable "rap sessions" to widen the discussion. When he realized that his department lacked the resources to undertake such an effort, he went outside the corporation for help.

In early January 1982 Management Analysis Center (MAC) was retained to interview a select group of 35 managers and to analyze their responses on the proposed statement of beliefs. According to Morris, MAC did a good job of categorizing the issues and, most importantly, helped build the perception that this statement was being developed in a democratic fashion.

Beré's List. Meanwhile, Beré was developing his own list of items that he thought should be in the statement of beliefs: He kept an index card in his pocket during the day and would often jot down words or phrases that he felt belonged with the company's philosophy. His words were then combined with the suggestions generated by management. For Morris, Beré's list proved critical in drafting a specific statement from what was originally an abstract concept:

- Sense of belonging
- Work ethic
- Competitive zeal
- Company loyalty
- Rational decision making
- Employee ideas
- Risk taking
- Agents of change
- Citizenship
- Share power
- Gratitude
- Belief in the economic system
- The whole person
- Diversity

Morris and his staff worked feverishly to prepare a draft of the beliefs since only a few months remained to the chairman's meeting. When Beré resisted words in one draft that were attributable to Socrates, Morris and his staff had to begin anew. Beré insisted that the statement be grounded in Judeo-Christian values.

To arouse enthusiasm for the development of the beliefs, Morris had an expert on corporate culture address an officers' luncheon on the subject of institutional values. It turned out to be a disaster. The top circle of management left the session more confused than ever about how values and beliefs would affect their strategic thinking.

Morris enlisted help from a philosopher at a well-known university whose teaching and research centered on ethics and business. The philosopher helped Beré and his staff find a historical springboard for each of the principles included in the draft statement. Beré later said: "He was a real catalyst—he boosted my confidence that we could finally articulate a meaningful statement of philosophy for Borg-Warner."

The Chairman's Meeting. By early March, the agenda for the May 1982 chairman's meeting had been established (see Exhibit 5). Guests would hear prominent speakers from industry and academia address issues on shared values and corporate policy. Yet the beliefs, to be released at that meeting's conclusion, were still not fully formulated.

When the actual principles in the statement started to come together, Beré realized that a preamble—a philosophical foundation—was needed to properly introduce the company's beliefs. Two approaches were considered: one could talk about how an enterprise making money could do good things for the community; or, conversely, one could talk about how an enterprise could do good things for the community and then expect to find profits flow as a natural consequence of its behavior. When Borg-Warner settled on the second choice, the statement of beliefs was ready to be presented at the chairman's meeting.

Important questions were raised during the three-day session. Division management was concerned that a corporate-wide statement of philosophy might reduce division autonomy. Beré was convinced that the sharing of common values would allow operating personnel to make difficult decisions *without* looking to headquarters for help. Centralization, he insisted, came when people relied too heavily upon the "mystical powers" of their leader. In this instance, he thought, the "Beliefs" would give power to a broader base of management—sharing beliefs meant sharing power.

When asked what steps would follow the chairman's meeting, Beré talked in general terms:

> The starting point for communicating these beliefs begins here—how I practice what is written down in this statement "to reach beyond the minimal."
>
> These beliefs are signposts, guides, goals—a vehicle for discussion. We must tell our people that these are *not* schoolroom rules—after all, they are *not* a bunch of kids. We need to start a training program to explain why we have beliefs. We need to continue to discuss the operating implications of these beliefs—how it will affect management behavior. We will have to become a lot more selective in the type of people we bring in [to Borg-Warner]. We must come up forward to tell people—this is the culture of our company, this is what we believe in! Lastly, we have to make this a living document of our company

Exhibit 5 **Agenda for 1982 Chairman's Meeting**

Monday, May 17		Tuesday, May 18		Wednesday, May 19	
7:45 AM	Continental breakfast	7:45 AM	Continental breakfast	7:45 AM	Continental breakfast
8:30 AM	General meeting session Peter Valli, moderator	8:30 AM	General meeting session Bill Blalock, moderator	8:30 AM	General meeting session Len Harvey, moderator
	"Shared Values" Jim Beré		"Choices" Jerry Dempsey		"What Businesses Can Do" Amitai Etzioni, professor of sociology George Washington University, founder and director of Center for Policy Research
	"The Power of Belief" Professor John R. Hale University College, London		"What Americans Believe" Florence Skelly, president Yankelovich, Skelly & White Inc.		"Beliefs at Work" Robert Patchin director of productivity programs Northrop Corporation
	"The Spirit of Democratic Capitalism" Michael Novak American Enterprise Institute		"Running Scared" Thomas J. Watson, Jr., chairman emeritus, IBM Corporation		"The Entrepreneurial Spirit" Bob LaRoche
	"Personal Values" Dr. Robert Kelly professor and consultant to business		"Gossamer Aircraft and Creativity" Dr. Paul MacCready, founder and president, AeroVironment Inc.		"Marketing and Moral Vision" Professor Peter E. Gibson Harvard University
	Lunch and afternoon free		Lunch and afternoon free		Closing remarks Jim Beré
					Lunch and afternoon free
6:00 PM	Reception	5:45 PM	Trip to Rawhide	6:00 PM	Reception
7:00 PM	Mexican fiesta			7:00 PM	Dinner dance

activity—no different than our accounting system. To me, the "Beliefs" are another professional tool of management to be utilized to reach our common goals.

He also reminded everyone of the relationship between philosophy and profit making:

I contend that unless you do what we are doing in terms of beliefs, you will *not* have a profitable company. Therefore, to those who attack me and say 'this is none of your business—your job is to make money for the stockholders', I say I am optimizing the stockholder's holdings. If I do what I am now doing, I will attract talent and release creativity to the point of making this a better company. This is what I believe.

The chairman's meeting was termed a great success. The invited speakers had triggered thoughtful management discussions on the subject of corporate philosophy and ethics. As the company's senior managers filed out of the conference room following the closing remarks, each received a portfolio of the "Beliefs," personally signed by Beré. It was a gratifying moment for Beré and his staff. Yet, he knew that the real job of sharing and communicating the "Beliefs" had just begun.

Incorporating the "Beliefs." A plan would have to be developed over the next several months that would move "The Beliefs of Borg-Warner" beyond the status of high-sounding rhetoric. Steps would need to be taken to clarify, communicate, and put into practice such phrases as "to reach beyond the minimal." It was important, as one officer put it, "that these words not disappear like spit on sand."

Almost everyone in the company recognized that Beré was deeply committed to the "Beliefs", but many wondered how such principles could meaningfully be shared in a large and decentralized organization whose divisions treasured their operating independence.

The axiom that policy formulation is empty without careful attention to implementation was something that Beré understood very well; however, the "Beliefs" of Borg-Warner were not just ordinary policies.

CASE NOTES

1. Copyright © 1983 by the President and Fellows of Harvard College. Harvard Business School case 383-091. Reprinted by permission of Harvard Business School.

2. Dekkers L. Davidson, research associate, prepared this case under the supervision of Kenneth E. Goodpaster as a basis for class discussion rather than to illustrate either effective or ineffective handling of an administrative situation.

3. References throughout the case to company history and documents come from H. Lee Geist's *Borg-Warner: The First Fifty Years*, Borg-Warner Corporation, Chicago, 1978.

Lessons from Borg-Warner

The Borg-Warner case is different from the other cases in this book because we have little information on what people within the company thought or on how far behavior in the company matched the beliefs. Moreover Borg-Warner is a diverse multibusiness company for which the formulation of a central strategy and values has to be tempered by the need to formulate different strategies and values for different subsidiaries. Nevertheless, some important lessons can be learned from this experience.

1. A written mission statement is meaningless unless the basic concepts are widely understood and accepted within the organization. Beré made three attempts to create a written statement of beliefs and recognized on each of the first two occasions that it would be a pointless document because there was too little agreement between management.

2. A mission takes time to develop. Beré was chief executive of Borg-Warner for ten years before he felt the organization was ready to accept a statement of beliefs. Many newly appointed chief executives seek to put their stamp on an organization by developing a new mission statement within a year of their appointment. The Borg-Warner story suggests that leaders need to take a longer view of the process of developing a new mission, remaining sensitive to the existing culture while they work to create a new one.

3. It is possible to develop a mission for a multibusiness company. We address the issue of multibusiness companies more

directly in Chapter 12. But the Borg-Warner case shows that it can be useful to create a mission for a multibusiness company. It is possible to define some common values that not only match the corporate-level strategy, forming a central mission, but also dovetail with the missions of subsidiary companies. A central mission of this kind is, we believe, necessary. It provides the rationale, both strategic and philosophical, for why managers in subsidiaries should be proud to be part of the larger organization.

Transplanting Philosophy at Dist, Inc.

• • • • • • • • • • • • • • •

In October 1981 the company we call Dist, Inc., acquired Albert, the U.S. industrial controls distributor, for $100 million in the biggest deal that Dist had ever done.[1] It represented a major strategic departure, taking the company into an unfamiliar technology in a growing service market.

In the late 1970s, under the guidance of chief executive Harry Smith, Dist had developed a management philosophy that it believed would be the foundation for its future strategy. This philosophy was propagated among the subsidiaries with a fair degree of success, particularly at the white goods distribution business. Dist saw the venture as an ideal opportunity to transplant its philosophy into a newly acquired company. In the event, however, the acquisition proved to be a major challenge for the philosophy, both for its content and for the way in which it was implemented.

The Growth of Dist

Dist, Inc., is a U.S.-based company that had a turnover in 1988 of over $1 billion. Three-quarters of its sales come from white goods distribution, but the company also has interests in the distribution of industrial equipment in the United States and Europe.

Originally a string of retail shops, the company was incorporated in 1940, and acquired by the Smith family in 1950. It was launched as a public company in 1951, and by 1982 the Smith family owned less than 10 percent of the shares.

Under Smith's leadership, Dist began a long series of acquisitions. In the 1950s and early 1960s Dist's new subsidiaries bore some relationship to the historical origins of the firm: retailing was expanded, and an exclusive franchise to import and distribute a European brand of white goods was obtained. In 1969 Harry Smith became chief executive at the age of 31 upon the retirement of his father. By 1970 Dist was the fourth largest white goods distributor in the United States. Over the next three years, Dist diversified into businesses in the distribution of catering and office equipment, property development, and even an advertising agency.

By the mid-1970s, however, the company was forced to rationalize its operations in order to survive the worldwide economic crisis. To avoid a repeat of this experience, Dist resolved to diversify its operations further. It expanded into leisure activities and in 1979 it acquired two white goods distributors in Germany. The acquisition of the industrial controls distributor, Albert, in 1981 furthered Dist's commitment to diversification. More acquisitions followed in the United States and Europe, but by 1988 the leisure and property development activities and most of the retail shops had been divested and European activities represented less than 25 percent of sales and less than 10 percent of trading profits.

From the outset of his leadership, Harry Smith played a very strong role in Dist's strategic and organizational decision making, particularly during the mid-1970s crisis. He believed, however, that as the company became more diversified and its financial position more stable, he could reduce his involvement in the business's operational decisions.

While Dist had nominally adopted a divisional, decentralized structure as early as 1970, it was not until 1978 that the company fully addressed the issue of decentralization and formally devolved into six divisions, each with a "division president" and its own functional staff. Corporate staff were centered in Los Angeles. Harry Smith led the company through an executive committee comprising the two chief operating officers, who supervised the U.S. and European groups respectively, and the vice presidents of finance, human resources, and corporate strategy. Like Smith, the company's senior management were unusually young: one of the chief operating officers and several division presidents were under 40, and none was over 50. All of them had been with Dist during its unstable strategic and organizational shifts in the 1970s.

In 1979 Smith and his senior managers worked with a professor from Stanford Business School to review the company's decentralization policy and planning processes in the light of the problems of the 1970s. They agreed that they needed some formal means for ensuring that the corporation maintained a cohesive character and strategy as its decisions became less dependent on the chief executive's personal judgement. To provide a focus, Smith and his executive committee drafted a set of statements that summarized the values and financial objectives of the company as they perceived them. The statement was circulated to the senior managers for comment and a final draft was reviewed at length at a meeting of the division presidents and senior corporate staff in September 1979. Revised guidelines were adopted a short while later.

A core concept in the guidelines was the belief that performance would come from a mutual sense of commitment between the company and its employees, and security of employment was to be a fundamental principle for generating that commitment. These principles were practical expressions of Harry Smith's profound religious beliefs. In his private life he was an active church member and also served on several secular public service committees; as chief executive of Dist, he had always emphasized concern for customer service and employee welfare. The guidelines seemed to be a consistent, if somewhat idealized, articulation of those same beliefs, and most of the group managers did not find it difficult to agree to comply with the statements for a trial period.

Not everybody felt comfortable with the guidelines, however. Jerry Martin, vice president of human resources, recounts:

> The effort began with looking at the decision making and planning processes that had failed in the past, and got into the decision-making scene and how responsibilities should be divided. Then we said, "Hold on a minute, isn't there a piece of this that we all share anyway, an attitude to being strategic . . . and an attitude to service positioning?" Harry Smith thought that on both counts it was game, set, and match, that everybody believed in the same attitudes and that there wasn't much need to talk about them, only to discover there was a lot of need, that there was very little buy in, particularly to the customer service posture.

One senior manager felt so strongly that he could not accept the kind of organization implied by the guidelines that he subsequently resigned.

The guidelines were reviewed at the 1980 senior managers' meeting and, despite the difficulties, they were retained. The original guidelines made specific statements about return on shareholders' funds, the geographical balance of the business, and the shape of the balance sheet, but later versions replaced them with a more extensive presentation of Dist's principles. The revised guidelines became known as "Our Principles," or OP.[2]

White Goods Distribution

One of the Dist subsidiaries where the implementation of "Our Principles" was most successful was the white goods business Cortone. It had been a Dist subsidiary since 1955. In its eight locations it employed around 500 people, 60 of whom were responsible for the interface with the retailers. Cortone had been very profitable over a number of years and consequently earned itself a relatively independent position within the group. Management style was warm and relaxed, first names being the norm. The managers were generally very young, with an average age of only 33, but they were loyal, many having been with the company for over ten years. The company had a reputation as an excellent employer offering above average conditions.

Dist's introduction of OP into Cortone resulted in a number of administrative and behavioral changes in the subsidiary. There was some initial reticence on the part of the managers, but basically the subsidiary was already sympathetic to the values and philosophy. The initiative therefore had the effect of clarifying, reinforcing, and institutionalizing existing beliefs rather than changing the organization's culture.

The new philosophy was introduced with the help of the division president. He had been a member of the senior Dist group that developed the OP "code of ethics," and it was he who made the initial presentations at Cortone, first at a preview meeting for managers and then at informal meetings at each of the sites. A video featuring Harry Smith supported the presentations and copies of the new code were distributed. Question and answer sessions enabled managers and employees to express their views.

The initial presentations were followed up with a number of actions that reinforced the OP messages. Some of these were deliberate measures to demonstrate the subsidiary's commitment to the new guidelines, while others were responses to specific problems. They had the effect of making OP part of the formal and informal systems, which influenced the behavior of the managers and work force. The informal site meetings proved successful and they were continued on a cyclical basis. They demonstrated the company's commitment to people and helped the division president to develop a better relationship with his employees. Over time, the meetings became more relaxed and the division president became more confident and approachable. He encouraged his directors and managers to conduct similar meetings at regular intervals. Harry Smith also became more visible. He frequently addressed various groups on OP and his enthusiasm brushed off on his audiences. People at Cortone came to like him.

OP was adopted as the basis for judging what kind of people Cortone should employ and how they should behave. In recruitment it became both the standard for defining the ideal candidate and a vehicle for explaining the business outlook to potential employees.

All new employees went through a personalized induction program which featured OP. They were given a copy of the statement to study and then discussed it with their managers. New managers attended an induction program focusing on OP and including a session with Harry Smith. Sally Andrews, then vice president of management development, described the reactions: "When introduced as an outsider to this concept most managers were very cynical. But in nearly all the cases which I followed up, the cynicism was replaced by incredulity within a few months of joining as they started to see and believe what they read [in the OP statement] was actually happening."

The appraisal system embraced OP, using it as a yardstick in a new appraisal format. The style of the new format was very much in the spirit of OP, involving an employee, his or her supervisor, and the supervisor's superior in a highly participative exercise. The aim was to find out about an individual's efforts and aims as well as achievement. Standards were not simply technical and financial, but related to attitudes and personal and interpersonal behavior.

OP set new standards, and the performance appraisal system encouraged people to meet those standards. Some employees were unable to meet the standards immediately, often because of their attitude to what they were doing rather than their actual work performance. Counseling and training were available to help them, but, unfortunately, not everyone was able to respond and sometimes people left as a consequence. These individuals inevitably felt a degree of bitterness about OP.

Some of the greatest challenges for OP were the tensions that arose during a number of internal reorganizations. During the period that OP was being introduced, Cortone reorganized its field structure with new team leaders operating at a higher level. The reorganization made many people feel insecure and to combat this a series of team-building events were organized for field personnel and retailers. The "outward bound" style of the events helped to create confidence and shared aims, and enhanced the status of the new team leaders. OP, with its emphasis on people, professionalism and personal development, was an explicit theme in the programs.

OP's ideals of service could not always be applied without problems, however. A practical example arose over the conflicts between meeting the needs of the buying public and those of the retailers. The central customer service department sometimes found itself arbitrating between a customer and a retailer, a process in which Cortone tended to side with the customer. This inevitably led to friction with the retailers.

To try to resolve these types of problems, the customer service department was reorganized and became the subject of a long-term development program involving the personnel and training functions, external trainers, and an industrial psychologist. Sally Andrews explained: "It was a long hard campaign, with casualties. The lesson learned, perhaps, could be that you don't restructure in immediate response to a mission statement. Like performance appraisal and salary review, the two should be seen to be separate and distinct activities, spaced apart by several months."

Cortone also had to work hard in the early days of OP's introduction to overcome some initial unease and cynicism among employees. This centered on the concern that a pious statement of values would be hard to live up to in the real world. At the initial meetings many of the managers expressed support for OP's ideas (although they had some regrets about not being involved in its development) and misgivings. Sally Andrews remembered particular phrases in the OP code that attracted comment:

"A workplace where people enjoy themselves by helping each other"—a tall order!

"Lifetime careers"—is this a promise of security of jobs or of employment? What will the unions make of it?

"Customer service standards will be more important than financial measures"—How do we define these?

"We believe that . . . our employees will devote themselves to our corporation and its aspirations"—causing human resource managers around the group to shake their heads and worry inwardly about dead wood, mediocrity, and those stuck in a rut.

Managers doubted whether they could apply the philosophy to real customers (especially the difficult ones), real employees (especially the demotivated ones), and real colleagues (who were not necessarily liked and respected).

Part of the initial resentment was linked to the feeling of many managers that they were already following the precepts of OP, albeit unconsciously. It is thus not surprising that, over time, unease and cynicism turned to support in most cases. Sally Andrews commented: "OP has become incorporated in the Cortone lifestyle. It is still a subject to be discussed at interviews, a yardstick, a statement of intent. It still forms the basis of a Cortone manager's induction. It matters and it works."

The Acquisition of Albert

The acquisition of Albert was a much more severe test of Dist's philosophy than the experience at Cortone.

Industrial controls distribution is a service industry, and in this respect similar to Dist's other businesses, but it is in an unfamiliar technology. A consultant's report explained the challenges facing the company:

The management skills required in this industry—marketing, customer service, logistics, multilocational management—are extremely compatible with Dist's current strengths. However the added dimension of supplying technical products to a sophisticated industrial customer base creates a somewhat more complex managerial environment than that to which Dist has been accustomed. . . .

Dist must be prepared for the managerial implications involved—recruitment and training of management at rates perhaps in excess of the growth in revenues; the necessity for extremely rapid (and accurate) decision making; the ability to manage the combination of growth; and constant technical change.

From very early in the project, it was believed that human resources would be the critical factor in success or failure. As Sam Calvert, Dist's vice president of strategic planning recounted:

> When Harry Smith decided to appoint someone to be our top man at Albert, there were several hats in the ring. I asked him why he chose Willy McCall—then Dist's vice president of human resources. Harry explained that he regarded the "people" issues—organization and management development and all that—as the most critical issues we would be facing in this new venture.

Dist felt that Albert had a strong competitive position in the distribution of industrial control equipment but that its full profit potential was not being reached. The quality of management came in for particular comment from the project team: "Simon Albert is 60 years old, with a longstanding electronics background. His management style is entrepreneurial and this is reflected in the organizational structure whereby the branches are run by managers who stand or fall by their own successes with relatively little corporate interaction." Albert's own director of human resources saw the same fragmentation: "Albert was essentially many different cultures . . . Chicago from where Simon and the Albert family ran the business, and seven regions, all operating pretty well autonomously."

Dist saw an opportunity to use its own skills to develop Albert, a process that would be underpinned by the cohesive principles of OP. Jerry Martin, the then Dist vice president of human resources, remembers:

> We saw a tremendous opportunity to use Dist managers to help build new management skills and approaches, provided we could do this without driving away the existing managers.
>
> To us at the time the competitive advantage represented by Dist's commitment to management development was a critical strategic issue.

Getting to Grips with Albert's Management

Albert's culture at the time of the acquisition was markedly different from that of Dist. The business's devolved style and emphasis on the here and now clashed with Dist's vision of an integrated management approach with a shared culture and long-term commitment to and from its employees. To quote one of Albert's regional vice presidents:

It was our job to make the sales numbers for the territory. We got no help from Chicago [Albert's headquarters]. If we wanted to hire or fire, we just did it. If we needed a new manager, we knew everybody who was anybody in the industry, so we called him up and made him an offer. Speaking personally, if you wanted to get on in your career, you could forget moving in Albert unless you belonged to the inner circle. I saw my career as being in the industry rather than in any particular company. Someone offers you a better deal and you go.

Given the differences in culture it was perhaps inevitable that there would have to be radical changes in Albert's management in the longer term. In the short term, however, Dist had to contend with its own ignorance of the industry. It had to attempt to get to grips with Albert without frightening off the key figures.

Initially, the approach was fairly gentle. In April 1984 Jerry Martin wrote from Dist corporate office to Mark Albert, Simon Albert's son and then president of the company, the following letter:

As we discussed last week, there are several areas in which I would like Stephen [Albert's vice president of human resources] to provide information and help. . . . I believe that Dist should take considerable care in managing the integration of Albert. . . . We need to understand the differences between our companies and the industries in which we have been working. There are three particular aspects which we must begin to understand now:

The first is the overall approach to running the businesses in industrial controls distribution. This would include their organization and responsibilities, their attitudes to risk taking and innovation, the industry and management skills which seem important, the measurement, reward, and motivation systems. . . .

The second is to understand the specific cultural and attitude similarities and differences between Dist and Albert. . . .

The third is to understand the types of management positions in Albert for which Dist managers may be suitable. This was one of the benefits which was anticipated from the merger but one which needs a lot of care and subtlety to bring about successfully. . . .

These are all areas in which Stephen and the senior managers can help me. I am conscious that Stephen is already very busy and I am more than happy to make available Rob Paulson, one of our most experienced management trainers in Dist, to help with the workload.

Rob Paulson was seconded to Albert from Dist's management
training center in Los Angeles. He targeted the regional managers as
the priority group both for training and for the implementation of
the company's long-term management development goals. The
approach was outlined during a regional managers meeting in July
1984 when an extensive training and development program was
introduced. Paulson was also confirmed as director of training and
development, reporting to the vice president of Human Resources.

In September 1984, in the run up to the 1985 planning process,
they identified the following management development problems:

- Key managers were highly valued financially, but poorly
  valued in terms of trust, responsibility, and management
  development.
- Managers were not regarded as a resource common to all of
  the regions.
- The focus was upon technical knowledge and sales rather than
  on the overall management of all the resources of the business.

High management turnover was seen as a symptom of these
problems.

The prescription included the establishment of a biographical
data base, the introduction of an appraisal system and a relocation
policy, and the transfer of a number of Dist managers into Albert
over the following years. At the end of 1984, Dist strengthened its
control over Albert with Willy McCall assuming day-to-day control.

Dist's approach did not go down well with everyone at Albert.
Mark Albert resigned in 1984, and in July 1985 the vice president of
sales and operations resigned, taking several key managers from
Chicago with him. He explained: "I'm getting too much interference. Not one of these Dist managers is a real industry man, none of
them have the long years of experience they need to understand
this business. Yet they keep pushing me to put in all sorts of new
things for my people to do, like planning, which I don't find any
help at all in doing my job." Simon Albert, the founder, left at about
the same time, clearly having similar feelings.

The impact of these conflicts over management was mitigated by
the commercial success that came from a strongly growing market
in the second half of 1985. Willy McCall saw the good profits as an
opportunity to build a unique business on the back of Dist's
philosophy and its approach to human resources.

The human resources function doubled in size to 16 people. The budget for 1986 was $4 million, supporting a heavy commitment to training, a move that appeared to be well received at the time. Comments from employees included: "It is good to see Dist doing what they say—caring about people and investing in them." "It was great that one of the presidents of Dist came and spent half a day with us. That showed real commitment."

In retrospect some managers had more mixed reactions: "We were pleased to get some training, it was a new concept, and we didn't really know what we wanted. This white file arrived, it was like a hypermarket. You just ticked the boxes and got your manager to sign. It was a thing that was totally new to us. I didn't really know what I needed. Training was such a hype thing that most managers just signed it off." "Sometimes managers were on courses that were inappropriate—we felt 'what's that dummy doing here?' It made an uncomfortable situation for all."

The five-year plan that was finalized in July 1986 identified a number of employee development initiatives. Its main focus was to ensure the recruitment of top performers in every area of Albert's activity and their retention while being systematically developed. At the Dist corporate office, this plan was well received, being in tune with both OP and with the strategic approach of building up management resources, capabilities, and attitudes in pursuit of customer service and competitive advantage.

The Downturn of 1986–88

"Our Principles" and the commitment to human resources were soon to be tested. Throughout 1986 the forward order rate had been declining. Willy McCall and his team made a tactical decision to try to hold on to sales and increase market share under the slogan "Hold Your Ground," but by the end of 1986 it was clear that costs would have to be cut to avoid losses. The usual industry practice of layoffs was to be avoided as being contrary to the high-quality culture that Albert was trying to create. Instead, recruitment was suspended, the training program was reduced, and there was an across-the-board pay cut. Senior managers lost 10 percent.

From the end of February to the end of August, the head count was reduced from 2,000 to 1,700. Unfortunately, the pay cuts and the hiring freeze had undesirable side effects. Some of the better managers left to join competitors for more money, and it became difficult to find internal recruits to fill the vacancies.

By 1988, it was clear that the U.S. industrial controls industry was experiencing more than a short-term recession. The "hollowing of America," coupled with increased Japanese competition, had resulted in a prolonged and severe downturn for distributors of U.S.-manufactured industrial control equipment. Budgets for all "discretionary" expenditure were severely restricted and the human resource function budget was cut back to $1.5 million. The headcount fell from 1,600 in November 1988 to 1,500 at the end of March 1989. In 1989 only four training courses were run; in effect training had ceased in the interests of short-term profitability.

Inevitably, cutbacks caused a backlash against Dist. The contrast between what happened during the downturn of 1986–88 and the high-profile human resources activity of 1985–86 inevitably brought Dist's commitment to its declared philosophy into question. As an experienced branch manager saw it: "The record speaks for itself. Dist is clearly not committed to developing its staff. The whole thing swung on profitability. It's obvious that the rest of Dist could afford to support training here." A product manager at Chicago commented: "What management development? It's a series of courses that stop and start. If I get one more training assessment form! What do these people think we've got time to do?" An MIS manager said:

> The last appraisal I had was in 1987. I don't really get the feeling that except on a one-to-one basis there's any real plan around here of where people would like to go and are capable of going. The whole system was compromised in the downturn—effectively appraisals weren't being done. If I went tomorrow, they'd be screwing around for a long time for a replacement and in all honesty I couldn't hand it over to any of my existing staff.

So were the concepts of OP a success at Albert? OP was a codification of beliefs at the top of Dist about the fundamental importance of quality and commitment as core values to drive the strategy of the organization. There appeared to be a moral foundation to OP. Smith and at least some of his fellow senior managers seem to have believed that the security of employment was not just a practical manifestation of the commitment "deal" with employees but was a moral imperative. The strength of feeling comes across in the comments of Jerry Martin, then Dist's vice president of human resources, on the crisis of 1987 and the cutbacks that were endemic in the industry. He said:

> The real trauma started when they completely switched round and came back to us saying "We'll have to follow the industry and do what they're doing. We're going to cut back. We regret it and all that but the commercial reality is that you've got to cut headcount and fast." This was the big test of the culture: what we'd been talking about in job security and all that stuff. It was really traumatic because we thought there was widespread commitment to employment security as a cornerstone . . . and we were desperately disappointed. We felt very let down when Willy and his people seemed to be throwing all that aside. It was actually a very personal thing. Employment security was really to be our last stopping point and the hurt was that there had been, we felt, no real evaluation, assessment, and deliberate implementation of all the other steps that you could implement along the way . . . [no consideration of] why we had spent this number of years talking through this posture that fits so well with a quality position. So that was it—a feeling that in a trice they'd come to something which they didn't seem to appreciate was undermining the whole thing that we'd been doing.

Harry Smith took the cutbacks equally hard, and there was some feeling that the pressure for cuts was coming from people who did not fully understand the philosophy. Sam Calvert recalled:

> I remember Harry walking in looking absolutely shocked saying that Willy was talking about laying off 200 people. We clearly knew that things weren't going well. One realized there would be some reaction. So I wasn't totally shocked but I was a little surprised at Willy and the people involved in proposing it . . . I could well believe even now, that they were under some pressure from below, from people in Albert who'd been there for many years . . . but I would have thought that having been involved in all these discussions, there would have been more resistance to carrying that proposal forward to say the least, let alone accept it.

Even among the long-standing Albert employees there appears to have been some appreciation for what Dist was trying to do. A senior manager who had been recruited in the 1970s and who had been based in Dallas during the recession in the industrial controls industry recounted the impact of Dist on his fortunes:

Those guys from Chicago just didn't seem to like Texas! With us in recession ahead of the rest of the country I thought I would have to start looking for a new job somewhere else with a competitor.

Then Dist came along and things changed. They seemed interested in us managers and in building up our jobs. At least the Californians did not seem frightened to visit Texas! At first I thought they were way out of line with their ideas about caring for people and even for customers, but after a few years it struck me, they're really on to something that could change this industry.

Anyway, instead of being fired because of Dallas' problems, after a while I was transferred from Albert to a new subsidiary to do a senior operations job. This gave me a chance to learn a whole lot of new things about operations management—we were all learning together.

Nevertheless, the experiences with the 1986–88 recession show that Dist had some difficulty in squaring its philosophy with the commercial pressures of the business. Possibly the real problem with Albert was Dist's inability to impart its approach in a very different business. The high-profile exposition of Dist's ideas in Albert was almost guaranteed to produce a backlash when the senior managers were unable to follow the philosophy through during the industry downturn.

Since the 1986–88 recession, Albert has partly recovered and is now performing well. However, less emphasis has been placed on the principles of OP. As Sam Calvert, Dist's vice president of strategic planning explained: "We still don't really know whether the quality strategy will work in all parts of industrial controls distribution. Maybe much of it is a true commodity industry."

Lessons from the Experience

The lessons drawn from Dist's experience in Cortone and Albert include the following.

1. The relative success of OP in the Cortone operations appears to have been due to the work force's familiarity with the practical aspects of the philosophy before its introduction as a formal expression of company policy. The OP statement, and its propagation within the group, were a means of clarifying, reinforcing, and institutionalizing a philosophy that largely preexisted.

2. In Cortone the management went to some lengths to make sure that the philosophy really did affect the way that people behaved. Recruitment, training, performance appraisal, and reorganization initiatives were all linked in some way to OP.

3. Mission management takes years not months. Dist has been learning about which parts of its original mission concept have true practical relevance for the long-term future of the company. By the nature of issues such as employee security, it is necessary to experience a severe recession before the principle can be fully tested. With an economic cycle of four or five years it will take at least that long to understand how far the principle is practical.

4. Dist's policy of allowing the philosophy to trickle down into the organization helped. The white goods business used OP quickly and effectively; the Albert managers were more cautious. Although with hindsight Dist managers were overenthusiastic in attempting to implement OP in the new company, they did not stick to its principles in the face of a change in the business environment.

5. Management's continuing concern about the relevance of OP to the industrial controls business shows the importance of achieving a fit between the strategic needs of the business and the mission.

NOTES

1. This case has been disguised as part of the company's normal policy of protecting commercially sensitive information.

2. Quotations from this statement have been edited in minor ways to maintain the disguise sought by senior management.

The Jewel Concepts—
Revitalizing a Company's Traditions

•   •   •   •   •   •   •   •   •   •   •   •   •

Jewel was started in 1899 with a horse and wagon delivering tea and spices in Chicago's Stockyards area. (The word "jewel" was contemporary slang for superior quality.) The company's development into a nationwide retail food chain began in the 1930s with the purchase of the Loblaw stores in the Chicago area. Beginning in the 1950s, Jewel Companies, Inc., diversified into drug stores, discount stores, convenience food stores, ice cream shops, and retail operations in Belgium and Mexico. By 1983 the corporation owned more than 1,100 retail stores in 29 states, including the original Jewel Food Stores and Osco drugstores; it was the sixth-largest supermarket company in the United States, with sales of $5.7 billion and net income of $83.1 million.

From its beginning, the company was characterized by an innovative responsiveness to customer desires. In the 1970s Jewel was among the first chain stores to introduce discount food pricing, to post prices for prescription drugs, to display unit prices, and to offer inexpensive generic-label products. No less important was the company's sense of community responsibility. Jewel had taken on a number of social causes—from boycotting grapes in 1969 to retaining uniform pricing among suburban supermarkets and stores in deteriorating neighborhoods from which other large chains had pulled out in the same period.

In 1980 Wes Christopherson became the Jewel Companies' chairman after serving as chief operating officer for ten years. As one of his first projects, he initiated an update of "The Jewel Concepts," the company's statement of its management philosophy. Though the project involved a much more extensive change of format and text than the revision of Johnson & Johnson's Credo (discussed in Chapter 6), there were many similarities in the goals and processes undertaken. Neither mission revision was intended to effect radical change in the company's core value system. Rather, executives sought to reaffirm long and successful traditions in light of new market conditions and a changing population of managers. In both cases, managers already had a strong commitment to ethical values, and understood public trust to be an essential component of their continued success. The mission statements were a way of putting these values on record for the whole company to follow. The results of each revision effort, however, were very different, and it is therefore valuable to compare the processes by which executives updated their mission statements and the eventual fates of these documents.

Jewel's Long-standing Beliefs

Jewel's earliest statement of mission consisted of a Jewel Motto, written in the 1930s by the company's management on the basis of a customer survey of 18,000 households around Chicago, and the so-called "Ten Commandments." These commandments, once prominently displayed in the stores, were regarded as a covenant with the customer to run an honest business and to make shopping a pleasant experience. Though still widely accepted in theory, this particular document was removed from the store walls when Father Raymond Baumhart, president of Loyola University in Chicago, became a company director; Baumhart suggested that while the commitments were valid, the quasi-biblical form of the document was inappropriate, even offensive.

In 1950 chairman Franklin Lunding, who had been with Jewel since 1931, wrote a formal reflection on his 12 years of leadership in a small book entitled *The Sharing of a Business*. As the title suggests, Lunding felt that Jewel's success had been molded from a management philosophy that emphasized a "spirit of sharing." This spirit was manifested in such policies as employee profit-sharing programs, an emphasis on two-way communication between management and Jewel people, and a mission to represent Jewel's customers' interests to the fullest extent possible. Lunding summarized these ideals as follows:

> The company has one simple overriding mission, as we see it, and that is to serve as an efficient purchasing agent for Mrs. Brown, the housewife. Jewel's real function is not to distribute food products and merchandise. It is to go into the marketplace as representative of the Mrs. Browns who give us their business and see that they get the greatest possible value and service for their money. Our loyalty and orientation is toward them and their needs, above all.

In the late 1960s Jewel's president Donald Perkins and chairman George Clements worked with Lunding to expand his booklet into a corporate credo titled "The Jewel Concepts." It took the form of a series of "concepts"—short precepts or phrases like "Sharing the Business"—each followed by a page of elaborative comments (see Figure 9.1). This statement was very much a sharing of wisdom between generations of management: Lunding was about to retire from the corporation, while Perkins had become president in 1964 at the age of 37.

As chairman, Wes Christopherson felt that while "The Jewel Concepts" was a familiar document in the company, it needed to be revitalized and made more meaningful for the newest generation of managers as well as for experienced managers who were facing new challenges in the food-retailing industry. He also wanted to communicate his own commitment to the spirit of these principles in a meaningful way. "Mostly," Christopherson said, "we wanted to remind people, ourselves included, that there's been a value system here and that these are appropriate standards by which to measure our leadership."

The words of the document were also beginning to sound arcane. As Christopherson put it, "Words wear out." Such phrases as "restless unsatisfaction" were outmoded or personally annoying. While he was not looking for a dramatic change in values, Christopherson believed that a reexamination of the Concepts from the ground up would stimulate managers to take a forthright look at how the old way of doing business applied to future market needs.

Figure 9.1 **Excerpt from the Jewel Concepts**

This version of one of the oldest concepts in the document, "sharing," grew out of managers' concerns that it had applied only to prosperous times and profits. The rewritten concept below describes many other forms of "sharing" as well.

SHARING THE BUSINESS

The more each strives to excel in serving the customer the more there will be to share.

Through sharing the obligations and the rewards of the business, Jewel people work toward common goals to the advantage of the stockholder, the supplier, the customer, and the public at large.

A business enterprise does not exist solely to make money for its owners or stockholders, although profit is essential if the business is to continue its function of serving society. Neither does business exist solely to provide jobs and income for its people. Profits and jobs result from providing service.

The owners and members of an enterprise have a common interest in rendering the utmost in satisfaction and value to the public they serve. Jewel is committed to this concept of a common interest in service. Jewel consciously seeks growth, satisfactory net profit, and increased income for its people.

Whether we are talking about the Chairman of the Board of Directors or the newest Jewel person, the more each strives to excel in serving the customer the more there will be to share. Whether the sharing is in the form of cash today or retirement benefits for the future, management must see that everyone shares fairly in monetary as well as other personal rewards which are the fruits of our service.

Two objectives support this broad spirit of sharing the success of a business with all concerned:

A better place to work

A better place to trade

"A better place to work" involves the obligation of the business to do more than just pay well. It must also provide

continued

---

satisfactions of the mind and spirit, the opprotunity for development and self-expression, peace of mind, and a share of the profits created.

Providing "a better place to work" means sharing the stress and cost of life's hazards by providing protection against unexpected adversity, and by providing funds for retirement years. It also involves sharing responsibilities broadly throughout the organization, sharing both successes and failures, sharing information and knowledge, and all the rest.

When "Sharing the Business" is at work in all its facets, the public is quick to sense and respond to this spirit and the service it fosters. As a result, there is more profit to share, greater job security and greater income for all. There are also greater satisfactions of the mind which spark the human spirit.

The Revision Process

When Christopherson conceived the idea of updating the Concepts, he did not plan to invite senior management participation. Christopherson liked to write, and he had planned to complete the update on his own and then disseminate its ideas through a new booklet and speeches. He quickly realized, however, that this would be impossible:

> I personally did not have the insight which a senior officer in marketing had on such values as customer service. What's more, I have my own personal biases about words, and I needed to hear from everyone else about what seemed outmoded.

Christopherson sent a written invitation to the 25 top managers in the company and to former chairman Don Perkins to send in their thoughts about the Concepts. He made it clear he was not putting the company's values up for auction, that he felt the principles behind the Concepts were still relevant. Updating the document was meant to be an exercise in self-analysis rather than a hunting expedition for moral failures in the past. Christopherson would write the final version himself.

Christopherson summed up his goals in the following way in his letter to the top management group:

"The Jewel Concepts" is ten years old in terms of being the written documentation of Jewel's management and leadership philosophies. While the concepts are still valid, or at least substantially so, they are not as well written for the 1980s as they may have been for the 1970s. It seems timely to adapt the ideas and the words to today's Jewel and in a way that might endure for another decade.

Like Johnson & Johnson's Credo revision in which some of the *words* of General Robert Wood Johnson were altered or deleted, the main thrust of Jewel's revision attempt was to put the current generation of managers in touch with the values that had made the company successful, and, by rewording them, to make the values touch on the current generation of business problems.

Rather than giving his managers the gargantuan task of revising the entire document, Christopherson put two people to work on each particular concept. Some were assigned topics close to their functional expertise, but most were given a concept at random. The managers were asked to rewrite the sections assigned to them in their own words or in collaboration with their partners. Having a statement and a coherent value system in place was particularly helpful in moving the discussion along. Jewel employees already had a common language for talking about their obligations and management philosophy, and the many values involved had been neatly categorized.

In thinking about the Concepts, managers were asked to consider three questions:

1. Is the principle still valid?
2. If so, how would you rewrite it for today and in this decade?
3. Are there any additional concepts which deserve to be included in the new version?

Within the month, Christopherson received replies from every manager who had been solicited. Each drew up a revised version of the concept in question, and some had added new material as well. Replies ranged from two to five single-spaced typed pages.

An interesting discovery of the revision process was how the company's values tended to overlap. One could not understand the full force of a concept like "Merchants of Empathy" unless one also considered such values as honesty and trust. In trying to address the one value assigned to them, managers made the important discovery that the concepts could not be put into separate compartments. One Jewel manager wrote, "As I read the Jewel Concepts, admittedly more thoroughly than ever before, it struck me that many are quite closely related." This discovery seemed to heighten Jewel managers' awareness of the potential fragility of the company ethic. Wes Christopherson summed up this phenomenon as follows: "I realized that you could not scrap any one concept for very long before the rest would be made obsolete. They were all interrelated and mutually reinforcing." Christopherson's comment echoes Johnson & Johnson managers' insistence that all four of their Credo responsibilities must be kept continually in balance for any to work effectively.

Writing It Down

There is an old saying that once you ask for a person's opinion, you'd better make use of it. Wes Christopherson was delighted with the extensive effort that his top managers put into their replies, but their comments also made rewriting the booklet more difficult. Comparing the letters and final draft of the Concepts shows that Christopherson used many of his colleagues' suggestions but often clarified them or rearranged the points. In some cases—especially the more flowery ones—he made very little use of the wording itself. In others, a manager's wording played a significant role in Christopherson's rewrite.

Christopherson wanted to retain the substance and spirit of Jewel's traditional values and yet revamp the document into a compact and immediate format. Anyone who has ever tried drafting a corporate mission statement can understand the magnitude of this challenge. There are no clear guidelines on how much tinkering with the tradition might be appropriate, nor is there a standard form of language for every occasion. One company's management loves nothing more than contemplating abstractions, while another will insist that everything be expressed through concrete examples and numerical objectives. Get the wording too legalistic and the statement becomes as cumbersome as a set of law books on the shelf. Get too moralistic and the document sounds overly pious.

Christopherson reorganized the earlier miscellany of precepts and comments into five sections that summarized Jewel's values into the

Concepts of organizations, leadership, people, marketing, and responsibility. Like Johnson & Johnson's Credo, "The Jewel Concepts" did not categorize ethics and business in separate departments. The language of the final version displayed Christopherson's stylistic taste while using many of the company catch phrases that had appeared in the responses from the management group. As he remarked:

> I've seen a lot of anonymous scrolls purporting to capture the business philosophy of the company, and you can't even get a clue as to which company they describe.
>
> Managers who read these documents are going to ask, "What meaning does this document have *for us*?" And some of the answers should be right there on paper in the kind of language we use everyday.

Christopherson's decision to keep the statement distinctive to Jewel's culture was a critical factor in how the company welcomed it.

Reaffirming Results

A description of corporate character seems to be an inevitable product of the self-examination that a mission program prompts. "The Jewel Concepts" remained a celebration of the company's history and culture as well as a commitment to uphold long-standing ethical values. The updated statement began with a description of the company and responsibilities implied in its structure. This section, entitled "A Federation of Independent Companies," was a miniature portrait of the major questions that most large companies were facing about decentralization and participatory management. Problems of communication, division of responsibility between operating centers and corporate services, and the creation of profit centers were all included. The old Concepts had clearly idolized Jewel's record of marketing innovations. For the 1980s, when company loyalty and managerial traditions were less in evidence elsewhere, the document deliberately spelled out and celebrated these values more explicitly than before.

The Concepts then went on to discuss the importance of placing customers first and empathizing with them. Customers remained the honored guest at Jewel's table. Interestingly, the document described empathy as having less to do with immediate instrumental value than with attitudinal, or spiritual, importance. A few items drawn from several parts of the document serve as illustration:

> Jewel people serve millions of customers each week yet must approach the task as that of satisfying each need individually. . . . We distribute thousands of tons of product daily yet must think in terms of providing a single item that is perfect for the customer. . . . We are challenged to devote ourselves to productivity improvements while preserving the quality of each human interaction.

Jewel's retailing orientation made it particularly sensitive to the crucial role that empathy plays in achieving business success, but empathy was more than a marketing concept at the company. One heard throughout the managers' responses a moral commitment of the heart. Christopherson called adherence to the Concepts a "basic Christianity," understood to mean not that everyone had to be fundamentalist Protestants, but rather that the Golden Rule—do unto others as you would have them do unto you—was a dominant theme in Jewel's value system.

The new Concepts laid out a balance between individual dignity and team responsibility. Jewel's management clearly placed a premium on respect for all people working in the company and for outsiders. The business implications of this ethic were explicitly addressed in a newly added section called "A Spirit of Initiative," beginning:

> The human spirit is motivated by considerations beyond the expectation of material rewards. . . . An organization which builds on individual initiative will achieve far more than one which relies on compulsion and fear.

At the same time, individual autonomy was counterbalanced with a strong emphasis on group effort. Christopherson felt that a key part of Jewel's management philosophy was the deliberate channeling of individual initiative into contribution to the group as a whole:

> Jewel's philosophy is based on the premise that no greater desire exists than that of an individual to achieve goals, those that are for the individual and those that are for the team.

Though he recognized that this statement bore some resemblance to Japanese management techniques, Christopherson saw this concept as a homegrown effort going back at least as far as Franklin Lunding.

Finally, "The Jewel Concepts" reasserted the stores' traditional sense of responsibility to community. Any large grocery chain is part of daily life in its region, a highly visible corporation. Therefore, it made good business sense to provide responsible maintenance of the physical plant, fair employment and pricing policies, and participation in the health of the local community. Good corporate citizenship does not come automatically, however. Jewel had always played an active, positive role in its communities, but management also knew very well that such participation was always controversial. The updated Concepts provided a thoughtful and much deeper statement of community responsibility than in the former document.

When a mission statement is revised to be more explicit, as with Jewel's reaffirmations of the values of company loyalty and community responsibility, the implications are unclear. The new explicitness might mean a heightened commitment to the value articulated, or it could show that the value was under assault and needed to be reaffirmed. In the 1940s teamwork and company loyalty might have been assumed, and thus needed no voice. In the 1980s they were seen as unusual enough to be special qualities of Jewel's management.

The Pitfalls of Profit and Profit Sharing

Though the new Jewel Concepts reaffirmed company traditions, the exercise also became a catalyst for change. Many managers had commented in their letters about "the real Jewel," a politic way of implying that Jewel's existing mission statement did not adequately describe this culture. As noted before, such reality tests are the decisive factor in whether a mission program provides a focal point for skepticism or demonstrates strong personal commitment by top management.

Many of the characteristics of the "real," formerly taboo aspects of Jewel's identity had to do with acknowledging the role of profit. As one manager put it, "We don't really like to think about these things, or, when we do, we don't like to talk about them." Apparently managers had come to believe that their mission to conduct business ethically precluded frank discussion of money-making. Christopherson received many suggestions on this issue. Former chairman Don Perkins wrote:

> As for additional concepts, one occurs to me. It might be called Oriented to Produce Results. . . . There is no conflict between being thoughtful and considerate of people and expecting and achieving results.

One executive suggested stating the company's commitment to "watching the bottom line" and ensuring that all assets were productively employed. Another manager offered a concept to be entitled "Profit is our Report Card." A third, who had written a highly abstract discussion of ethical obligations, ended his letter with a brief paragraph on how he felt about the concepts as a whole:

> In my judgment, it is extremely important that we rewrite the Concepts because in their current form we may foster an attitude of cynicism toward them that will destroy their value. The problem, as I see it, is that they don't have a strong enough "results" message presently; yet we are an extremely results-oriented company.

These managers did not demand that Jewel's mission be radically changed to include profit, simply that the words of the new mission statement reflect concerns that had always existed but were taken for granted.

Though the comments on profit were brief, their message was clear. Christopherson himself felt the original document had not placed enough attention on financial management for the contemporary manager. Eventually he added two new sections to the document to address these points: "We Expect to Succeed" and "Managing Our Assets." The first speaks eloquently to the concept of profit and a results orientation, and the second addresses financial reporting and stewardship.

This insistence on including profit as a positive and driving value in the company was of critical importance to the success of the updating process. Philosophies of business ethics are totally irrelevant if they assume that ethics is confined exclusively to "people values" and not money-making.[1] By facing up to their own profit motive, Jewel managers brought the Concepts more directly into their business lives. Doing so did *not* dilute other ethical beliefs which they held; it put them into a realistic context.

Another important result of Jewel's revision exercise was a renewed discussion of Franklin Lunding's key concept, "Sharing of a Business." When the original document was written, sharing of the business stood for many things, from sharing information about the stores with hourly employees to sharing in the homemaker's responsibility to provide good food for the family. Over time, however, sharing of the business began to stand in many managers' minds for good salaries and special perks. Jewel had been at the forefront of such employee benefits as health coverage and a profit-sharing retirement trust fund (instituted in 1938). At the time of Christopherson's update, cost squeezes had begun to take hold, and some managers participating in the rewrite foresaw a constriction on perks and salaries.

Several managers commented that, if left in its simplistic form, a value like "sharing of a business" worked well in a growth period when you could "afford" ethics, but was a cause for embarrassment in times of constriction. This kind of "situational ethic" disturbed them. As one Jewel manager insisted: "We have to face the fact that sharing of the business raises problems in hard times. We cannot try to slip it through. That just won't work for anybody." On first glance, the impending cuts in personnel, perks, and salary increases were widely perceived as betrayals of the company philosophy. How could you reconcile the Jewel Concepts about rewarding employee participation with the obvious managerial obligation to use good judgment and cut expenses?

Jewel's credo update process became an effective way for managers to demand explanations of this human fallout.[2] Most people had been reluctant to discuss and analyze these changes. One manager commented on their reticence as follows:

> In good times we are very willing to discuss our ethics, but in bad times we lose sight of the values by simply looking the other way. For example, EEOC [Equal Employment Opportunity Commission] guidelines receive a lot of attention in management reviews when times are good. But when profits are down, we never mention the guidelines *even if the report is favorable.*

As with profit, revising the mission document provided an opportunity to bring up fundamental issues managers had avoided before.

In the resulting discussions, the group eventually reaffirmed the concept "Sharing the Business," but with a new contextual perspective: Sharing of the business meant sharing adversity as well as prosperity. Rather than turning this value on and off depending on whether managers could "afford" it, they found it essential to integrate the concept into their managerial thinking *all the time.* The revised "Sharing the Business" concept appears in Figure 9.1. The new explication breaks out of the cost-benefit view of ethics that had bothered many of the managers. It further emphasized Jewel's long-term commitment to values in both good times and bad.

Spreading the Word

When the time came to introduce the new version of the Concepts, Christopherson did not try to gloss over the more difficult challenges that the process had brought to the surface. He wrote:

> We are tough-minded when it comes to what we expect of ourselves and of the whole Jewel team. We use our hearts, but we also use our brains, and we are not going to let ourselves get away with poor performance. We'll be patient when that is appropriate, but when the report card is finally in, we will do what it says we should.
>
> Sharing the business is a whopper! It says that Jewel people have a right to expect that part of the revenues of the business will go for decent wages and salaries and benefits, and that some of the profits belong in bonuses and JCRE [Jewel's profit-sharing plan]. But it also says that the material rewards depend on sharing the work and responsibilities, sharing the failures and the successes. And it calls for sharing the human burden both within and outside the Company.

Christopherson introduced the new document to all employees through a videotape. "Also," he added, "I think you'll see it creeping into a lot of presidential talks and the management development programs." Division personnel staff were asked to devise ways to create discussions of the Concepts as well.

Judging from interviews with managers, the mission update strengthened a new generation's understanding of Jewel's business philosophy. When the expected wage cuts and revision of employee benefits were carried out, heightened understanding of "Sharing the Business" seemed to prevent some embarrassment and internal disagreements about policies. The process also prevented a wholesale abandonment of the values. As one manager pointed out, just having reviewed the concepts in the way they did kept many of them from jumping too quickly on people issues in hard times.

One sign of a strong mission program is that managers see it as a practical guide to their work that they refer to spontaneously. This study of Jewel's updating program was initiated after a seafood buyer at Star Markets in New England, one of Jewel's largest chains, stated during an interview that he had a personal responsibility to act in the customer's best interests, even when the customer could not distinguish between good and poor seafood quality. He pointed to "The Jewel Concepts" on his coffee table and said, "There's something in here on anticipating customer needs. I really believe we mean this."

In many respects Wes Christopherson's efforts at promulgating the revised Concepts differed from James Burke's more elaborate methods at Johnson & Johnson, and those differences probably affected responses to the statements. To begin with, the management group at Jewel never formally engaged in a conversation about the Concepts, although many division managers held informal discussions with their own staff as they were rewriting their assignments. The process of thinking through revisions was conducted on paper, with all opinions flowing to the chairman's office.

In their suggestions for the revised Concepts, several managers reported that there were multiple cultures within Jewel, which is not surprising since the corporation had grown from many locally rooted businesses. Not all parts of the company held equally strongly to the same value system, and potentially they might have responded to particular phrases and challenges in different ways. It would have been enlightening to have had representatives from these different cultures sit down together to confront the differences that emerged during the updating exercise, in the manner of J&J's Credo Challenge Meetings.

As the process worked at Jewel, each manager was "showing off" his or her belief in the Concepts for the chairman, who clearly was looking for an affirmation of the document. With no anonymity or outside facilitators to encourage them to probe more deeply, it would be unrealistic to expect the managers to write something very controversial. Some of the letters, though eloquent in the abstract, avoided relating the values to anything real at Jewel. A few were simply "throwaways," ill-considered or politically motivated pieces of fluff with sycophantic nods to the Concepts' importance. Most replies, however, indicated that the managers had taken the program seriously by reworking some old concepts in major ways and adding new ones. No matter how skilled a manager might be at hypocrisy, the difference between those who had really confronted the Concepts and those who had not was clear. How much more insight could have been gained if the motivated executives had been able to bounce ideas off each other?

Just as Wes Christopherson kept the revision process inside his office, he publicized the results less widely than Johnson & Johnson's executives. "The Jewel Concepts" was not distributed to outsiders despite its readability and obvious public-relations value. The covenant between employees and the public remained unpublicized. The Concepts had the potential to become the public embodiment of Jewel's reputation for service, but it remained an internal document.

Finally, the mission inquiry at Jewel never reached the stage of conducting further reality tests. The updating stopped short of asking, "How are we doing?" as J&J's Credo survey did. For years, managers had quietly perceived that the Concepts did not reflect "the real Jewel"; after enough time and change that feeling would resurface and threaten the value of the document. In addition, the company was fortunate never to have to face a crisis like the Tylenol poisonings that struck Johnson & Johnson (though, ironically, the original tampered capsules were sold at a store owned by Jewel), and thus could not point to passing such a crucial test with honors. Instead, the corporation was challenged in a different way.

Up for Auction

On May 31, 1984, American Stores publicly offered $70 per share for 70 percent of Jewel's stock (then selling at $49 per share), a takeover bid valued at more than one billion dollars. Though the companies had very different corporate cultures, American Stores was also a retail chain, based in Salt Lake City and encompassing more than one thousand stores. The two companies had even discussed a merger earlier. American Stores' offer made clear that Wes Christopherson could become chairman of the combined company, but he recommended that Jewel not agree to the buyout. His record never came under criticism during the tender negotiations; indeed, his building of Jewel was frequently mentioned as a reason why the company was so attractive to American Stores.

At Jewel's annual shareholders' meeting, Christopherson and the board avoided bringing up American Stores' offer for discussion. "When will we hear about it?" a woman called out from the audience.

"You can read it in the press," replied Christopherson. He did not offer the assembled shareholders an argument in favor of keeping Jewel independent. At no point during the public discussion did anyone bring up "The Jewel Concepts"; as in the revision process, the company's value system and culture as represented by the document were not presented for public debate. Unlike Johnson & Johnson's Credo, the Jewel mission was not used as a yardstick for the public to measure the corporation. Managers and employees who had long supported the company mission saw it fade into irrelevancy as stockholders decided the company's future.

Jewel's board and shareholders were deeply divided on American Stores' offer. One family holding 10 percent of Jewel stock had already come out in favor of the buyout. In an all-night bargaining session on June 14, the president of Jewel and the chairman and CEO of American Stores came to an agreement for American to buy Jewel stock at $75 per share. Within a week it was announced that the contracts of Wes Christopherson and ten other top Jewel executives had been severed; Jewel's president remained on the combined company's board. By the end of the year, Wes Christopherson was once again in a chairman's seat, at Northern Trust Bank in Chicago, where he went on to build an outstanding performance record for the bank.

According to executives at the restructured Jewel, "The Jewel Concepts" are no longer in circulation. "They wouldn't fit with the new culture," one executive explained. The fate of the Concepts is an eloquent reminder of how fragile traditional values can be when a change of ownership occurs. Obviously, the values embodied in Jewel's mission have not been thrown out wholesale, yet their very association with the previous corporate culture put them in danger of becoming obsolete when a new chairman and management were introduced.

Lessons from the Experience

As both the comments of some managers and later events confirmed, updating "The Jewel Concepts" was above all an exercise in idealism. That is not necessarily a bad thing even if reality proved to be disappointing. The update of the company's mission statement captured the ethical impulse of many managers and prompted them to conduct a thoughtful exploration of what the corporation should be. In a time of great and often-justified cynicism about business ethics, this is very good news indeed. Reflecting on the entire incident, Wes Christopherson uncannily echoed Jim Burke's statement about the update of Johnson & Johnson's Credo. Jewel's former chairman confidently said, "You'd be amazed how much our employees want a document like this. People feel good about attaching themselves to decent values."

It is unfortunate that Jewel's revised Concepts had such a short life to be studied. Drawing conclusions from comparing different companies, or from projecting hypothetical outcomes if certain paths had not been followed, is always dangerous. Nevertheless, we can find some lessons in the story of "The Jewel Concepts."

1. Obviously, a mission program cannot protect a corporation from hostile takeover bids and similar challenges. Indeed, a company perceived as having a focused strategy, a strong public identity, and dedicated employees—all of which are cultivated by mission programs—may be seen as a more inviting target. Yet the more a company values its culture, the more integral that culture is to its success and the more likely it will be to survive intact.

2. An updated mission statement is only one benefit of the rewriting process. Discussions prompted by the effort are equally valuable in instilling a sense of mission among the managers involved. Reissuing the document provides an opportunity to publicize it and reinforce the mission's value to employees and the organization as a whole.

3. In far-flung companies, open, face-to-face discussions of mission and corporate identity may be more valuable than written responses, however well considered. Such meetings allow managers from different corporate subcultures to compare views, and they encourage executives to build on each others' ideas. Nevertheless, it is necessary for the chief executive to act as final arbiter, resolving difficult questions and taking responsibility for the results of the meetings.

4. Mission revisions provide opportunities for companies to discuss the real challenges they face, as opposed to possibly unrealistic ideals, and to bring up "taboo" subjects that the corporate culture

normally keeps underground. At the same time, executives should recognize that values may go unstated simply because everyone agrees about them.

5. Mission statements are not just useful for strategizing or "for internal consumption only." Each company has its own tastes in public relations, but any clearly written statement of methods and ideals has value in the public arena.

NOTES

1. For a more complete discussion of the interaction of commercial and ethical responsibilities, see Laura L. Nash, *Good Intentions Aside* (Boston: Harvard Business School Press, 1990). For further discussion of phases in corporate ethics statements and programs, see Laura L. Nash, "Addendum to the Report on the Conference Board Ethics Survey," European Business Ethics Network, London, 1992.

2. Sociologist and philosopher Max Weber noted that most people seem to need a formal explanation and answers to the problem of suffering, to the "human fallout" of hard times. In many companies top management has a strong disinclination to raise issues of mission and values during times of constrained finances, yet it is then that explanations and responses are most valuable.

Shell UK—
A Courageous Experiment

· · · · · · · · · · · · · ·

In the mid-1960s Shell UK Refining launched a program of change that, at the time, was unique in the history of management. In common with much of British industry, Shell was suffering from poor industrial relations practices. Negotiations were confused, with the different unions constantly attempting to leapfrog each other's deals. Labor costs were being forced up by demarcation disputes, excessive overtime, reluctance to agree to more effective staffing arrangements, and the erosion of the authority of supervisors. Management had made many attempts to resolve the industrial relations problem, but little progress had been made.

Against this background, Shell UK Refining welcomed the help that was offered by social scientists from the Tavistock Institute of Human Relations. The Tavistock academics suggested that the company should formulate and implement a new philosophy and that it should use it to bring about a fundamental change in the attitudes of company employees. The objective was to create an atmosphere of mutual trust and confidence in which the industrial relations and manning problems could be tackled.

The events at Shell were recognized as being a bold experiment. As a result, they attracted widespread attention and publicity. Paul Hill, one of those intimately involved in the work, said in his account of the episode published in 1971:[1] "Whether, therefore, the values and concepts of the philosophy statement are now sufficiently well embodied in the organization to withstand any future setbacks it is too early to judge. The indications are that they are, but the next five years will show."

Six years later, Frank Blackler and Colin Brown, both of the Department of Behaviour in Organizations at the University of Lancaster, interviewed many of the managers, staff, and union officials who had been involved at the Stanlow, Shell Haven, and Teesport refineries, and at the company's head office. The objective was to establish what had happened in the intervening period.

Their study, which was described at length in a book published in 1980,[2] concluded that the philosophy program had not achieved the full change in attitudes that had been hoped for. The following account of their work is taken from a summary published in 1981.[3]

CASE STUDY

A New Philosophy of Management: Shell Revisited

Background to the Philosophy Exercise

In the early 1960s the oil industry was changing rapidly. The Suez Canal crisis, the beginning of OPEC, the nationalization of oil companies by oil producing countries, and price wars in the UK provided the background to this story. At Shell UK Refining attempts to improve financial performance had led to an unprecedented program of voluntary and compulsory layoffs. Furthermore, Shell's main rival Esso was known to have negotiated far-reaching productivity deals with employees.[a] Within Shell, however, no such deal had yet been agreed and job demarcations and wages drift were serious and continuing problems for management. To deal with manpower difficulties, an advisory group, Employee Relations Planning (ERP), was established in the company in 1964. This group was formed to initiate long-term thinking on industrial relations issues and initial analysis led to recommendations that unfavorable worker attitudes and inefficient restrictive practices could be overcome if the company adopted a participatory management style and introduced a series of productivity bargains. To restore the effectiveness of management's calls to collective endeavors, the ERP recommended that emerging behavioral science ideas should be incorporated into a specially written philosophy of management.

At the Tavistock Institute these proposals found receptive ears. At that time Emery and Trist had been working on a wide-ranging analysis of social and organizational problems and on ways to combat them. Their views were that modern organizations function increasingly under conditions of great instability.[b] Collaboration, they felt, rather than the traditional competition between different organizations was necessary to overcome the resulting managerial problems. New values needed to be instilled in organizations through, for example, socio-technical job redesign. Further, Emery and Trist believed that urgent research was needed to study the processes associated with the successful introduction of social changes of these kinds. For the Tavistock team, therefore, the Shell project offered them the exciting opportunity to draft a statement outlining a new role and new approaches to management for major companies in the modern world, and to be closely involved in the first attempt to introduce such thinking in a technologically advanced "post-industrial" organization.

The Launching of the Philosophy Program

Between 1965 and 1967 the philosophy the Tavistock theorists outlined was debated in the company. Early indications suggested that it was being well received. Later, four "channels of implementation" emerged through which it was hoped the philosophy would be put into practice. Figure 1 indicates the nature of these channels and presents a comparison of comments Hill made about progress of the philosophy with those made by people we spoke to in our retrospective study.

Although Hill's report makes it clear that both the Tavistock consultants and the ERP personnel who ran the conferences were impressed with the philosophy's initial reception, it would appear with the benefit of hindsight that this reception was much less positive than had first appeared. A senior manager from Shell Haven, present at the very first conference (that for the managing director and his immediate subordinates), described how people from the Stanlow refinery had been immediately enthusiastic but that those from Shell Haven were far less so. He said:

> We had to do something. The ideas had been sold well to the boss of manufacturing. We had to do something as the top man wanted to go this way. Given a free choice I'm not sure what we would have done.

Yet while top management's views had been divided, at later conferences many junior staff were either to feel ambivalent toward

Figure 1

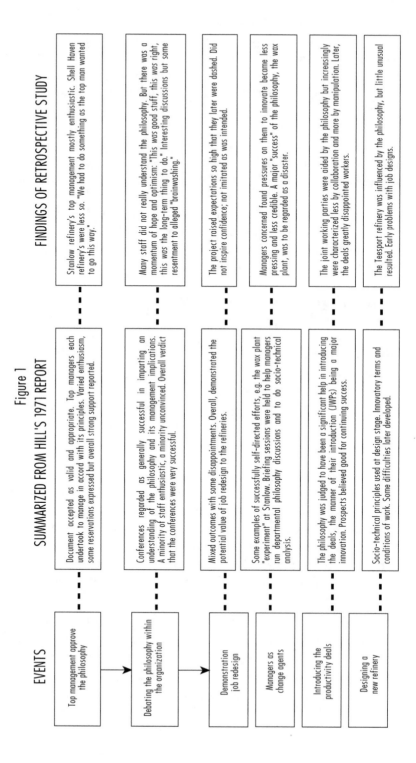

EVENTS

Top management approve the philosophy

Debating the philosophy within the organization

Demonstration job redesign

Managers as change agents

Introducing the productivity deals

Designing a new refinery

SUMMARIZED FROM HILL'S 1971 REPORT

Document accepted as valid and appropriate. Top managers each undertook to manage in accord with its principles. Varied enthusiasm, some reservations expressed but overall strong support reported.

Conferences regarded as generally successful in imparting an understanding of the philosophy and its management implications. A minority of staff enthusiastic, a minority unconvinced. Overall verdict that the conferences were very successful.

Mixed outcomes with some disappointments. Overall, demonstrated the potential value of job redesign to the refineries.

Some examples of successfully self-directed efforts, e.g. the wax plant "experiment" at Stanlow. Briefing sessions were held to help managers run departmental philosophy discussions and to do socio-technical analysis.

The philosophy was judged to have been a significant help in introducing the deals, the manner of their introduction (JWPs) being a major innovation. Prospects believed good for continuing success.

Socio-technical principles used at design stage. Innovatory terms and conditions of work. Some difficulties later developed.

FINDINGS OF RETROSPECTIVE STUDY

Stanlow refinery's top management mostly enthusiastic. Shell Haven refinery's were less so. "We had to do something as the top man wanted to go this way."

Many staff did not really understand the philosophy. But there was a momentum of hope and optimism: "This was good stuff, this was right, this was the long-term thing to do." Interesting discussions but some resentment to alleged "brainwashing."

The project raised expectations so high that they later were dashed. Did not inspire confidence, not imitated as was intended.

Managers concerned found pressures on them to innovate became less pressing and less credible. A major "success" of the philosophy, the wax plant, was to be regarded as a disaster.

The joint working parties were aided by the philosophy but increasingly were characterized less by collaboration and more by manipulation. Later, the deals greatly disappointed workers.

The Teesport refinery was influenced by the philosophy, but little unusual resulted. Early problems with job designs.

or to resent the exercise. The following two quotations are not atypical. One section head said:

> The ideals, then, were above my head. All I was interested in was how it affected my section, what I could get out of it. I came away with the feeling I got nothing out of it. It was not presented at a low enough level. There was a lot of mistrust at that level of management. What was the need for it? Was there something to be found? Is the mileage that we are putting in not adequate? I suppose it was done to provide the spurt via a rest-cure holiday. Generally it was not accepted by people at that level. There was a feeling it was brain washing. It did not reduce the barriers between management and the rest. In fact it did exactly the opposite. It led to a polarization.

A shift supervisor commented:

> A little bit must stick whatever you feel at the time. I don't remember what I thought was good but I was not very impressed. The general reaction of people was "it's a bit of a giggle." The only enthusiastic people there were the lecturers. Possibly other people were enthusiastic but I didn't meet any. We were there for a purpose. We were being indoctrinated on the role of Shell in the community, to shareholders, to employees. Some of the ideas were good but whether they are ever followed up when you get back from these courses is questionable. I was suspicious because the 1964 "Golden Handshake" (a redundancy program to reduce manning levels) had been preceded by consultants doing something, and other company exercises were followed by reductions.

Despite the reservations one might have about the factual accuracy of such comments describing how people had reacted (they were made over a decade after the conferences), there can be no doubt that the conference program did not convince people as it initially appeared. Here are two sets of comments by managers who, with ERP and advisors from the Tavistock, had helped to run the conferences. The first, a manager at Shell Haven, describes in this quotation from the interview he gave us the basic position argued in the philosophy document. He then speculates about the extent of people's actual (as against apparent) commitment to it:

> The whole basis was, what business are we in? What is the philosophy of the company? "We are here to make a profit," that was basically (what we called) Position I. "We are here to make a profit, but realizing there are social constraints of society and employees which will impose a limit on our profits." That was Position II. And Position III was: "We

are custodians of the assets of society and we may not even make profits at its expense." The implication being you had to be successful at making profits but within that framework. And I wondered in retrospect whether that was understood. According to Positions I, II and III there would be some overall and specific objectives which recognize the characteristics of the oil industry, and certain kinds of recognizable actions to meet these. So, the first thing to debate was, do we believe that Position III (or II, or I) is what we are in and where we should be? Now that's where I believe that however many hands went up the consensus was never more than Position 2H, perhaps only Position 2.1! But we all said we believed in Position III . . . I would put it this way. There were probably 50 percent who really wanted to make Position III a go and thought they could. There were 25 percent who would like to but didn't think it had much hope. And there were 25 percent who didn't think it was right anyway, but weren't going to say so . . . although you had better not take this as literally as I have said it.

The second manager we quote here helped run many of the conferences for people in the Stanlow refinery. In what follows, he speculates about the extent to which people there fully understood the concept of the "Joint Optimization" of the social and technical systems, the second key element in the philosophy statement.

Looking back I would say that really only about 5 percent of the people who attended the conferences really understood it. My manager kept saying "It is not a 'be nice' policy, but it is a philosophy for getting the best out of people." But the idea of Joint Optimization was not really understood. Engineers could not grasp the idea of optimizing what can't be measured! It actually did become a "be nice to people" philosophy I suppose. Then later on when this manager retired, there was a rumor he was studying for a degree in social work or something similar. This confirmed the image of "being nice" in people's minds . . . If you mention the notion of Joint Optimization now, you get a snort of laughter.

Why, we wondered, had the conferences initially appeared to be more successful? The first of the two managers we have just quoted (and who emphasized to us that at the time the conferences were running, he himself had felt they were going rather well) made further observations relevant to this point. Why did people say they went along with "Position III" if they did not actually agree with it?

If you go along to one of Billy Graham's meetings and you're the only one who hasn't gone down to be saved do you think you can sit there? They were, I would think, a bit like that. I mean it wasn't revivalist. But that was the pressure. That's what I meant when I said "hands went up."

Where then was this pressure coming from?

> I would think the pressure, I would certainly like to think this, the pressure was from people who felt, like me, that this *was* good stuff, this *was* right, this *was* the long-term thing to do.

It is fair to say that this was the only time any of the people we spoke to about the conferences described the pressures on people in quite such terms, yet other similar observations were made to us. Two other people associated with running the conferences, one at that time with the ERP Unit the other with the Tavistock Institute, agreed that while dissent was discussed, as a general rule its persistence was not fully recognized as legitimate. It does seem that expressions of disagreement with the philosophy tended to be given the status of "problems" that people were having with it, rather than being respected as expressions of legitimate alternatives.

The euphoria that seems to have characterized some of these conferences is perhaps illustrated in this recollection by a (then) shift supervisor:

> Most of us found it very convincing. We felt it was good, it could be a very good thing. The bit about responsibility to the community was sensible you know. And there were some good ideas coming out of it, like no clocking on, and the idea we are all professional people. Remember, Shell used to be paternalistic, anti-union. In those days the "boss man" counted. But at the conference they said, "You call me Eddie, I'll call you Jack." We thought, what the bloody hell is going on here? But it made you feel good. Then we all got drunk!

Putting the Philosophy into Practice

It was not intended that the philosophy conferences should be regarded as ends in themselves. It was hoped that significant advances would come after the theory of the philosophy was realized in everyday actions.

Four main channels of implementation of the philosophy emerged. In his 1971 account, Hill acknowledges problems with two of these: demonstration job redesign projects and the design of a new refinery at Teesport, although evidence we collected suggests he did not fully appreciate their significance. In this paper, however, we wish to concentrate on the other two aspects. These were the expectation that managers should act as change agents (i.e., manage their departments by the principles of the philosophy) and the introduction of joint working parties of management and

worker representatives (to explore possible new working arrangements prior to negotiating productivity deals). Both were clearly
crucial for the success of the program.

(a) Managers as Change Agents

Hill's comments on this include reference to some successes but
mainly include descriptions of how briefing sessions were run to
help managers discuss the philosophy with their staff and to
understand the socio-technical theory of job design. He later notes
how top level support for the whole exercise was to wane and how
rapid staff movements mitigated against the consolidation of new
ideas. Our study indicated this "channel of implementation" was
soon to dry up and Figure 2 summarizes how the hope that
departmental managers would transform the company was not to
be realized.

(b) Progress toward the Productivity Deals

As Hill suggested, and our inquiries confirmed, the philosophy
exercise did help the introduction of the productivity deals. Joint
working parties of management and worker representatives were a
new departure in the company. To an unprecedented degree, management were discussing and explaining their plans to workers in
these committees. Yet our study produced strong evidence that all
was not what it may have appeared in this respect. The JWPs first
met in 1966, were halted because of industrial action in 1967, then
met again through 1968. (The deals were signed in 1969 and 1970.)
Reflecting on the slow progress of 1966, a management representative was later to say in a paper to his colleagues:

> It is as well to remind you that at this stage the company had not fed in
> the concepts it had in mind, in other words we went into bat with the
> working parties with the blank piece of paper approach, except that the
> management representatives declared what they felt were impediments
> to efficiency, e.g. restriction practices, overtime. In hindsight we feel it
> would have speeded up the discussion had we exposed the concepts we
> had in mind at the outset and used the working parties to ferret out
> other concepts and to graft flesh onto bones. However, you will recall
> that at this time the wage freeze was imposed upon us and perhaps this
> gave us a false impression that we had all the time in the world to allow
> participation/involvement to take its natural course. For the first few
> months of the meetings which took place once a week (half day), most

Figure 2 **Events Associated with Managers as Change Agents**

The philosophy had been launched with a "fanfare of trumpets." The support of top management had been carefully wooed, though even here was *some* evidence of bulldozer tactics. Later certainly the sell was to become harder.

Reactions to the philosophy varied, though supporters seemed to be winning the day. Some people did not understand it. Others saw it in the context of the period of relative austerity the company had just passed through.

Managers were encouraged to become more participative. Problems here led to a feeling that early experiences were patchy in their success.

In the absence of social skills training all people were given were exhortations and the impression that failures were not respectable.

Many managers involved were technical men. For them the immense work load put on them after the conferences seemed to be producing slow results.

People thought there may have been more for those paid weekly (in, e.g., equal status) from the philosophy than was true for staff, but it was difficult to get those paid weekly to see this.

The demonstration job redesign projects did not inspire confidence.

People looked to their supervisors' behavior to assess how worthwhile continued effort would be. Important inconsistencies were seen.

Rapid staff movements were taking place at this time. Commitment to the philosophy was not a relevant factor for appointment at senior level in Shell Refining, nor for success in a career in the broader Royal Dutch/Shell group.

By 1970 the refinery managers at both Stanlow and Shell Haven were known as unsympathetic to the philosophy. No support from higher levels was visible.

In 1972 reports were published of an alleged success in participation in the Stanlow wax plant. At this time serious problems at the plant led many to believe that, on the contrary, the wax plant was an example of the "be nice" philosophy coming unstuck.

of the ideas being generated came from the management representatives, some of whom, you will recall, were present on all working
parties. Obviously, they were gently feeding in the concepts of the
embryo plan and ensuring that cross fertilization between the JWPs was
taking place.

To describe this as "participation" sounds somewhat dubious, even
allowing for the fact that the level of openness between management and the workers that did exist at this time was greater than
ever before. By 1968, however, delays had been such that management had been spurred on, secretly and unilaterally, to decide what
it wanted. The manager from whose report we have just quoted
said to us in an interview:

> From about 1968 management took the initiative. We went along to the
> meetings with blank sheets of paper, just like before. Our minds too had
> to appear to be blank! But it was really a process of re-education we
> were in from now on. Management knew what they wanted by now,
> but we had to lead the men. Change had to emanate from the same
> union as the men belonged to. A number of items appeared on the
> agenda, but we presented ideas as if they were off the top of our heads.
> Really, the second set of working parties was just a gimmick. They were
> just a way of moving toward the productivity deals.

Comments by a union representative about this period provide a
clue as to how this apparent spontaneity was engineered. While he
fully understood that the philosophy had been launched in 1966,
this interviewee nevertheless maintained that as a real influence it
did not emerge until after an industrial dispute in mid-1967. "After
that," he said, "it led to the productivity deal." Reports such as
these, taken with the close links most people we interviewed saw
between the philosophy and the productivity deals, tend to suggest
that references to the "spirit of the philosophy" were regularly
being made at that time as part of a management effort to formulate
and implement the revised union agreements it desired; a manipulative rather than a collaborative element was predominant in
management dealings with the unions.

Later, that goodwill which had been built up through the
productivity deals was not to last. At the time of our survey in most
ways the "pre-deal orthodoxy" had been reestablished in shop-floor
working. Commenting on such developments an ex-union
negotiator said:

Up till 1969 there had been wage freezes. So the pressures were great to sign for money. But many people believed in the deal then because it was a change in our position and status in the company, and because the company assured us "this was not the end, but the beginning!" But look at the value of the productivity deals then, and now! And look at the erosion of the differentials! The company was not willing to try to keep it alive. . . . The company doing nothing has left a bitter taste. We [operators at Shell Haven] have had only one strike in all this time, but that is not due to the company being good!

Included in the deals was the provision that employees should be paid an annual salary rather than a weekly wage. As part of this change, paid overtime was replaced by a "time off in lieu of overtime" provision. The abolition of paid overtime ended any mechanism by which shop-floor employees could be paid more money short of increasing their annual salaries. Successive years of U.K. government pay policy prevented this latter course of action, and early reviews of annual salary levels (conducted in 1971 and 1972 between governmental pay pauses) produced settlements described as "penny-pinching." While Shell's original deal had made them leaders, within 12 months or so other companies caught and passed them without requiring concessions of workers that were built into Shell's deals and, importantly, without abolishing paid overtime. "In the early days the operators made it work," said a plant manager, "then they looked for the rewards and did not get them."

CASE NOTES:

a. Flanders, A., *The Fawley Productivity Agreements*, Faber and Faber, London, 1964.

b. Emery, F. E. and Trist, E. L., "The Causal Texture of Organizational Environments," *Human Relations* 18 (1965), pp. 12–32.

Blackler and Brown's Conclusions

Blackler and Brown summarize the points emerging from their interviews:

1. Top management and their social science advisers had somewhat different perspectives on the activities in which they were jointly engaged.

2. In contradiction to early optimistic reports of the project, it never became a force for widespread change.

3. Despite the good intentions of the architects of the philosophy, championing the values of mutual respect and partnership, a manipulative element became a feature of the exercise.

The emphasis Blackler and Brown place on the word "manipulation" says as much about their value judgments and their academic disagreements with the Tavistock Institute as it does about the activities at Shell.

Given the nature of the project, it is not surprising that many employees felt pressured or uncomfortable. Several interviewees mention the pressure they felt at the conferences and point out that as a result doubters acquiesced or suspended judgment rather than voice their objections.

It is also apparent that some site managers were uncomfortable with the consultants. The consultants were reluctant to adopt a directive style, implying that managers had a choice. In practice, managers felt they had to support the philosophy or reject it in total. This led to a good deal of frustration. As one manager at Shell Haven commented:

> We were more sluggish getting off the mark than Stanlow was. We weren't sure how to handle it. We had the Tavistock people over for a few days, but I blew my top at them! They wouldn't give us an opinion as to what we ought to do. "What are we paying you for?" I exploded! They explained that they were working only as catalysts and we had to take responsibility for any program.

One further point emerging from Blackler and Brown's study concerns the philosophy itself. With the encouragement of Tavistock and the Employee Relations Planning (ERP) group, Shell UK Refining had espoused some values over which, with hindsight, it is clear that it could not exercise real control. A pivotal notion in the philosophy was that the company should act as "the custodian of the assets of society and should not make a profit at its expense." Such a role would have involved a political balancing act to resolve the conflicting needs of governments and other interest groups. Shell UK Refining, in view of its subsidiary position within Royal Dutch Shell, would not have had the freedom of action to make such a concept a reality.

What Can the Shell Experience Teach Us?

It is easy with hindsight to be critical of the way that the exercise was handled, but it should be remembered that Shell was largely breaking new ground. Moreover, Shell was unlucky in the timing of its initiative. The government's pay freezes in the 1970s undermined the benefits that had been gained from the new approach to industrial relations and the efforts to eliminate overtime. The question today is whether the Shell experience can tell us anything useful about what or what not to do.

The new philosophy had been worked out on an intellectual plane by the Tavistock Institute and Shell's ERP group and this seems to have been the source of some of the problems. The philosophy statement itself ran to around 2,000 words and embraced concepts that might have been difficult to communicate in a way that related to the day-to-day issues facing managers and employees (see Appendix on page 235). Management changes and the industrial relations climate appear to have made it difficult to sustain support for the philosophy for long enough for it to become part of the culture.

These appear to be the chief lessons:

1. *Philosophy should not be too far from reality and the operational problems facing the company.* Shell was attempting a radical departure in its philosophy but it was doing so from a "cold start." This created a credibility gap. The new philosophy laid out a comprehensive view of how the company should run its affairs but it was labored and intellectual in style and therefore difficult to translate into action.

2. *There should be a clear theme with which everyone can identify.* While senior managers probably saw Shell's industrial relations difficulties as the key issue, these problems did not make a very good common cause for the rest of the organization. The objective of stewardship of the "social resources" might have filled this role, but it was probably insufficiently practical to motivate people's immediate actions; and the theme of "joint optimization" was too elusive to appeal to most of the managers.

3. *Changing philosophy and culture needs stamina.* We have noted in other cases that people react badly to the initial communication

of a philosophy. Cynicism can be widespread and some people will feel manipulated or brainwashed. If the words are subsequently turned into action and the effort is sustained for a period of years, then cynicism dissolves and real emotional support develops. For a variety of reasons—external pressures, union difficulties and management changes—the effort was not sustained for long enough to overcome the initial resistance.

4. *Philosophy and action have to be consistent to be accepted.* Shell's philosophy proclaimed participation and openness. Yet the implementation process inevitably involved some top-down pressure, and negotiations within the joint working parties were not always able to live up to the true spirit of openness. The conflict between the philosophy's espoused values and management action generated concern and some cynicism.

The fact that employees remembered this conflict as much as six years later points to the importance of making values and action consistent.

NOTES

1. C. P. Hill, *Towards a New Philosophy of Management* (London: Gower Press, 1971).

2. F. H. M. Blackler and C. A. Brown, *Whatever Happened to Shell's New Philosophy of Management* (Aldershot, England: Saxon House, 1980).

3. F. H. M. Blackler and C. A. Brown, "A New Philosophy of Management: Shell Revisited," *Personnel Review* 10, no. 1 (1981), pp. 15–21. Reproduced with the permission of the authors.

Draft Statement of Objectives and Philosophy (May 1966)

. . . .

I Primary objective

Shell Refining Company is primarily concerned to maximize its contribution to the long-term profitability of the Shell Group insofar as this arises from the efficiency with which it uses the Group's resources of men, money, and material.

The resources to which it has legal rights of privileged access are nonetheless part of the total resources of society as a whole and are, in this sense, social resources; the Company believes that they must be protected, developed, and managed as such. It furthermore believes that its use of these resources must be such as to contribute to meeting society's requirements for products and services.

The Company recognizes, however, that ultimate discretion for what can be done to maximize Group profitability cannot properly be exercised without having a total picture of the exploration, production, transportation, manufacturing, marketing, and research functions. Since the activities of Shell Refining Company lie mainly within the manufacturing function, this makes necessary the statement of its specific objectives in terms of the minimum expenditure of resources appropriate to the discharge of its responsibilities to the Group.

II Specific objectives

Specifically this commits the Company to:

(a) meeting the current market requirements for refined petroleum products with minimum expenditure of total resources per unit of quantity of given quality, and

(b) ensuring the Company's ability to meet emerging market requirements with decreasing expenditure of total resources per unit of quantity of specified quality.

An essential task of Management is to seek at all times optimal solutions to (a) and (b).

In addition, the Company is specifically committed by its position in the Group to:

(c) seeking continually from the Group the power and the information necessary to enable it to meet its responsibilities.

In certain circumstances it may be necessary to seek a redefinition of its responsibilities in order that the Company's capabilities may be best used on behalf of the Group.

Implicit in these three specific objectives and in the fact that the Company's resources are part of the total resources of society, are the following additional specific objectives:

(d) creating conditions in which employees at all levels will be encouraged and enabled to develop and to realize their potentialities while contributing toward the Company's objectives;

(e) carrying out its productive and other operations in such a way as to safeguard the health and safety of its employees and the public;

(f) seeking to reduce any interference that may be caused by its activities to the amenities of the community, accepting the measures practised under comparable conditions in British industry as a minimum standard and making use of the expertise and knowledge available within the Group.

III The principle of joint-optimization as a guide to implementation

The Company must manage both a social system, of people and their organization, and a technical system, of physical equipment and resources. Optimization of its overall operations can be achieved only by jointly optimizing the operation of these two systems; attempts to optimize the two independently of each other, or undue emphasis upon one of them at the expense or the neglect of the other, must fail to achieve optimization for the Company as a whole.

IV Key characteristics of the evolving technical system

In order to create appropriate conditions for the optimization of the overall system, it is necessary to design the social system jointly with the technical system recognizing that the latter has certain key persistent characteristics which must be taken into account. These characteristics are:

(a) The Company forms part of a complex, science-based industry subject to rapid technical change. This rate of change can be expected to increase in the future.

(b) There is a wide measure of flexibility available in all the main processes involved in oil refining, i.e. distillation, conversion, and blending. The added value which results from refining operations depends to a high degree upon the skillful use of this flexibility in plant design and operation and the programming of refinery and overall Company operations in order to meet variable market requirements from given and variable inputs.

(c) The Company is capital-intensive and it follows that adequate criteria of overall Company performance must be sought mainly in measures of efficiency of plant utilization. The importance to overall Company performance of efficient plant utilization makes necessary a high degree of plant reliability.

(d) The Company's refineries are already highly involved with automation and instrumentation. Pressure for a very much higher level of automation and instrumentation arises from the development of new processes and the drive toward optimal use of the flexibility described in (b) above, and the need to improve the ability to control, identify, and account for the large number of movements through the technical system at any one time.

(e) There is considerable variation in the degree of automation of different operations in the Company. Labor-intensive activities exist side by side with highly automated ones. Despite the trends noted in (a) and (b) above, some variation is likely to persist.

(f) The Company's process operations are carried out on a continuous 24 hours per day, seven day week basis, by a number of shift teams, while many associated service activities are carried out discontinuously on a day working basis.

(g) The refineries and Head Office are geographically widely separated and within refineries there is a considerable dispersion of the various activities. For economic and technical reasons this characteristic is likely to persist.

V Implications for the social system

The rapid and increasing rate of change in the technical system defined in characteristic (a) creates a special need for new expertise, skills, and knowledge at all levels, and new forms of organization to cope with changing requirements. It also increases the rate at which skills and knowledge are rendered obsolete. The Company believes that its objectives in relation to the social nature of its resources commit it to train its employees in new skills and new knowledge where obsolescence of skills and knowledge has resulted from its own or the industry's technical development. These effects require the Company to plan for the development of appropriate skills and forms of organization in parallel with the planning of technical change.

The most significant consequence of characteristics (b), (c), (d), (f), and (g) is that economic production within our process technology is critically dependent upon people effectively dealing with information yielded by the technical system and contributing the most appropriate information to the control and guidance of that system. Some of these informational flows are confined to individuals who take information from the technical system and feed back guidance directly into it. Other informational flows must be carried at any one time by a network of many people at many different organizational levels. The effectiveness of this social informational network depends upon the recognition by all those involved in its design and operation that it is made up of people and is therefore affected by the factors that influence human behavior.

The wide geographical dispersion of the refineries and the extensive layout within the refineries themselves present an impediment to effective communications. This makes it even more necessary for the Company to design efficient informational flows.

A further consequence of characteristic (c), namely the need for a high degree of plant reliability, is that economic production is also highly dependent upon the application of craft skills and knowledge.

In information handling and to a large degree in the exercise of craft skills, the problem is to avoid lapses of attention and errors in observing, diagnosing and communicating or acting upon information. Information handling work in the refining industry is such that lapses and errors are likely to result in heavy costs, both from delay in recognizing errors and taking corrective action and from the nature of the equipment and the processes involved. The only promising way of avoiding these faults is for the individual to be *internally* motivated to exercise responsibility and initiative. Any *external* control can only act after the error has occurred or had its effect.

In contrast, in those jobs where the main human contribution is manual labor, there is some choice as to how control may be achieved. Although optimal control requires internal motivation, the shortcomings associated with mainly manual tasks do not normally result in heavy costs and it is possible to achieve an economic degree of control by external incentives and supervision. For these reasons, the exercise of personal responsibility and initiative in such work, although desirable, may be considered less significant.

However, the manual jobs in the refineries [characteristic (e)] exist mainly amongst service activities ancillary to the operating and engineering activities which are central to the task of oil refining. It is considered essential that the Company's philosophy should be appropriate to the nature of these central activities. For those activities of a different nature it may be necessary to modify them through technical developments, e.g. the introduction of mechanization or automation, or to develop other social systems appropriate to them, in keeping with the values of the Company's philosophy.

Despite the complication arising from characteristic (e) therefore, the major implication of this group of technical characteristics emerges as the need to develop a high level of personal responsibility and initiative.

VI Responsibility and commitment

People cannot be expected to develop within themselves and to exercise the level of responsibility and initiative that is required unless they can be involved in their task and unless, in the long run, it is possible to develop commitment to the objectives served by their task.

The Company recognizes that it cannot expect its employees at all levels to develop adequate involvement and commitment spontaneously or in response to mere exhortation. It must set out to create the conditions under which such commitment may develop.

The work of social scientists has shown that the creation of such conditions cannot be achieved simply by the provision of satisfactory terms of service, including remuneration. The provision of such terms of service is essential, but is not in itself sufficient; for involvement and commitment at all levels it is necessary to go beyond this, to meet the general psychological requirements that men have of their work.

The following are some of the psychological requirements that relate to the content of a job:

(a) The need for the content of the work to be reasonably demanding of the individual in terms other than those of sheer endurance, and for it to provide some variety.

(b) The need for an individual to know what his job is and how he is performing in it.

(c) The need to be able to learn on the job and go on learning.

(d) The need for some area of decision making where the individual can exercise his discretion.

(e) The need for some degree of social support and recognition within the organization.

(f) The need for an individual to be able to relate what he does and what he produces to the objectives of the Company and to his life in the community.

(g) The need to feel that the job leads to some sort of desirable future which does not necessarily imply promotion.

These requirements exist in some form for the large majority of men and at all levels of employment. Their relative significance, however, will clearly vary from individual to individual and it is not possible to provide for their fulfillment in the same way for all kinds of people. Similarly, different jobs will provide varying degrees of opportunity for the fulfillment of particular requirements.

They cannot generally be met, however, simply by redesigning individual jobs. Most tasks involve more than one person and, in any case, all jobs must be organizationally related to the Company's objectives. If the efforts to meet the above requirements for individuals are not to be frustrated, the Company must observe certain principles in developing its organizational form. Thus, the individual must know not only what he is required to do, but also the way in which his work ties in with what others are doing, the part he plays in the communications network, and the limits within which he has genuine discretionary powers. Furthermore, the individual's responsibilities should be defined in terms of objectives to be pursued; although procedural rules are necessary for coordination, they must be reviewed regularly in the light of experience gained in pursuing these objectives.

Responsibility and authority must go hand in hand in order to avoid situations in which people are delegated responsibility but do not have the means to exercise it. Likewise, the Company must be ready to redefine responsibilities where there are capabilities which are unused.

Not least, the Company must seek to ensure that the distribution of status and reward is consistent with the level of responsibility carried by the individual.

In following this course the Company will seek the fullest involvement of all employees and will make the best use of available knowledge and experience of the social sciences.

VII Principle of implementation of the philosophy

The effective implementation and communication of the philosophy throughout the Company can be achieved only if its mode of implementation manifests the spirit of the philosophy. Verbal or written communication alone will not suffice; it is essential that all employees be enabled to relate the philosophy to themselves by participating in the implementation of the philosophy in their particular parts of the Company.

A special burden of responsibility must rest with the senior managers, who alone are in a position to exercise the leadership and provide the necessary impetus to translate the philosophy into a living reality. Starting with their commitment, it will be possible to involve progressively the other levels of the employees in searching out the implications for themselves. As the philosophy begins to shape the activities of the Company, it will be able more effectively to pursue its objectives.

CHAPTER
11

Do You Have a Good
Mission Statement?

. . . .

A division planning manager recently produced a nicely bound, 52-page document simply headed *Our Mission*. Although it included an eight-page summary of the mission statement for the division and subsidiary statements for each function, including one for marketing, sales, export, production, technical, finance, personnel, and planning, it lacked liveliness and gave few insights into the business. The statements did not demonstrate that the company had a sound strategy. The functional statements did not fit easily together. The company values did not shine through to give a sense of pride in the company. Lastly, there was no tangible guidance for behavior. It would be difficult for an individual manager to know what day-to-day behavior was expected.

The document had been put together with a considerable amount of effort, involving all members of senior management. Each function had written its own section and the management committee had worked together on the overall statement. Yet each member of the management committee agreed with our judgment that as a whole it was ineffective. Although each manager had his or her own criticisms, the real problem was that the committee had no objective criteria against which to judge the quality of the document. The planner, who was administering the process, had no basis for saying that the quality was poor. All agreed that it was a first draft effort, and that if they repeated the exercise next year it would probably be better; but there was no agreement about what would constitute a better document.

The need to assess the quality of a mission statement is a problem that is being faced by many management teams and consultants. Mission statements have become an important tool of management. They are believed to help clarify management thinking and improve communication with the organization, and they now get regular attention in texts on strategic management. It is not unusual for managers in management development courses to be asked to develop a mission statement for their business. Recent research by Fred David, associate professor of management at Alabama's Auburn University, gives an insight into the scale of usage of mission statements in U.S. firms.[1] David sent questionnaires about the use of statements to all *Business Week* 1,000 firms. A total of 181 responses were received: 41 percent had developed a mission statement while 59 percent had not. Of the 75 organizations with statements, 30 were manufacturing businesses and 45 service firms. Research we have carried out in Britain suggests that almost half the large businesses in that country have a mission statement or something similar. The extent of the use of mission statements in Britain was a surprise to the research team. Many British managers still find the word distasteful, associating it with hype and insincerity. In addition, we have found that mission statements are more evident at the division and business unit level than at the corporate level in large companies. All told, we have collected almost 200 mission statements from U.S., European, and Japanese companies (see Table 11.1).

Despite the large-scale use of mission statements, little guidance is available on what constitutes a high-quality statement. Our work has given us a definition of mission, and we have turned this understanding into a questionnaire entitled "Do you have a good mission statement?" (see Figure 11.1). The questionnaire is based on the four elements of mission described in Chapter 1: purpose, strategy, values, and behavioral standards.

Purpose

Why does the organization exist? For what end result is all the effort being expended? Purpose is the ultimate rationale for the organization and provides people with a justification for their work. It is something that lies behind specific objectives or goals; it deals with the philosophical question of the role of business in society.

We have defined two questions that should assist managers in deciding whether they have created a satisfactory purpose.

Table 11.1 **Mission and Philosophy Statements Collected**

3i plc
Abbey Life Assurance
    Company, Ltd.
AB Electronic Products
    Group plc
Akzo
AMEC plc
Appleyard Group plc
Arizona Bank
Arkla, Inc.
Armstrong World
    Industries
Ashridge Management
    College
Association of
    Management
    Consulting Firms
Atlantic Electric
BAA plc
Ball Corporation
Bank America Corporation
Bank South
BASF Aktiengesellschaft
BBA Group plc
Beatrice Companies, Inc.
BICC plc
Black & Decker
Blue Circle Industries plc
Boeing Company
Borg-Warner Corporation
BPB Industries plc
British Gas plc
British Petroleum
    Company plc
British United Provident
    Association, Ltd.
Bunzl plc
Leo Burnett USA
Burson-Marsteller
Cadbury Schweppes plc
Capital Holding
    Corporation

Carteret Savings and Loan
    Association
Caterpillar, Inc.
Celestial Seasonings
Center for Creative
    Leadership
Charter Consolidated plc
Chevron Corporation
Chloride Group plc
Ciba-Geigy
Citizens and Southern
    Georgia Corporation
Clark
Coats Viyella plc
Colorado National
    Bankshares, Inc.
Columbia Gas System
Commerce Union
    Corporation
Corning Glass Works
Costain Group plc
Dana Corporation
Dayton-Hudson
    Corporation
Delmarva Power
DRG plc
ECC International, Ltd.
El Du Pont de Nemours &
    Company
Electro Scientific
    Industries, Inc.
Eli Lilley and Company
Elswick plc
Emhart Corporation
Excess Insurance Group
FI Group plc
Ford Motor Company
Gencor
General Electric Company
General Motors
    Corporation
Gerber Foods

Glaxo Holdings plc
Glynwed International plc
Grumann Corporation
GTE Corporation
Guardian Royal Exchange
Guinness plc
Hanson Trust plc
Hewlett-Packard
    Company
Hickson Group
Hitachi Shipbuilding &
    Engineering Co., Ltd.
Honda Motor Co., Ltd.
Hormel
Hunting Associated
    Industries plc
Imperial Taverns
Inchcape plc
Intel
International Business
    Machines Corporation
ITT Barton
ITT Corporation
Jaguar Cars, Ltd.
Jewel Companies
Jewish Institute for
    Geriatric Care
Johnson & Johnson
The Kaye Organization,
    Ltd.
Laporte Industries, Ltd.
Libbey-Owens-Ford
    Company
The Limited, Inc.
Lloyds Bank plc
London International
    Group plc
Low & Bonar plc
Lucas Group
Marion Laboratories, Inc.
Macarthy plc
continued

Table 11.1 (continued)

Mars
Mary Kay Cosmetics
Matsushita Electric
 Corporation
McDonald's Corporation
John Menzies plc
Metropolitan Police
Monsanto
Motorola, Inc.
National City Corporation
NCR Corporation
New York State
 Electricity & Gas
 Corporation
Norcros plc
Northern Foods plc
Norton Company
Ohio Edison and Penn
 Power
Olston Corporation
Pacific Gas and Electric
 Company
J. C. Penney Company,
 Inc.
Pilkington plc
Plessey Company plc
Polly Peck International
 plc
Port Authority of New
 York & New Jersey
Portsmouth & Sunderland
 Newspapers plc
PPG Industries
Price Waterhouse
 International
Procter & Gamble
 Company
Public Service Company
 of Colorado
Public Service Electric

and Gas Company
Quad/Graphics
Quaker Oats Company
Raychem Corporation
Redland plc
Richardson Sheffield
Rockwell International
 Corporation
Rover Group plc
Rowntree plc
Royal Dutch/Shell Group
 of Companies
Royal Insurance (UK), Ltd.
RTZ Corporation plc
J. Sainsbury plc
St. Paul's Cathedral
Security Pacific
 Corporation
Shell New Zealand
Smith & Nephew
 Associated Companies
 plc
W. H. Smith, Ltd.
Society Corporation
Southeast Banking
 Corporation
Southern Company
 Services, Inc.
Sunwest Bank of
 Albuquerque
Tarmac plc
Tesco Stores, Ltd.
Texaco, Inc.
Texas American
 Bancshares, Inc.
Texas Instruments
TI Group plc
Tioxide Group plc
FH Tomkins plc
Tootal Group plc

Toshiba Corporation
Toshiba UK, Ltd.
Toyota Motors
 Corporation
Trafalgar House plc
Transport Development
 Group plc
Trusthouse Forte plc
Ultramar plc
United Biscuits plc
United Kingdon Central
 Council for Nursing,
 Midwifery, and Health
 Visiting
United Technologies
 Corporation
U.S. Postal Service
USX Corporation
Vaux Group plc
Wachovia Corporation
Washington Mutual
 Savings Bank
Washington Water Power
 Company
Watts Blake Bearne & Co.
 plc
Wellcome Foundation,
 Ltd.
Whirlpool Corporation
Whitbread & Co. plc
Williams Holdings plc
Willis Faber plc
Wisconsin Electric Power
 Company
F.W. Woolworth Company
Woolworth Holdings plc
Xerox Corporation
Zale Corporation

Figure 11.1 **Do You Have a Good Mission Statement?**

Answer each question: 0 = No   1 = To some degree   2 = Yes

1. Purpose

(a)   Does the statement describe an inspiring purpose that avoids playing to the selfish interest of the stakeholders—shareholders, customers, employees, suppliers?

0   1   2

(b)   Does the statement describe the company's responsibility to its stakeholders?

0   1   2

2. Strategy

(a)   Does the statement define a business domain and explain why it is attractive?

0   1   2

(b)   Does the statement describe the strategic positioning that the company prefers in a way that helps to identify the type of competitive advantage it will look for?

0   1   2

3. Values

(a)   Does the statement identify values that form a link with the organization's purpose and act as beliefs that employees can feel proud of?

0   1   2

(b)   Do the values "resonate" with and reinforce the organization's strategy?

0   1   2

4. Behavioral Standards

(a)   Does the statement describe important behavioral standards that serve as beacons of the strategy and the values?

0   1   2

continued

Figure 11.1 (continued)

(b)   Are the behavioral standards described in a way that
      enables individual employees to judge whether they have
      behaved correctly or not?

                          0   1   2

5. Character

(a)   Does the statement give a portrait of the company that
      captures the culture of the organization?

                          0   1   2

(b)   Is the statement easy to read?

                          0   1   2

Maximum score 20; good score 15; poor score less than 10.

> 1. *Does the statement describe an inspiring purpose that avoids
>   playing to the selfish interests of the stakeholders—shareholders,
>   customers, employees, suppliers?*

All stakeholders—shareholders, customers, employees, suppliers,
and even the community—have a claim on the company. It is,
therefore, legitimate to ask whether the company is in business to
maximize the return to shareholders, to produce the highest-quality
products for customers, or to provide the most rewarding jobs for
employees. Which stakeholder has the greatest claim?

The most common answer is that the shareholders, as owners of
the business, have the greatest claim. Companies such as Hanson,
Britain's largest diversified conglomerate, have made this choice
explicit. Lord Hanson says that: "The central tenet of my faith is
that the shareholder is king." In other such companies it is not
uncommon to hear the chairman say: "Managers should realize that
we are in business to make profits."

It is perfectly possible to build a purpose around each of the
other stakeholders. A consumer cooperative would be unabashed
about stressing its consumer–members; a farm cooperative views its
owner–suppliers as being paramount; and a professional partnership might legitimately argue that the working partners have the
greatest claim on the business.

What our research has shown is that some companies have defined a purpose that rises above the interests of any one stakeholder: a higher ideal. These companies have defined a cause that *all* the stakeholders can feel proud of supporting. By refusing to identify any one stakeholder as having the greatest claim on the business, these companies are able to play down self-interest and emphasize the greater good that all stakeholders are supporting. By creating a higher cause, these companies are able to argue that each stakeholder should take from the business only what is reasonable. Surpluses are then applied to furthering the cause.

An excellent example of an organization with a purpose aimed at a higher ideal is London's St. Paul's Cathedral, whose mission statement defines its purpose clearly: "to proclaim the Christian gospel according to the practices and traditions of the Church of England, and, in an environment of excellence and beauty, to uplift the minds of men, women and children to the things of the spirit." It is, however, equally possible to have an uplifting purpose in a conventional business. Matsushita, the world's largest producer of electrical products, has probably developed the most coherent philosophy based on a higher ideal. In the words of Konosuke Matsushita, the company's 88-year-old founder:

> Happiness of man is built on mental stability and material affluence. To serve the foundation of happiness, through making man's life affluent with inexpensive and inexhaustible supply of necessities like water inflow, is the duty of the manufacturer. Profit comes in compensation for contribution to society. Profit is a yardstick with which to measure the degree of social contribution made by an enterprise. Thus profit is a result rather than a goal. An enterprise in the red will make all co-operating people poor, and ultimately the whole society poor. If the enterprise tries to earn a reasonable profit but fails to do so, the reason is because the degree of its social contribution is still insufficient.

Matsushita sees the purpose of his company as being to serve society. Profit is merely a by-product and provides the means for making further social contributions.

Noble statements such as these may initially seem out of place in a U.S. or European context. Yet some of these countries' most successful companies have purposes aimed at a high ideal. Sainsbury's, Britain's most successful grocer, states that its primary objective is "to discharge the responsibility as leaders in our trade by acting with complete integrity, by carrying out our work to the highest standards, and by contributing to the public good and to the quality of life in the community." Sainsbury's final objective, intentionally placed last, is "to generate sufficient profit to finance continual improvement and growth of the business whilst providing our shareholders with an excellent return on their investment." Like Matsushita, the Sainsbury philosophy sees profit as an engine for growth rather than as an end in itself.

2. *Does the statement describe the company's responsibility to its stakeholders?*

While a purpose statement should avoid legitimizing the selfish interests of stakeholders, it must clarify the company's responsibility to each stakeholder. The company defines a cause (a purpose) that is inspiring and worthy of the support of its stakeholders. The stakeholders join the cause by giving their loyalty to the company. In return, the company needs to define what each stakeholder should expect to gain from the relationship. On the surface, defining the company's responsibility is a reasonably straightforward process. Shareholders will get better-than-average returns; employees will get better-than-average compensation and working conditions; customers will get superior products; and suppliers will get fair dealing and loyalty from the company.

However, at a deeper level, a company needs to think through what is the nature of its preferred relationship with each stakeholder. It wishes to gain the loyalty of each stakeholder, but it may not be in a position to buy that loyalty by offering better financial terms. It may not choose to pay top rates to employees, commit to long term relationships with suppliers, or guarantee to provide continuous supply to customers; but it must think through what it can offer each of those groups that will retain their loyalty.

The engineering company BICC's mission statement describes explicitly the company's response to each of its stakeholders: shareholders, customers, employees, and the wider community. For example: "BICC aims to develop and maintain good relationships with all its customers and deal at all times ethically and in good faith." Awareness of the broader environment in which the company operates is seen to be important, hence: "BICC endeavors to ensure that its employees have the opportunity to contribute in practical ways to local community interests." By delineating in detail its preferred relationship with each stakeholder, the company explains the benefits that the stakeholders should expect to gain from a relationship with the company. The statement becomes the company's commitment to deliver something to the stakeholders: to "ensure rapid response to meet customer's needs"; or to "provide an open, challenging and involving environment for all who work in the company."

Johnson & Johnson's mission statement is called *Our Credo* and in fact reads very like a religious creed. It is set out in four verses, each dealing with the company's responsibility to a different stakeholder. It gives pride of place to the customer: "to the doctors, nurses and patients, to mothers and all others who use our products and services." Last in the list come the stockholders. This verse of the Credo describes the principles the company aims to follow in order that "the stockholders should realize a fair return."

Every company is unique and each one will have a different set of statements about its responsibilities to its stakeholders. The best mission statements make these commitments clear so that each stakeholder knows what to expect from its relationship with the company.

Strategy

Strategy is the commercial rationale for how the business is going to achieve its purpose. The subject of strategy has been much analyzed and written about. The classic works are Michael Porter's two books,[2] *Competitive Strategy* and *Competitive Advantage*.

Good strategy is about finding a way to run the business that is better than its immediate competitors. Good strategy is also about choosing a market that is attractive, where competitors and customers will not force prices down too low or insist on cost levels that are uneconomic. Articulating a particular strategy can be difficult and will need a full description to capture the detailed reasons why a market is attractive or why a set of activities will lead to better performance than the competitors. All of these details cannot be included in a mission statement; yet the mission does need to describe the central elements of strategy. From examining companies' statements we have judged that two questions help managers include the appropriate level of detail about strategy in their mission statement:

1. Does the statement define a business domain and explain why it is attractive?

A mission statement needs to make clear what business the company is in. The Limited, Inc. is in the business of apparel retailing; the London International Group's statement says the company's "principal activities will continue to be the manufacture and marketing of high quality branded consumer goods and services." In describing the nature of the business, the statement should be as specific as possible. It should define not only a general industry but also what part of the industry the company prefers to compete in and why. The statement should give its readers confidence that the company knows clearly the type of business environment in which it can perform well.

Coca-Cola's mission statement is a good example. It explains the businesses the company is involved in: soft drinks, foods, and packaged consumer goods. It defines the company's strengths in these businesses: "an impeccable and positive image with the consumer; a unique franchise system second to none; and the intimate knowledge of, and contacts with, local business conditions around the world." It further defines conditions for entry into new markets—that there should be "sufficient inherent real growth potential." The reader is left with the impression of a company that knows what it is good at and where it wants to be.

Another company that gives a clear definition of its business domain is the heavy textiles company BBA, based in Yorkshire, Britain. In a document called *BBA—A Corporate Philosophy* (see Figure 11.2), famous for its blunt phrasing, Dr. John Whyte, the chief executive, has stated: "We shall concentrate in markets where: (a) The products are in a state of maturity or decline—'Sunset Industries' . . . (c) The capital cost of market entry is high, (d) Fragmentation of ownership on the supply side facilitates rapid earnings growth by acquisition of contribution flows." The statements about high barriers to entry and fragmented ownership explain why sunset industries of this type are attractive.

Both Coca-Cola and BBA have clearly stated the business domains that they want to compete in and why these domains are likely to be attractive. Their mission statements have more credibility as a result. The users of the statement can be confident that management have thought through an important element of strategy.

Figure 11.2 **BBA's Mission Statement**

BBA—A CORPORATE PHILOSOPHY

The inertia of history is a powerful influence on corporate philosophy. BBA in its 103 years of existence has strayed little from:

i. Yorkshire paternalism
ii. Weaving of heavy textiles
iii. Friction technology via woven or pressed resin media

The philosophy of BBA for the next few years will be to adapt rather than abandon the inert.

Management
(a) Grit and gumption are preferable to inertia and intellect.
(b) The Victorian work ethic is not an antique.
(c) One man can only serve one master, to whom he is responsible for a minimum number of succinctly defined tasks.
(d) Most companies owned or yet to be acquired possess adequate people waiting to be transformed by dedicated leadership.
(e) The effectiveness of an organization is in inverse proportion to the number of hierarchical layers.

Markets
We shall concentrate in markets where:

(a) The products are in a state of maturity or decline—"Sunset Industries."
(b) The scale of our presence in a market segment will allow price leadership.
(c) The capital cost of market entry is high.
(d) Fragmentation of ownership on the supply side facilitates rapid earnings growth by acquisition of contribution flows.

Money
(a) The longer run belongs to Oscar Wilde, who is dead.
(b) The key macro and micro variables of our business are so dynamic that poker becomes more predictable than planning and reactivity more profitable than rumination.

continued

Figure 11.2 **(continued)**

(c) Budgets are personal commitments made by management to their superiors, subordinates, shareholders and their self respect.

(d) The cheapest producer will win.

(e) The investment of money on average return of less than three points above market should be restricted to Ascot.

(f) Gearing should not exceed 40%. The location from which funds emanate should be matched to the location from which the profit stream permits their service.

(g) We are not currency speculators, even when we win.

(h) Tax is a direct cost to the business and, accordingly, should be eschewed.

(i) Victorian thrift is not an antique.

(j) Nothing comes free, cheap assets are often expensive utilities.

Monday

Our tactic is to:

  i. Increase the metabolic rate of BBA through directed endeavor.

 ii. To increase profit margins by drastic cost reduction.

iii. To massage and thereby extend the life cycle of the products in which we are engaged.

 iv. To become market dominant in our market niches by:
   (a) outproducing the competition.
   (b) transforming general markets where we are nobody to market niches where we are somebody.
   (c) buying competitors.

  v. Use less money in total and keep more money away from the tax man and the usurer.

 vi. Avoid the belief that dealing is preferable to working.

vii. Go home tired.

Maybe

(a) The replication of our day to day tactic provides long term growth.

continued

> (b) We need to address "Monday" this week and what our
>   reaction will be to what may be on "Monday" for the next
>   three years.
> (c) Three years is, in the current environment, the limit of
>   man's comprehension of what may be.
> (d) Long term growth necessitates:
>   i. Resource—notably men and money
>   ii. Sustained performance rather than superficial genius.

2. *Does the statement describe the strategic positioning that the
company prefers in a way that helps to identify the sort of competitive advantage it will look for?*

The strategic positioning of a company is the role it takes on relative
to its competitors. Within the business domain of food retailing,
some companies seek to gain advantage from cost leadership, offering a cash and carry service. Others aim to be a quality supplier
gaining economies of scale through volume and through brand
leadership. Others position themselves as specialist delicatessens,
offering a limited range to a narrow customer segment. Others
stress convenience for local customers, often opening at unusual
times. Each type of company has chosen a different positioning in
the food retailing business.

In many mission statements the description of a company's
strategic position is intermingled with the description of its business
domain. By defining the business domain, the mission statement
will often also make clear the positioning that the company prefers.
Nevertheless, a good mission statement should explicitly address
both questions, making sure that both are adequately answered.
Doing so gives the mission statement more credibility and gives its
users confidence that the basic elements of strategy have been
addressed by management.

Where the description of business domain does not address
strategic positioning, a separate paragraph or sentence is needed in
the statement. In *BBA—A Corporate Philosophy*, Dr. Whyte describes
the position that the company prefers to take up: the largest competitor with the lowest cost. He explains that BBA seeks "market niches
where we are somebody," where "the scale of our presence

. . . will allow price leadership." The company also seeks cost leadership: "to increase profit margins by drastic cost reduction" and "to become market dominant . . . by . . . outproducing the competition." At one point the document bluntly states: "The cheapest producer will win."

The F.I. Group is an information systems company that uses a network of computer professionals throughout the United Kingdom, working in flexibly organized work centers or at home. Its mission statement contains a succinct description of the strategic position it is aiming for: "F.I. Group's strategy is to maximize the value of its unusual asset base by establishing a competitive advantage over conventionally organized firms, and imitators of its approach, through cost and quality competitiveness." It will achieve this strategy by "developing, through modern telecommunications, the unutilized intellectual energy of individuals and groups unable to work in a conventional environment." Readers of the statement are immediately aware that this company has given considerable thought to identifying its competitive advantage and how this can best be exploited.

Values

Values are the morally based beliefs of the organization. They are the cornerstones of the corporate religion. Although they are hard to articulate because they are the assumptions lying behind many of the rules and behavioral standards in the company, it is vital that they are understood.

A company's values are often built on the personal values of its senior management. Where these personal values happen to fit the organization's purpose and its strategy, all is well. This fit normally occurs at the time an organization is founded. The founding managers create a natural fit between all three elements, rejecting strategies that do not blend easily with their values and defining a purpose that captures their deeply held beliefs. However, when the founders retire and professional managers take their place, the fit between the personal beliefs of the senior managers and the organization's values can be broken. Only by making the organization's values explicit can this potential mismatch be avoided.

Two questions help to ensure that the organization's values fit with its strategy and purpose.

1. Does the statement identify values that link with the organization's purpose and act as beliefs that employees can feel proud of?

We have pointed out that the best mission statements describe a purpose aimed at a high ideal. The purpose also clarifies the responsibility of the organization to its stakeholders. The company's values must link with these elements of its purpose.

Sainsbury's has a purpose of being a leader in its trade and of contributing to the quality of life. Quality is, therefore, one of its central values. This value applies to the products, shopping environment, and the high standards to which people throughout the organization work. It is a value everyone can feel proud of because it can be seen to be good in itself. To strive for the best quality is to achieve something worthwhile.

Matsushita is another company with an elevating purpose: the happiness of the individual through material affluence. Konosuke Matsushita took great care to articulate the company's values, describing them as the "Seven Spiritual Values":

- National service through industry
- Fairness
- Harmony and cooperation
- Struggle for betterment
- Courtesy and humility
- Adjustment and assimilation
- Gratitude

These are not values that are normally associated with hard-driving companies fighting to win in the international marketplace, yet they were carefully selected by Konosuke Matsushita for their moral content as well as their good business sense. He wanted employees to feel morally nourished by their work. By working to principles that they could be proud of, he felt they would find work more fulfilling. These values also link well with the Matsushita purpose. Fairness, betterment and harmony are all values that fit well with thoughts of the happiness of man.

Portsmouth & Sunderland Newspapers plc, a British independent publishing, printing, and retailing company, has a mission statement that makes clear the company's dedication to serving local communities. It sets out such values as customer service, quality and being market driven, in a way that explains how following them will ensure that the company "adds to and protects the quality of local life." The pride that the company takes in its activities and its history shines through this statement.

   2. *Do the values "resonate" with and reinforce the organization's strategy?*

For the best performance, strategy and values need to work together. If the strategy is cost driven, the value system needs to emphasize frugality. If the strategy is about coordination and team-work, the value system should give high regard to helpfulness and harmony.

Defining an organization's values is not about making a long list of all the good things in the business that have a moral content. It is about setting priorities. It is about, for example, whether frugality is more important than helpfulness. Day to day, these two values frequently conflict. "Should I be extra helpful and courier this document because I know the person wants it urgently? Or should I send it the cheapest way?" is a mundane issue, but one where the values conflict. It is possible to develop a rational answer to this dilemma, but in the day-to-day rush, most decisions are made on the basis of the value system rather than on a careful weighing of the pros and cons. Choosing the values that have the highest priority is therefore an essential part of managing the organization.

Honda's purpose is to be "Number One in terms of customer satisfaction," and its strategy is based on developing a broad spectrum of truly unique and innovative products, all designed from a global perspective. To achieve this, Honda promotes competition between different parts of the company as well as with rival manufacturers and encourages its employees to come up with new ideas and developments in technology. Its values of quality and efficiency—"respect sound theory, develop fresh ideas, and make the most effective use of time"—fit well with this strategy.

BBA's mission provides a second example of a good link between values and strategy. BBA's strategy is based on cost leadership in niche markets in sunset industries. Its values support this strategy well. The mission statement explains that in BBA "Grit and gumption are preferable to inertia and intellect" and "Victorian thrift is not an antique." This is reinforced by "Our tactic is to . . . use less money in total."

For some managers these puritan values might not seem uplift-ing or particularly moral. Their fit with strategy is clear, but their ability to make employees feel that work is worthwhile is less obvious. BBA operates from Yorkshire in the north of England and many managers brought up in this part of the country understand and value frugality. For these managers, BBA's values have a moral content, bringing added fulfillment to their work.

BBA and Honda are examples of companies with values that fit. For them, their values guide day-to-day behavior; act as an inspiration, help to make work more fulfilling; and also link more closely with strategy and purpose.

Behavioral Standards

A mission is made real only when it affects behavior: when it guides people's actions by helping them decide what to do and what not to do. Strategy and values both have behavioral messages. Strategy contains messages about what should be achieved—for example, low-cost production, excellent service. Values contain messages about how things should be done—for example, frugally, or harmoniously, or with quality.

When strategy and values support each other, the behavioral messages are doubly powerful. However, these messages don't achieve anything until they are translated by managers into behavioral standards. Behavioral standards are the organization's rules of thumb: "the way we do things around here," or the "ten commandments."

There are two questions that the mission statement writer should answer to be sure that the statement clarifies the behavioral standards.

1. *Does the statement describe important behavioral standards that serve as beacons of the strategy and the values?*

Companies with clear missions have a few behavioral standards that have come to symbolize the purpose, strategy, and values. If you ask managers why they like working for the company, or what is important about the way the company does business, it is these behavioral standards that they will most often refer to. Although they may be seemingly insignificant management actions, such as the holding of regular staff briefings or a policy of open accounting so that employees and customers can examine the figures, the company's culture has identified them as beacons of the mission.

We believe that good mission statements identify these behavioral standards and emphasize their importance.

Most mission statements describe behavior in a loose way, wrapped up in a statement of values. Sainsbury's, for example, states as one of its objectives: "In our stores, to achieve the highest standards of cleanliness and hygiene, efficiency of operation, convenience, and customer service, and thereby create as attractive and friendly a shopping environment as possible." There are plenty of behavioral messages in this statement, but there are no clear behavioral standards. A behavioral standard for Sainsbury's might read: "Store managers meet with their staff weekly to discuss cleanliness, efficiency and customer service. Junior staff and customers join in these standard-raising meetings." Or it might be a more simple behavioral standard, such as: "Every day store managers ask themselves, each other and staff, 'What have you done for the customer today?'"

Most mission statements do not contain behavioral standards as explicit as these because managers feel awkward about being so prescriptive. They do not want to tell people exactly how to behave. They would rather give guidelines that individual managers can fit to their own circumstances. They are right; as a general rule it is better to use the creativity of the individual to make the best of the situation.

However, some behavioral standards have a special importance that far outweighs the disadvantage of being over-prescriptive. Just like the ten commandments, these behaviors capture the essence of a company's religion. By making a few behavioral standards explicit, senior managers can attempt to control which behaviors become the beacons of their mission. In this way they create a tighter link between the mission statement and what is happening day to day in the company.

Insisting that these behavioral standards are described in the mission statement has other benefits. It demonstrates to the users that senior managers have thought about how they are going to translate the strategy and the values into action. It also gives a mandate to managers throughout the company to demand compliance with these behaviors.

The most famous examples of behavioral standards come from two of the world's best-known companies: Hewlett-Packard and

IBM. Hewlett-Packard (HP) coined the phrase, "Management by Wandering Around" (MBWA). This is a behavior standard at HP. The rationale for it was clearly described when the practice was introduced in *The HP Way*:

> To have a well managed operation it is essential that managers/supervisors be aware of what is happening in their areas—not just at their immediate level, but also at several levels below that. Our people are our most important resource and the managers have direct responsibility for their training, performance and well-being. To do this, managers must get around to find out how their people feel about their jobs and what they feel will make their work more productive and worthwhile.

HP's strategy is to focus on high-value niches in the industrial electronics market and to gain advantage through innovation. Its strategy depends on attracting quality people and encouraging them to contribute to the organization. Linking with the HP strategy is a value of supportiveness based on a belief that all employees will be doing their best. MBWA acts as a beacon, both of the strategy of innovation and of the value of supportiveness. HP has found that managers who wander around are more likely to be supportive and encourage innovation. By insisting on MBWA, HP is helping to implement its mission. (Figure 11.3 presents the current version of *The HP Way*; note that it now includes specific examples of what MBWA looks like.)

IBM is famous for its open door policy. Thomas Watson, Jr., in *A Business and its Beliefs*,[3] describes this behavior standard, which encourages employees to appeal directly to a higher authority when they are dissatisfied: "The Open Door grew out of T. J. Watson's close and frequent association with individuals in the plant and field offices. It became a natural thing for them to bring their problems to him and in time was established as a regular procedure."

The open door is now a deeply held belief at IBM. Managers feel that their doors should be open both physically and metaphorically to any employee wishing to talk to them. The open door is a beacon of IBM's strategy and values. It reinforces IBM's value of respect for the individual. It also links to strategy. Like HP, IBM needs to attract high-quality people to execute its service-led strategy. Such people prefer a working environment where their concerns and

Figure 11.3 **The HP Way**

"MANAGEMENT BY WANDERING AROUND" AND "OPEN DOOR POLICY"

Purpose

Through the years a fundamental strength of the company has been the effectiveness of communications both upward and downward within the organization. Two key ingredients for making this happen are:

1. Management by Wandering Around
- To have a well managed operation it is essential that the managers/supervisors be aware of what is happening in their areas—not just at their immediate level, but also at several levels below that.
- Our people are our most important resource and the managers have direct responsibility for their training, for their performance, and for their well-being. To do this, managers must get around to find out how their people feel about their jobs and what they feel will make their work more productive and more meaningful.

2. Open Door Policy
- At times there are legitimate dissatisfactions and cases where employees feel they are blocked by the "system," or have a serious misunderstanding with their manager/supervisor, or for a variety of other reasons.
- In these cases, all employees have the right, if in their opinion they feel such steps ultimately are necessary, to discuss their concerns with higher-level managers (starting with first level above their immediate manager) until their problems are resolved. Any effort to prevent an employee from going "up the line" through intimidation or any other means is absolutely contrary to company policy and will be dealt with accordingly.
- Invoking the Open Door Policy will not in any way impact any evaluation of the employee or subject him/her to any other negative reactions.

continued

- Employees also have responsibilities—particularly in keeping their presentations to upper level managers focused on specific events which impacted them as individuals.

Business Related

1. Pay As You Go—No Long-Term Borrowing
- Helps to maintain a stable financial environment during depressed business periods.
- Serves as an excellent self-regulating mechanism for HP managers.

2. Market Expansion and Leadership Based on New Product Contributions
- Engineering excellence determines market recognition of our new products.
- Novel new product ideas and implementations serve as the basis for expansion of existing markets or diversification into new markets.

3. Customer Satisfaction Second to None
- We sell only what has been thoroughly designed, tested, and specified.
- Our products have lasting value—they are highly reliable (quality) and our customers discover additional benefits while using them.
- Best after-sales service and support in the industry.

4. Honesty and Integrity in All Matters
- No tolerance for dishonest dealings with vendors or customers (e.g., bribes, kickbacks).
- Open and honest communication with employees and stockholders alike. Conservative financial reporting.

People Related

1. Belief in Our People
- Confidence in, and respect for, our people as opposed to depending upon extensive rules, procedures, etc.
- Depend upon people to do their job right (individual freedom) without constant directives.
- Opportunity for meaningful participation (job dignity).

continued

Figure 11.3 **(continued)**

---

2. *Emphasis on Working Together and Sharing Rewards (Teamwork and Partnership)*

- Share responsibilities; help each other; learn from each other; chance to make mistakes.
- Recognition based on contribution to results—sense of achievement and self-esteem.
- Profit sharing; stock purchase plan; retirement program, etc. aimed at employees and company sharing in each other's successes.
- Company financial management emphasis on protecting employee's job security.

3. *A Superior Working Environment which Other Companies Seek but Few Achieve*

- Informality—open, honest communications; no artificial distinctions between employees (first-name basis); management by walking around; and open door communication policy.
- Develop and promote from within—life-time training, education, career counseling to help employees get maximum opportunity to grow and develop with the company.
- Decentralization—emphasis on keeping work groups as small as possible for maximum employee identification with our business and customers.
- Management-by-objectives (MBO)—provides a sound basis for measuring performance by employees as well as managers and is objective, not political.

---

contributions can be freely voiced. The open door policy demonstrates IBM's commitment to an open working environment.

Another computer company that has clear behavioral standards well related to its strategy and values is ICL. Its strategy is: "To succeed in the international marketplace by applying information technology to provide high-value customer solutions for improved operational and management effectiveness." There are "seven basic commitments," which highlight the company's overriding values:

commitment to change, to customers, to excellence, to teamwork, to achievement, to people development, and to creating a productivity showcase. Underpinning these values are the "ten obligations of the ICL manager" expressed under the following headings: business manager, people manager, direction, strategic thinking, high-value outputs, teamwork, and development. In the booklet *The ICL Way* there are well-defined behavioral standards to enable ICL's values to be put into practice. For example, under development: "Managers must first ensure that optimum use is being made of current skills and that individuals are given tasks which 'stretch' them in their existing jobs. They must then agree development and career progression plans with their staff and rigorously monitor the implementation of these plans to make sure they are effective."

These companies have made their missions easier to manage by identifying these behavioral standards. Because the behaviors are explicit they can be referred to in training, they can be used in assessment discussions and promotion decisions, and they can be a useful framework for disciplinary procedures.

   2. *Are the behavioral standards described in a way that enables individual employees to judge whether they have behaved correctly or not?*

Where behavioral standards are included in a mission statement they are frequently too vague to be useful. A typical statement might read: "Ensure rapid response to meet customers' needs." It is hard for employees to know whether their actions are complying with this standard or not. The real benefit of a behavioral standard is that it gives clear guidance for behavior. To reinforce this point, it is only necessary to consider the Ten Commandments in the Bible. Each of these is clear about the difference between good and bad behavior.

One mission statement we collected provides a particularly good example of how to move from a broad statement of values to a clear statement of the behavioral standards (see Figure 11.4). BUPA is the largest private health insurance company in Britain, and it also runs hospitals and a number of other activities. The health insurance division of BUPA identified "caring" as one of its most important values. As might be expected, this value links well with BUPA's strategy of being the service leader. It is also an attractive value for

Figure 11.4 **BUPA's Mission Statement**

BUPA MISSION STATEMENT

- To deliver the "best value" independent health financing and insurance.
- To provide an unrivalled service to our customers.
- To pursue excellence and superior performance.
- To care for customers, staff, suppliers, and the community within where we operate.

"Best Value" means:
- Making efficient and effective use of technology.
- A commitment to delivering and planning product innovations and services which satisfy customer needs.
- Using market leader position to reinforce initiatives on behalf of customers.

Unrivalled Service to the Customer means:
- Ensuring staff are well trained, informed, and skillful.
- Courteous and prompt attention to Customer, Doctor, and Hospital enquiries.
- Personal commitment by everybody to serve the customer.

The Pursuit of Excellence and Superior Performance means:
- Defining and achieving the highest standards of performance.
- Understanding and responding to customer needs.
- Rewarding superior staff performance and not accepting excuses for failure.
- Ensuring that underachievers receive help, counseling, and training to reach the required standards.

Caring means:
- Delivering to the customer more than we promise.
- Recognizing the contribution of each member of staff.
- Treating all our suppliers as we would wish them to treat us.
- Paying attention to the needs of the whole community.

---

the type of person that BUPA would like to have working for it. The problem is how to translate both the service strategy and the caring value into behavioral standards. BUPA's solution was to set about defining what caring means at the company. The definitions it came up with are not brilliantly full of insight, nor do they score particularly highly against our criteria, but they do illustrate the process of searching for behavioral standards that meet the two criteria in this section—that they should be beacons of strategy and values, and clearly indicate good and bad behavior. Part of BUPA's mission statement reads:

Caring means:
- Delivering to the customer more than we promise.
- Recognizing the contribution of each member of staff.
- Treating all our suppliers as we would wish them to treat us.
- Paying attention to the needs of the whole community.

BUPA's kind of caring is not an "all-you-need-is-love" type of caring. It is a more commercially based kind of caring that links back to the company's purpose, its responsibility to its stakeholders and its strategy.

BASF, a German-based international chemical company, has as an objective: "the goal of generating products which can be produced, used and disposed of safely." One of the values it stresses in its mission statement is that of social responsibility. Reinforcing both the strategy and the values are several explicit behavioral standards that leave employees in no doubt about what is expected of them in terms of environmental protection. These start with the broad brush: "Each employee must cooperate in working toward optimum environmental protection"; but they become more specific, for example: "The amount of waste water produced must be constantly reduced by internal measures," and "the impact of noise at the workplace and on adjoining residential areas is to be kept as low as possible." BASF's behavioral standards are clear guides to employees and act as beacons for the company's strategy and values.

Character

Our final advice to the writer of a mission statement is to make it readable. The examples we have collected vary from a straight-talking, thumbnail sketch written by the chairman over a weekend to smooth, jargon-filled, advertising copy prepared for the annual general meeting by communication consultants. We have examples of mission statements that contain as few as 200 words and others that amount to books of more than 10,000 words.

Two questions will help the writer to assess his or her work:

1. *Does the statement give a portrait of the company and capture the culture of the organization?*

We do not advise writers to construct their mission statements around the four sections we have defined as important: purpose, strategy, values, and behavioral standards. In preparing to write the statement each of these areas needs to be considered, but the statement itself should be designed to fit with the company's style.

The statement is a work of art that should capture the essence of the company in its size, format, and wording. If the company is a no-nonsense, frugal, cost-driven organization based in Yorkshire, then the mission statement should be a few gruff words on one side of a piece of paper—and BBA's mission statement is an excellent example of just that. Photocopied, neatly typed, on one page, the document *BBA—A Corporate Philosophy* begins:

> The inertia of history is a powerful influence on corporate philosophy. BBA in its 103 years of existence has strayed little from:
>
> i. Yorkshire paternalism
> ii. Weaving of heavy textiles
> iii. Friction technology via woven pressed resin media
>
> The philosophy of BBA for the next few years will be to adapt rather than abandon the inert.

The rest of the document is divided into five headings: Management, Markets, Money, Monday, and Maybe. Each section consists of four to ten terse sentences such as, "The cheapest producer will win"; "Avoid the belief that dealing is preferable to working"; "Three years is, in the current environment, the limit of man's comprehension of what may be"; "Go home tired."

It is clearly a document written by the chief executive, John Whyte, containing his important messages for the people in BBA. In presentation, in style, in the language it uses, and in its content, the statement captures BBA. It does not attempt to separate purpose, strategy, values, and behavioral standards; they are all bound up together in phrases that touch on the most important issues at BBA.

For example, under the heading of money, the statement says: "Budgets are personal commitments made by management to their superiors, subordinates, shareholders, and their self respect." On the face of it, this sentence is a behavioral standard—managers must meet budgets. But it is also a value statement—at BBA we believe in doing what we say we are going to do; we believe in living up to our promises. And the statement also describes some of the detail of BBA's strategy: to manage its diverse businesses in a decentralized structure controlled through demanding profit targets.

Another example of a mission statement that fits the organization is *The HP Way*. It is just a well put together document with good copy and no glossy photographs or other communication props. It reflects the serious and no-nonsense nature of the HP culture. Many of the phrases have been crafted by Bill Hewlett or David Packard and are, therefore, well worn within the company. One page is devoted to HP's two central behavioral standards— "Management by Wandering Around" and the "Open Door Policy"; one page addresses four "Business Related" objectives such as "Pay As You Go—No Long Term Borrowing"; and the third page addresses "People Related" issues such as "Emphasis on Working Together and Sharing Rewards (Teamwork and Partnership)." As in BBA's statement, the purpose, strategy, values, and behavioral standards at HP are interwoven throughout the document. As a whole it answers all the questions, and it does so in a way that speaks to HP people. They can read it and say, "That really is my company."

Many companies want to develop a neat, one-page summary of their mission that can be framed and hung on the wall, enclosed in wallet-sized plastic folders or etched into the cover of the company's annual report. We counsel against producing such summaries. First, the real mission statement should be regarded as a work of art, and management should realize that a cut-down sketch will not have the same impact. If management want to tell shareholders or customers about the mission they should be prepared to give them the whole document so that they get the whole message. The second reason we are against shortened versions is because they normally become sanitized versions. The slang is removed; the sentences are polished by communications experts; and the final version reads like advertising copy. In this form the statement loses its essence and can become pious platitudes.

2. *Is the statement easy to read?*

Many writers of missions believe that the statement should be short enough and important enough to be memorized. "If you can't remember it, it can't be worth the paper it's written on," is a common piece of advice. The argument is that the mission should be a kind of corporate creed that can be intoned repeatedly as a form of management character-building.

Our view is quite different. Some of the best mission statements are much too long to remember: IBM's mission statement is best described in Watson's book, *A Business and Its Beliefs*. Brevity is not essential, but ease of reading is. Whether the statement is 200 words or 20,000, it must be a good read. The 200-word statement will include some day-to-day company slang to bring it alive and it will touch on some behaviors that managers would naturally describe when talking about the company. The 20,000-word statement will include anecdotes and stories, particularly ones that the chairman or the founder used to tell. It will describe major decisions and turning points in the recent past, explaining how they have moved the company closer to its mission. It will read like a conversation with the founder.

The Elswick business philosophy is an example of a short mission statement. It includes eight simple sentences that together provide a clear picture of a caring, forward-looking company. Statements such as "There is no substitute for the facts" and "We want to do today what others do tomorrow" are straightforward and easy to understand.

Undoubtedly, writing a mission statement is no easy task. It requires commitment, energy, vision, and, above all, endless patience. A management team that wants to create a meaningful and powerful statement will be forced to ask itself some searching questions. The statement that it eventually produces will not be perfect the first time. It will need further refining as employees throughout the organization gradually commit themselves to the statement's aims and values and attempt to translate these into tangible behavior. This is, however, exactly what *should* happen. Only through trial and error and a constant willingness to return to the drawing board will senior managers eventually create a mission statement that is truly a *statement*—a powerful assertion of all that is most prized by the organization. We wish every success to the managers who are about to embark on this ambitious, yet worthwhile, task.

NOTES

1. Fred R. David, "How Do Companies Define Their Mission?" *Long Range Planning* 22, no. 1 (1979), pp. 90–97.

2. Michael E. Porter, *Competitive Strategy: Techniques for Analyzing Industries and Competitors* (New York: Free Press, 1980); *Competitive Advantage: Creating and Sustaining Superior Performance* (New York: Free Press, 1985).

3. Thomas J. Watson, Jr., *A Business and Its Beliefs: The Ideas that Helped Build IBM* (New York: McGraw Hill, 1963).

A Passion for Mission

. . . .

It has probably become apparent by this stage that we have a sense of mission about mission: that we believe managers, employees, and organizations could improve their effectiveness, contribution to society, and fulfillment if more attention were devoted to mission. At the end of Chapter 1 we discussed the difference between vision, mission, and strategic intent. We pointed out that both vision and strategic intent are flawed concepts because they have an unbalanced view of organizations. Vision is too much focused on goals and on the future, and strategic intent is a left-brained concept missing the importance of elevating purposes and organizational values. Mission is, we believe, the best conceptual framework for thinking about organizational purpose and identity. By thinking mission managers can improve the way they manage.

We have a passion for mission because we see a great opportunity for improvement. Few Western companies and few Western managers think in the terms we have laid out in this book. Yet many of the audiences we have spoken to have responded warmly to our ideas. It is not that managers have rejected mission thinking, it is that they have never been given a tool or framework in which to organize their thoughts. The Ashridge mission model is that tool. Learning to work with it takes time, and the task of creating a mission is demanding. But it is the right way to think. Mission thinking leads to a better understanding of strategic as well as organizational problems and this leads to better decisions and better initiatives.

Although we have not done field research in Japan, we are aware that mission thinking is much more common among the business leaders in Japan than in Europe or America. One example of this has been a series of advertisements by Japanese companies in the *Financial Times*. These advertisements have taken the form of a half-page or quarter-page interview between a well-known journalist or management commentator and the chief executive of the business. While much of the interview was devoted to discussions of products and markets and major projects, in all cases the interviews included a section on company philosophy, in which the chief executive talked about the ultimate purpose of the company, the management style, and the company's attitudes to its people. In an equivalent advertisement from a British or American company, the section on philosophy would be missing. During the time of the research, two British electronic companies, Ferranti and GEC, did run advertisements of a similar style, in which the difference in focus and the lack of discussion of mission and philosophy were apparent.

As we were writing this chapter, a new book arrived in the mail emphasizing this aspect of Japanese management: *As I See It* by Konosuke Matsushita.[1] Published in 1989, this is the second book of Matsushita's personal philosophy. It contains a collection of 56 essays written by the founder of Matsushita Electric between 1985 and August 1989. The titles of some of these essays demonstrate the author's commitment to philosophy and its importance in business: "Sincerity Counts," "The Company as a Work of Art," "Spiritual Value Added."

Another example of the commitment by Japanese companies to mission is the way they define their purpose. We have already given the examples of Matsushita's purpose, "happiness of man," and Wacoal's purpose, "to promote the creation of feminine beauty and to improve the culture of living." These companies are not unique. Toyota has defined part of its purpose as "to make ever greater contributions toward the economic development of all nations and the realization of higher living standards for their peoples, through the manufacture of automobiles." The purpose of ASICS, a Japanese sporting goods manufacturer, is "to contribute to the advancement of the global sports culture." Purposes of this kind are commonplace in Japan and their importance is increasing rather than declining. The Japanese manager from a firm of communications and corporate identity consultants called Landor Associates explained that the attention being given to these issues under the banner of "inner identity" is growing. As domestic Japanese companies have ventured overseas, and focused companies have begun to diversify, they have felt the need to reexamine and redefine their mission, an exercise to which they devote considerable time and expense.

A doctoral thesis on corporate identity by a Japanese student, Kasuo Mishima,[2] includes the following:

> Since the beginning of the 1980s the number of companies which have introduced corporate identity programs has rapidly increased. The proportion of corporate identity programs which put stress on problems of internal management has increased in the 1980s. In addition to the development of a visual identity system, most corporate identity programs address such internal problems as the reconstruction of the corporate concept, in-company morale raising, the renovation of the organization, and the diffusion of corporate philosophy.

A third example of the Japanese commitment to mission is the words they use in their company songs. Employees of Nippon Telegraph and Telephone, Japan's largest company, sing:

> Words of love echo in the sky
> Let's deliver them over mountains and rivers.
> It's the task of NTT to transmit the text
> That lifts up hearts . . .

Employees at Toshiba are known for their hearty rendering of:

> Let the boon of science
> Spread our tide to towns and villages
> Planting new culture
> Toshiba the Honored, Fruits of Science
> May Toshiba prosper, for all eternity.

Western companies have devoted less attention to mission because they have for many years had a biased view of the task of management. The blame has been laid at the feet of Frederick Winslow Taylor, the father of the school of scientific management, and also the cold analytical approach adopted by U.S. business schools whose methods have been copied around the Western world. Whoever is to blame, the important realization is that there is an opportunity to change. And what is even more exciting is that we have found we are pushing against an open door. Much of the groundwork has been done by crusaders like Tom Peters, who have railed against outdated management thinking, yelled at audiences for ignoring the fact that people and passion are the key to success, and articulately demonstrated that organization theory is incompetent for the job of helping managers think about how to run their organizations. We are joining the Peters crusade and contributing with this book some theory that will help.

We have addressed the body of this book to a general audience of leaders, managers, consultants, and students of management. In this last chapter we would like to try to draw out the implications of our thinking for more tightly defined groups, such as leaders of multibusiness companies, middle managers, unions and other groups with a stake in the success of business. We start with a long section addressing the issues facing multibusiness companies and follow with some shorter sections aimed at other groups.

Leaders of Multibusiness Companies

Leaders of multibusiness companies should take away two messages from this book. First, they have a role in promoting mission thinking among managers and planners running business units. Second, they need to develop a mission for the corporate headquarters level.

We have tried to show in Chapters 1 and 11 that mission can be analyzed and discussed in as rigorous a way as strategy. In other words managers can do mission planning in the same way that they do strategic planning. In fact, strategic planning is a subset of mission planning. Mission planning is more sophisticated than strategic planning; it helps managers formulate strategies that will fit their organization.

One of the reasons so many strategies fail to get further than the pages of a beautifully bound planning document is that they are strategies not missions: They fail to build on the values and behavioral standards that already exist in the organization and they don't inspire the emotions of the managers and the employees who are expected to put them into practice.

Mission planning goes beyond strategic planning in three ways: It involves an analysis of employee values and organizational behavior to assess the changes needed; it focuses on identifying behavioral standards that are central to the implementation of strategy and symbolic of the new value system; and it encourages a discussion of the organization's commitment to its stakeholders and to some higher level purpose. Mission planning forces managers to think through the behavioral implications of their plans; it prompts them to articulate an inspirational reason for any new plans; and it prevents them from side-stepping the issue of whether existing managers and employees are capable of responding to the challenge. Mission planning is where strategy, organization, and human resource issues come together. It asks managers to take a holistic view of their organization and its environment before developing a plan of action.

The strength of the Ashridge mission model is that it helps managers to be analytical about issues that have previously been handled intuitively. The emphasis on policies and behavioral standards gives specificity and tangibility to the discussion of culture. Most managers find culture an elusive topic, but it becomes crystal clear when they are asked to define their three most critical behavioral standards and say why these behaviors are relevant to both strategy and values. Behavioral standards can be documented and analyzed against the two rationales for action: the strategic rationale and the values rationale. Moreover, a simple organizational survey can confirm how widely the behavioral standard is upheld, whether or not it fits with employee values, and whether or not it is likely to be acknowledged as a symbol of the organization's values.

The emphasis on achieving a fit between employee values and organizational values is a second tangible part of analyzing culture. Mismatches between the employees' values and the organization's values can be discovered through opinion surveys and small discussion groups. These immediately show up unrealistic strategies.

The chief executive of a confectionery company recognized the need to make quality a plank of the company's strategy. He was about to launch an expensive set of programs to indoctrinate his employees in a new philosophy of quality, but before he did so he carried out an employee survey with the intention of using it as a benchmark for measuring progress. He was surprised to find that, according to the survey, the employees were disillusioned with the company because of their belief that management did not care enough about quality. The survey showed that there was no mismatch between the employees' values and the organization's desired values. The problem, as it turned out, lay in the company's policies on production volumes. These policies and measurement systems were encouraging managers to ship product regardless of quality. Once the policies were changed the employees' natural desire to make a quality product was allowed to flourish, saving much of the expensive indoctrination effort.

Leaders of multibusiness companies should be encouraging analysis and planning of this type. They should be promoting mission planning at the business unit level in the same way that most companies currently promote strategic planning. The first step is to extend mission thinking into the periodic strategic planning process. Ask managers in charge of business units to include issues of purpose, values, and behavioral standards along with their presentation at the strategy review. Ask them whether or not their organization is culturally aligned with their strategy. And ask them what their three most important behavioral standards are.

Initially, these questions will get little attention, superficial discussion, and insufficient analysis. But the process will have started. Managers at the center will be able to identify issues of concern and ask for further clarification or follow up with the business unit informally. The mission questions at the next strategy review can be more targeted, moving the thinking forward yet again.

In a highly developed process it may become necessary to separate the mission discussion from the strategy discussion in the same way that most companies have found it beneficial to separate the strategy discussion from the budget discussion.

Currently, most multibusiness companies have what is loosely called an organization review or manpower review. This is usually a separate meeting where business heads talk through the people in their business and share their thoughts about succession. These manpower reviews could be extended to become mission reviews. The agenda would be expanded to include issues such as the congruence between organizational values and the values of different functions within the business and the issue of behavioral standards. The Ashridge mission model or the McKinsey 7S model would be excellent frameworks around which to organize these reviews.

The best way to promote mission planning, however, is by example. Yet many managers at headquarters have argued to us that although they can see the relevance and importance of mission thinking at the business unit level, they can see no value in it at the headquarters level of a diversified company. They point out that each business should have its own strategy and culture—its own mission. In a diversified company these missions will be and need to be different. A corporate level mission would be an imposition, discouraging diverse businesses from developing their own diverse missions.

This was forcefully put to us by the director of a diversified engineering company who said: "We run our business on a decentralized basis encouraging managers to feel a strong commitment to their businesses. It is not our role at the center to interfere with the values of these units. They must build their own tightly knit and committed teams, and each one will be different." We do not disagree with this comment, yet we still believe that diverse companies should have corporate-level missions. In other words, we see that it is possible to have a headquarters mission and a set of diverse business unit missions. Mission can be treated in the same way as strategy. Because it is possible, in fact necessary, to have a corporate strategy and a different strategy for each business unit, it is possible to have a corporate mission and a different mission for each business unit. With good strategic planning the strategies at different levels and between sister companies do not clash and can reinforce each other. In the same way, good mission planning ensures compatibility between the different missions.

Companies as diverse as Hanson, a conglomerate spread across the United States and the United Kingdom; Grand Metropolitan, a diverse food and drink company; and Hewlett-Packard all have central missions and many different business units with different cultural biases and different missions. Yet in all three cases the missions are complementary, drawing the company together rather than pulling it apart. It is the clarity of the central mission that makes this possible.

For Hanson, the corporate headquarters mission is clear. The organization exists to make money for shareholders. "It is the central tenet of my faith that the shareholder is king—for it is he or she who decides, on their assessment of a company's abilities and prospects, that they will entrust their money to your company. The shareholder is rarely out of my mind and we never forget who our shareholders are. Many of them are retired people or pensioners whose income is derived from their pension fund's investments in our shares," explained Lord Hanson.[3] The company's strategy is to focus on mature, stable businesses: "We avoid areas of very high technology. We do not want to be in businesses that are highly capital intensive, where decision making has to be centralized or that rely on huge and sometimes expensive research with a prospect of a return sometime or never."[4]

Hanson also preys on groups where senior management have lost direction, have over-diversified and have lost control. Hanson buys these diversified groups, closes unprofitable parts, and sells businesses that do not fit the Hanson style, keeping only the mature, stable businesses. The behaviors and values supporting this strategy are equally clear:

> We believed from the beginning—and 23 years has not led us to change this view—that the best results flow from three systems which operate simultaneously and continuously. The first is the identification of the man or woman on whose performance the business will succeed or fail—the Manager. If you are in very complex or highly technical businesses, it is hard to identify the one person who carries the can for success or failure.
>
> The second is financial discipline. We work hard to get our operating companies to understand the concept that budgets are something you intend to achieve, not something you hope to achieve.
>
> The third is motivation. I believe very firmly in the combination of carrot and stick. We make it crystal clear what the manager's task is, but don't just leave it to him or allow him to get on with it. We require him to do it. This has a dramatic effect on the individual. Possibly for the first time in his career he senses the meaning of personal responsibility.[5]

If we summarize these elements (see Figure 12.1), we can see that Hanson has a clear mission for the corporate headquarters team and the managers in immediate contact with headquarters. The financially based culture is driven from the center. It is certainly intrusive. It affects the culture in all of the businesses it acquires. Yet it does not prevent the subsidiaries like Embassy Cigarettes or Butterly Bricks from having their own strategies and their own culture focused on the needs of their own businesses.

One of the strengths of Hanson is that it is more than a holding company. The center has a clear sense of its distinctive competence

Figure 12.1 **A Summary of Hanson's Mission**

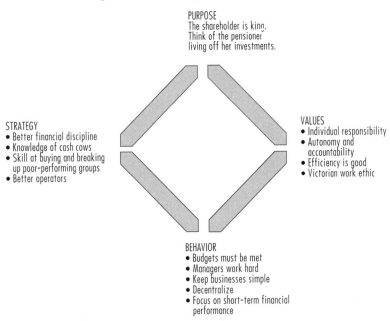

PURPOSE
The shareholder is king.
Think of the pensioner
living off her investments.

STRATEGY
• Better financial discipline
• Knowledge of cash cows
• Skill at buying and breaking
  up poor-performing groups
• Better operators

VALUES
• Individual responsibility
• Autonomy and
  accountability
• Efficiency is good
• Victorian work ethic

BEHAVIOR
• Budgets must be met
• Managers work hard
• Keep businesses simple
• Decentralize
• Focus on short-term financial
  performance

and the formula that has generated the company's remarkable success. It was a small family business in the 1960s and is now one of the largest companies on the London Stock Exchange.

The same strength of corporate-level mission exists in another company dedicated to decentralization, but with a completely different mission. Hewlett-Packard's mission is well documented in *The HP Way*. The company exists to succeed and success is to "be respected by our customers, our people and society." Its strategy in high-tech electronic and related products is to be more innovative, focusing on the high added-value products that need engineering excellence and outstanding after sales service.

The company has strong values about integrity, about caring for people, and about informality and creativity. These values are reinforced by behavior standards such as MBWA (Management by Wandering Around), MBO (Management by Objective), Open Door, and Team Work (see Figure 12.2).[6] Like Hanson, Hewlett-Packard's mission is intrusive: It lays down behavioral rules for people at headquarters and in the businesses; it defines the type of

Figure 12.2 **Hewlett-Packard's Mission**

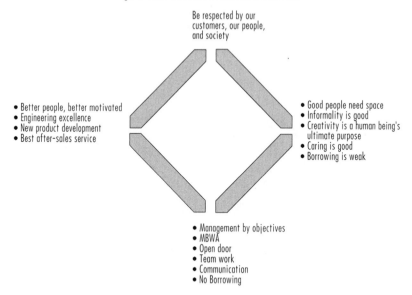

Be respected by our
customers, our people,
and society

• Better people, better motivated
• Engineering excellence
• New product development
• Best after-sales service

• Good people need space
• Informality is good
• Creativity is a human being's
  ultimate purpose
• Caring is good
• Borrowing is weak

• Management by objectives
• MBWA
• Open door
• Team work
• Communication
• No Borrowing

businesses that Hewlett-Packard seeks to focus on; and it even identifies the type of strategy (high value-added) that business units should pursue. Yet within Hewlett-Packard the computer products group will have a different mission from that of the medical group or the components group. The missions will be compatible and they will fit with the center's mission, but each group will have its own unique mission.

As at Hanson, the corporate-level mission at Hewlett-Packard provides a focus and some cultural rules within which the subsidiaries can develop their own missions. Other multibusiness companies should follow their example, clarifying their corporate-level strategy and their centrally determined cultural rules and so giving guidance to subsidiary managers as well as providing a demonstration of the benefits of mission thinking.

We know too many companies where the center avoids the issue of corporate mission, arguing that headquarters should not be dictating culture. The result is the creation of cultural "barons" at division or business levels and an emasculation of the center's ability to add value. For these companies, it is only a matter of time before a corporate raider such as Sir James Goldsmith or T. Boone Pickens exposes the failure of the center and breaks up the group.

Managers in Charge of Businesses

If you are in charge of a business, whether it is a small family business, a large focused business, or a business unit in a larger company, start to think about how you can make your business into a cause. Thomas Watson, Jr., had a saying that captures this: "Don't just put your heart into the business. Put the business into your heart." By doing this, managers can create a cause for themselves and for their employees.

Many managers feel this is unrealistic. They strive to win the diligent and creative involvement of employees and no more. Some even question the morality of seeking to engage the emotional interest, let alone the spiritual interest, of employees. We side with Watson. Managers who don't aim to persuade employees to take the business into their hearts are aiming for second best. They are missing the opportunity to help their employees find greater fulfillment from work and they are running less effective organizations. These passionless managers will find that their companies start to lose ground to those companies with leaders prepared to engage the emotions of their people.

The exciting part of our research was meeting employees and managers who already have the business in their hearts. It was apparent to us that these people feel a form of love for the organization they belong to. The feeling of belonging and of responsibility is evident. We could detect nothing unique about these people. They have no obvious personality differences. There is no reason to suppose that every employee could not feel the same sense of belonging. Some have the ability to express their commitment to an organization more strongly than others, but, in the same way as almost all people have the ability to love in its broadest meaning, almost everybody has the ability to feel a sense of belonging that amounts to what we have called a sense of mission.

So what should you do if you and your colleagues are convinced that working on mission is valuable? The first step is to meet together and talk through the four elements of mission—purpose, strategy, behavioral standards and values. The agenda item should be: "Do we (i.e., the group around the table) have a mission?" For most companies, the answer unfortunately is no, and this can be for many reasons. The members around the executive committee table have different values and different styles of management and they have never felt the need to reconcile them. The predominant values among the management team do not fit well with a strategy inherited from previous managers. The strategy has little substance when examined for its implications for behavior and values. The management team has been mouthing a devotion to shareholder wealth, but while acting to preserve or enlarge management's domain.

If you are in one of the few businesses where the management team does have a mission, this will become clear almost immediately. As you discuss each element of the model, the meeting will become more animated, the noise level will rise and the participants will become visibly excited. It will be like fitting the pieces of the jigsaw together—like showing the complete picture to everyone for the first time. As one manager explained, "It was one of the best sessions we have had together. It works. I don't know if I fully understand it, but it captured what we have all been working toward and it helped us focus on the three themes that we are all now agreed on. We are going to manage the business by them." The themes were communication, creativity, and quality.

This managing director had seen an early report of our research and used the model to focus the discussion at one of his planning meetings. The three themes they developed at the meeting became the banners of a management crusade that revitalized and created an identity for the newly formed division they had been put in charge of.

It was luck that the five managers involved had similar values and a strategy that fitted. But it was not luck that led them to the themes of communication, creativity, and quality. And it was hard work and persistence over the next 18 months that turned these themes into standards guiding management behavior throughout the company and giving the new organization and two subsequent acquisitions a sense of purpose and identity.

This manager's use of our model happened before we had researched the case studies in Chapters 5 through 10. We are now able to look back at this early example and acknowledge it as a model others should follow. So, if you and your colleagues have a mission, convert it into three themes and use these themes to drive management action, providing the logic for policies and behavioral standards.

If you and your colleagues do not have a mission, you should start to work on the problem. It is likely to take a year or two before the feelings of warmth and sense of common purpose and identity start to develop and it may be necessary for the team to change by releasing members with highly divergent views or values.

A good first step is to ask an outsider or objective insider to carry out an informal culture audit among the top two or three layers of management. This should involve interviews with a cross section of managers and can also include a simple values questionnaire. The interviews should include at least one question about how the person would like to see the business develop. Another powerful question is to ask managers whether or not they think the company is a good company. If they ask what is meant by good, tell them to answer against their own definition of good.

The results of the culture audit should be shared at a half-day or full-day meeting of the management team. After the results have been discussed, all team members should be asked to think about what they would most like the company to become. They should be asked to describe their ideal vision of the company in five or ten years' time, including as many behavioral descriptions as possible.

The outcome of this meeting is a clarification of areas of agreement and disagreement. Three types of agreement and disagreement are relevant: those that exist within the top team; those that exist between what the top team wants and what the organization currently is; and those that exist between what the top team wants and what other members of the organization want.

These areas of agreement and disagreement provide an agenda for further meetings. As soon as it is possible to define one important value that is central to the likely future mission, the management team should resolve to set about making the value a reality in the organization. This early action will give all concerned renewed enthusiasm to continue working on the development of a mission.

Middle Managers and Staff Functions

What can you do about mission if you are not part of the executive team in charge of a business? First you can lobby members of the executive team. You can send them a copy of this book. Or, referring back to the foreword to this book, you can press the chief executive to give a clear answer to the question of "where is our company going?"

One way to do this is through the management development process. A group of senior managers from a food manufacturing company was spending two weeks at the London Business School as part of a company program on strategic management. During the evening the company chairman spent with them, he invited them to let him know directly if they had any common concerns about the future of the business. The group took the opportunity and sent a memo to the chairman and the chief executive titled "The Future of the Company." The body of the note contained the following statement of the need that they felt for a mission.

> We do have a shared vision about what sort of company we would like to become. We would like to be recognized as the best (not necessarily the biggest) in the fields in which we compete. And we would like to be among the top companies (say the top 50) in the U.K. Our commercial skills, innovativeness, and professional management skills should be commented on by outside observers in the way that M&S, Unilever, P&G, and other top companies are seen as business exemplars.
>
> We would also like to be driven forward by the desire to be the best. We would like to be proud of having the best manufacturing, the best product, process, and packaging R&D, and the most feared marketing teams.
>
> We believe our future lies in building and maintaining product superiority. This will create both the brand franchise and the loyalty of private label customers that we need and it will provide us with the market share that will give us cost leadership.
>
> To have the best products and the best operations we need exceptionally strong managers. We envisage a management cadre that is praised for its professionalism, that is experienced in more than one company in the group, that works together in teams rather than hierarchical structures and is supported by a HQ recognized to be among the leaders in the complex task of managing a diversified group.
>
> These aspirations are bold. But our exposure to other companies at the LBS makes us realize that we can be among the best and that we should not settle for less.
>
> We recognize that it is our task at operating board level to make much of this vision come into being. It is our responsibility to make sure we have the best products, the most skilled marketing teams, and the finest manufacturing. But clearly the center has a vital part to play. It is in this context that we would like to pass up to you some messages about where we feel the center can make the most contribution.

One of the five messages in the memo was about values: "We would like to understand the center's approach to managing the culture, of setting the example and values that will make the Group strong in 20 or 50 years time."

As a result of the note, the whole group was invited for a discussion with the chairman and chief executive, and three years later almost all of the messages have been acted on. Aggressive lobbying of the executive team can have an impact.

However, middle managers and staff managers should not limit their efforts to lobbying. It is possible to develop a mission for a department or function. We were particularly impressed at Price Waterhouse by the mission statement and apparent commitment to its principles of the training function. Mike Philips, who was at that time in charge of the function, explained: "I carry the statement about with me all the time and refer to it frequently. It has helped me make decisions and focus my energy."

In another company the O&E department, responsible for implementing quality initiatives and industrial engineering improvements, has a detailed mission called, not surprisingly, *Our Mission*. It has influenced the way the function is managed and has the enthusiastic support of the small team involved. Having experienced the power of mission planning and mission thinking, the manager of the department is now lobbying his boss and his boss's boss to start working on a mission for the whole organization.

Wherever you are positioned in the hierarchy you can, as a manager in charge of people, start to think mission and start to manage values as well as commercial imperatives. In our experience many managers, like the example of Laura in Chapter 3, are instinctive users of values and frequently face the dilemma she faced between fairness and quality. Our advice is that you should actively seek these dilemmas, or at least be alive to them when they occur. By working through these dilemmas with the Ashridge mission model as an aid, you will be able to develop a mission for your area of responsibility.

Employees

As we have already repeated frequently throughout this book, we have met many people who love their work. Like the enthusiastic manager from the clothing manufacturer, these people feel that work is worthwhile and they get an emotional satisfaction from helping their organizations succeed. We therefore encourage you, the employee, to start looking for this extra ingredient at work.

If you recognize that what you are looking for is a company or a department that has values compatible with your own, you are more likely to find it. Some of you may need to think of moving organizations. For others, moving departments within the company may be sufficient. Others may have only a temporary problem caused by a values mismatch with your existing boss. Waiting for the boss to move on may be sufficient.

Unfortunately, we do not have a simple values questionnaire that you can complete and ask your prospective employer to complete to identify potential mismatches. But, with careful thought, you can develop some penetrating questions to ask in an interview that will help you screen out unsuitable employers. Think through your past job experiences and list events concerning other people's behavior, particularly that of superiors, that made you feel good and feel bad. Separate the good experiences from the bad and see if you can identify themes that are connected with behavioral standards or values important to you.

Once you have identified these themes, be creative about developing questions that will help you assess the values of the organization. You will find that managers with values are easy to identify because they respond to the right questions with enthusiasm in their voice and in their body language.

For example, we met a manager from a software consultancy looking for a new job. After some questioning, it emerged that he had left one of his previous jobs because he did not like the way the company exploited junior staff. Based on this experience and some others, he began to recognize that people development and fairness are important values to him. We were then able to develop questions to help him choose a compatible employer: What is your company's attitude to junior staff? How does the company balance the interests of staff, shareholders and customers? What policies do you have for development, particularly for junior staff?

As an employee you can also take an active part in trying to influence your company's values. The "green" revolution is one vehicle for doing this. Many office workers have, for example, lobbied their companies to create "greener" offices. Dual waste bins are appearing in many companies, one for recyclable waste and one for nonrecyclable waste. Certain brands of office equipment are being discouraged because they are not as good for the environment as competing products, recycled stationery is appearing, and other environmentally friendly policies are being developed. The importance of these initiatives is not being missed by sensitive managers. They are a signal that employees want a deeper relationship with their companies than the traditional pay-for-work relationship.

One event during our research surprised us and appeared initially to challenge our view that employees can create a close bond with their organizations. We had interviewed a senior consultant at Egon Zehnder who had been involved in the process of writing down the Zehnder mission. He obviously felt a strong sense of mission for the organization and took great trouble to articulate his understanding and his sense of commitment. We were therefore surprised when we received a letter from him saying that he had left the firm and was now working for another firm in a similar part of the professional service industry.

We knew that Egon Zehnder had an unusually low level of consultant turnover, particularly at senior levels. This man's decision to leave seemed to contradict all we had been thinking about the personal fulfillment that comes from a sense of mission. While we don't want to reveal, for reasons of privacy, the factors that led to his decision to leave, we were much reassured by talking to him. He obviously still feels a strong loyalty to the firm and a commitment to what Egon Zehnder stands for. It was apparent from talking to him that he felt a sense of loss and separation similar to that of losing a friend. At the same time he felt great hope and excitement about his new activity. What was reassuring was that he had found it difficult to break the emotional bond that he had with Egon Zehnder. It helped to confirm for us the existence of the emotional bond that can develop between an employee and his or her organization.

Government, Business Associations, Unions, and Financial Institutions

One of the advantages that Japanese companies have is the clear and stable understanding in Japanese society about the role of business. Business was seen as a means of rebuilding the country's self-esteem following the war. Outsiders talk fearfully of Japan, Inc., speculating that industry is being orchestrated by the powerful Ministry for International Trade and Industry (MITI). But much of the strength of Japanese industry stems from a commonly held belief about the importance of business success and how business can contribute to society.

No such stability of opinion about the role of business in society has existed in Britain or the United States. Government, business associations, unions, and financial institutions have an important responsibility to help business define its role in society. The Ashridge mission model, with its emphasis on purpose, is a valuable aid to each of these groups both in underlining the importance of the role business identifies for itself and in providing an insight into why business needs a role beyond that of making profits.

Britain has suffered most from the lack of a stable role for business. After the war, the role of business was to help rebuild Britain. Seeing business in this role caused many voters to support the nationalization of critical industries such as coal and steel because there was a lack of trust between capitalists and voters.

As the economy became more prosperous, this mistrust developed further. Profits and dividends were seen as part of the unacceptable face of capitalism. They were symbols of the capitalist exploitation of the worker. During the 1970s, it could be argued that the government discouraged a focus on profits and profitability and restrained a company's ability to pay dividends. Searching for an identity for industry, many businessmen and politicians argued that the role of business was to create employment. We spoke to one manager who was running a large chemical plant in the 1970s and he recalled with some embarrassment how strongly he had believed in his business's role in creating employment: "I even wrote a memorandum on the principle and circulated it to my staff." Without a clear identity for business and with profitability something of a dirty word, it was not surprising that business failed to compete effectively in international markets, creating a balance of payments crisis in the late 1970s that forced the government to seek help from the International Monetary Fund. It proved to be a turning point in thinking.

The new role of industry became "service to the shareholder" to generate wealth and "international competitiveness" to stem the tide of imports. During the 1980s, the shareholder crusade gathered momentum, and chairman after chairman now declares "we are in business to make money" or "we are here as servants of the share-holders."

However, the current emphasis on shareholders is no more solid as a role for business than the emphasis during the 1970s on employees. Undoubtedly, the pendulum will swing again as a new political group reacts to the unbalanced nature of existing attitudes. What is desperately needed in Britain is a stable view of the role of business in society.

The United States has been through a similar self-questioning about the role of business in society. In the mid-1970s American business was under attack. Society began to question the moral probity of business behavior. Ralph Nader formed a powerful political lobby to attack business. In a desperate defense managers began to talk about the social responsibility of business. They made large charitable donations and invested in their local communities. But it was not a reaction based on a new understanding of the role of business in society; it was an attempt to fend off criticism.

Business had lost its way and many senior executives were confused. A graduate of the Harvard Business School recalls sitting between two famous industrialists at his Baker Scholar dinner in 1978. When the conversation turned to broader issues of business and society, the student noted: "These were men who felt defensive. They didn't seem to understand what had happened to them. They had worked all their lives believing that business was good and now just at the pinnacle of their glory people were saying that business was bad. They didn't know how to cope. They did not seem to have any solid philosophy on which to rest their defense."

Like Britain, the United States took up the banner of shareholder value as the crusade of the 1980s and, as in Britain, this banner will in time be torn down because it is not sustainable. Managers in both countries are increasingly unhappy about the pressure to pursue the shareholders' bidding, and a counter-crusade against "short-termism" is under way.

Dick Giordano, the American-born chairman of BOC, a gas company based in Britain with a large position in the United States and plants all over the world, explains the problem. In a speech to the British business community in February 1990, he described the trends facing his industry and how these trends do not fit easily with short-term financial performance measures.

The common messages that emerge from these trends are higher costs, more intense competition, greater risk, and the demand for higher rewards from the providers of capital.

Any of you who have worked closely with financial analysis techniques, such as discounted cash flow, or present values, know that very high discounts driven either by greater risk or the higher cost of money, tend to diminish the present value of profits beyond the very near term *very substantially*.

The pejorative name of this phenomenon is short termism. Short termism has inspired a great deal of finger pointing. Industrialists blame bankers, bankers blame the stock market, the stock market blames pension fund managers, and everyone blames the government. There are no single villains, but the short-term bias has crept into every nook and cranny of our industrial and commercial life.[7]

As one of the most influential and highest-paid industrialists in Britain, Giordano's views demonstrate the widespread unease felt by those running businesses under the current shareholder-dominated philosophy.

The government, business associations, unions, and financial institutions have a responsibility to help formulate a more stable and more balanced philosophy. To expect business to thrive in an environment where business purpose is unclear or frequently changing is unrealistic. On the surface, financial institutions might like to encourage business to see the shareholder and the financier as the most important stakeholder. In the same way, unions might like to see the welfare of employees placed at the head of the list of priorities. The government might prefer the customer (the voter) to be the most important stakeholder in business. Lastly, business associations, staffed by retired executives, may want to argue that management should be the most influential group in business.

However, as we have argued earlier in the book, putting any one of these groups ahead of the others encourages instability. By acknowledging the selfish interests of one group, you encourage other groups to fight back. What business needs is a philosophical grounding that rises above the selfish interests of any group of stakeholders. Developing this philosophy is the responsibility of the representatives of all the stakeholder groups. Hence our belief that government, business associates, unions, and financial institutions need to join in an effort to agree on the role of business in society.

Developing a philosophy that all the stakeholder groups can support will not be easy. It could be similar to the Matsushita philosophy where business is seen as contributing to the happiness of each person through material affluence. An alternative philosophy could be built around the capitalist concept of wealth creation. The detail of the philosophy that is chosen is not in our view as critical as the stability and sense of common identity it can provide.

In discussions with managers we have noted how quickly they shy away from a discussion on purpose. Some see it as having little relevance. Others view it as a debate without resolution between those who support the shareholder and those who aspire to something more fulfilling. Hence most managers avoid the issue and limit their ambition to satisfying their responsibilities to the various stakeholder groups. To raise managers' ambitions and ignite enthusiasm behind purpose, government, unions, financiers, and other stakeholders need to come together and answer the question: "What is the purpose of business in society?"

Summary

Mission thinking has implications at all levels in business as well as for those connected to business. Our greatest hope is that this book will stimulate management teams to give the subject some executive time.

We are confident that the Ashridge mission model is a powerful analytical tool and we want managers to use it. It may be appropriate, therefore, to close this last chapter with a summary of why we think the model is so powerful.

First, the model states that organization values must be compatible with employee values. This compatibility or lack of it can be analyzed and measured, bringing objectivity to the discussion of culture and human resource issues. Will the executive team members have a values conflict with the proposed mission? Will the marketing department have a values conflict? While we recognize that the analysis of cultures and values has proved difficult and of limited managerial benefit, we believe values differences of the kind exposed by mission thinking can be analyzed and have important management implications. Techniques for interviewing, group discussions, and questionnaires will expose these value differences and confront managers with the need to change the values, change the people, or win the people to the new values.

Moreover, since values must be embedded in behavioral standards, values conflicts become exposed when managers or employees react to behavior instructions. It may be hard to analyze whether the managers of the chemical laboratory believe in "supportive management." It is much easier to decide whether these managers are likely to implement a standard of managing by wandering around. The model's strength, therefore, is that it defines the relationship managers need to create between organizational values and employees' values.

Second, the model demands that strategy and values resonate and reinforce each other. We pointed out in Chapter 2 that the link between strategy and values has been a central part of the McKinsey 7S model, but we know from personal experience using the 7S model that the link is hard to analyze. So it is possible to articulate values that are compatible with the strategy, but it is impossible to analyze whether they are the right values, whether they resonate with strategy sufficiently strongly.

The mission model's emphasis on behavioral standards helps to solve this analytical gap. By insisting that strategy and values are converted into a few behavioral standards acting as beacons of the mission, the degree of resonance between strategy and values is exposed. If it is possible to condense the mission into a few symbolically important behavioral standards, such as "Putting People First" or MBWA, then we can be confident that the strategy and the values resonate strongly. If no powerful behavioral standards can be identified, then the fault almost certainly lies in a lack of resonance between strategy and values. Further mission planning, further experimentation, and further insight are needed.

We can illustrate this with an example drawn from our own organization, Ashridge, whose largest activity is as a management center, based just outside London. Ashridge has identified two main planks of its future strategy: self-directed learning and internationalization. With the ambition of becoming Europe's best management school, Ashridge recognizes the need to become more international and eliminate elements of its culture and product-offering that have been focused on the British and Commonwealth market. It also feels the best way of achieving European preeminence is to become more learner-centered: to focus on the needs of managers. Since managers have different needs, a learner-centered focus demands that Ashridge develop ways of helping managers learn what they want to learn rather than what the lecturer wants to teach them.

Both of these thrusts are proving difficult to implement; not because the strategy is unclear or there is widespread disagreement about the values, but because the policies and behavioral standards that need to underpin the new mission are hard to identify. What behavior is required of a lecturer, program administrator, or member of hotel staff to ensure they contribute to the themes of internationalization or participant-centered learning? We don't yet know. It will take months, possibly years, to identify the appropriate behaviors and reach the point where the behavioral standards can be articulated. We have not yet found a resonance between the desired strategy and the organization's current values.

Managing mission is, therefore, an ongoing process. Companies will be able to articulate the behavioral standards that drive their mission only after a number of years. By being clear about the need to have a mission, to create a resonance between strategy and values, and to articulate behavior standards, managers can avoid a superficial attitude to mission and continue the analysis, thinking, and experimentation for long enough to develop the mission that will make them into a great company.

NOTES

1. Konosuke Matsushita, *As I See It* (Tokyo: PHP Institute, 1989).

2. Kasuo Mishima, "Corporate Identity Programmers in Japan." Ph.D. diss., 1988.

3. *The Treasurer* (June 1987), p. 10.

4. From *Management for Prosperity* (1984), a Hanson Trust document.

5. *The Treasurer* (June 1987), p. 10.

6. Based on *The HP Way*, reproduced on pp. 262–4.

7. Richard V. Giordano, KBE, "Strategy as a Tool for Renewal," *The Stockton Lectures* (February 1990).

Bibliography

Abegglen, James C., and George Stalk, Jr. *Kaisha: The Japanese Corporation.* New York: Basic Books, 1985.

Abell, D. F. *Defining the Business: The Starting Point for Strategic Planning.* Englewood Cliffs, N.J.: Prentice-Hall, 1980.

Ackerman, Laurence D. "The Psychology of Corporation: How Identity Influences Business." *Journal of Business Strategy* 5, no. 1 (Summer 1984).

Ackerman, Robert W. *The Social Challenge to Business.* Cambridge, Mass.: Harvard University Press, 1975.

Ackoff, Russel L. *Management in Small Doses.* New York: Wiley, 1986.

Adler, Patricia A. and Peter Adler. "Intense Loyalty in Organizations: A Case Study of College Athletics." *Administrative Science Quarterly* 33 (1988).

Alexis, M. and C. Wilson. *Organizational Decision Making.* Englewood Cliffs, N.J.: Prentice-Hall, 1967.

Andersen, Dan. "Vision Management." *European Management Journal* 5, no. 1 (1987).

Andrews, Kenneth R. *The Concept of Corporate Strategy.* Homewood, Ill.: Irwin, 1980.

Andrews, Kenneth R. "Ethics in Practice." *Harvard Business Review* (September-October 1989).

Andrews, R. R. *The Concept of Corporate Strategy.* Homewood, Ill.: Dow Jones–Irwin, 1971.

Ansoff, Igor. *Strategic Management.* New York: Halsted, 1979.

Argyris, C. *Integrating the Individual and the Organization.* New York: Wiley, 1964.

Arrow, Kenneth J. *The Limits of Organization.* New York: Norton, 1974.

Badaracco, Joseph L. and Richard R. Ellsworth. *Leadership and the Quest for Integrity.* Boston: Harvard Business School Press, 1989.

Barley, Stephen R., Gordon W. Meyer, and Debra G. Gash. "Cultures of Culture: Academics, Practitioners and the Pragmatics of Normative Control." *Administrative Science Quarterly* 33 (1988).

Barnard, Chester L. *The Functions of the Executive.* Cambridge, Mass.: Harvard University Press, 1938 and 1968.

Barry, Vincent. *Moral Issues in Business*. Belmont, Calif.: Wadsworth, 1979.

Beauchamp, Thomas. *Case Studies in Business, Society and Ethics*. Englewood Cliffs, N.J.: Prentice-Hall, 1983.

Beauchamp, Thomas and Norman Bowie. *Ethical Theory and Business*. Englewood Cliffs, N.J.: Prentice-Hall, 1983.

Beer, Michael. "The Critical Path for Change: Keys to Success and Failure in Six Companies." In *Corporate Transformation*, San Francisco: Jossey-Bass, 1988.

Behrman, Jack. *Discourses on Ethics and Business*. Weston, Mass.: Oelgeschlager, Gunn, and Hain, 1981.

Bell, Daniel. *The Cultural Contradictions of Capitalism*. New York: Basic Books, 1976.

Bennis, Warren and Burt Nanus. *Leaders: The Strategies for Taking Charge*. New York: Harper & Row, 1985.

Berger, Peter. *Pyramids of Sacrifice*. Garden City, N.Y.: Doubleday, 1976.

Bettinger, Cass. "Behind the Mission Statement." *ABA Banking Journal* 77, no. 10 (October 1985).

Bettinger, Cass. "Use Corporate Culture to Trigger High Performance." *Journal of Business Strategy* (March-April 1989).

Bettman, Ralph B. "Manage the Change Reaction." *Personnel Journal* (November 1989).

Bok, Sissela. *Lying: Moral Choice in Public and Private Life*. New York: Pantheon, 1978.

Boulding, Kenneth. *Beyond Economics*. Ann Arbor: University of Michigan Press, 1968.

Bower, Joseph. *Managing the Resource Allocation Process*. Homewood, Ill.: Irwin, 1972.

Bowie, Norman. *Business Ethics*. Englewood Cliffs, N.J.: Prentice-Hall, 1982.

Bradley, P. and P. Baird. *Communication for Business and the Professions*. Dubuque, Iowa: Wm. C. Brown, 1983.

Bradshaw, Thornton and David Vogel. *Corporations and Their Critics*. New York: McGraw-Hill, 1981.

Braybrooke, David. *Ethics in the World of Business*. Lanham, Md.: Rowman & Allanhead, 1983.

Brown, Lester R. *World Without Borders*. New York: Random House, 1972.

Brozen, Y. E. Johnson and C. Powers. *Can the Market Sustain an Ethic?* Chicago: University of Chicago Press, 1978.

Bruce, Mike. "Managing People First—Bringing the Service Concept to British Airways." *Industrial and Commercial Training* (March–April 1987).

Bumstead, Dennis and John Eckblad. "Developing Organisational Cultures." *Leadership and Organisation Development Journal* 5, no. 4 (1984).

Byars, Lloyd L. and Thomas C. Neil. "Organizational Philosophy and Mission Statements." *Planning Review* (July-August 1987).

Campbell, Andrew and Kiran Tawadey. *Mission and Business Philosophy.* Stoneham, Mass.: Butterworth-Heinemann, 1990.

Campbell, Andrew and Sally Yeung. *Do You Have a Good Mission Statement?* London: Economist Publications, 1990.

Carlzon, Jan. *Moments of Truth.* New York: HarperCollins, 1989.

Carr, Albert. "Is Business Bluffing Ethical?" *Harvard Business Review* (January-February 1968).

Carroll, Archie B. *Managing Corporate Social Responsibility.* Boston: Little, Brown, 1977.

Carroll A. and Frank Hoy. "Integrating Corporate Social Policy into Strategic Management." *Journal of Business Strategy* (Winter, 1984).

Cavanaugh, G. *American Business Values.* Englewood Cliffs, N.J.: Prentice-Hall, 1982.

Chandler, Alfred D. *Strategy and Structure.* Cambridge, Mass.: MIT Press, 1962.

Chandler, Alfred D. *The Visible Hand: The Managerial Revolution in American Business.* Cambridge, Mass.: Harvard University Press, 1977.

Chapman, Elwood. *Scrambling: Zig-Zagging Your Way to the Top.* Los Angeles: Tarcher, 1981.

Chewning, Richard C. *Business in a Changing Culture.* Reston, Va.: Reston Publishing, 1984.

Chrisman, J. J. and A. B. Carrol. "Corporate Responsibility: Reconciling Economic and Social Goals." *Sloan Management Review* (Winter 1984).

Ciulla, Joanne B. "Note on the Corporation As a Moral Environment." Harvard Business School Case No. 9-386-012 (1986).

Clifford, D. and Richard Cavanagh. *The Winning Performance: How America's High-Growth Midsize Companies Succeed.* New York: Bantam, 1985.

Clinard, M. and P. Yeager. *Corporate Crime.* New York: Free Press, 1980.

Collins, James C. and Jerry I. Porras. "Making Impossible Dreams Come True." *Stanford Business School Magazine* (July 1989).

Commoner, Barry. *The Poverty of Power.* New York: Knopf, 1976.

Cotter, John. "Designing Organizations That Work: An Open Sociotechnical Systems Perspective." John J. Cotter & Associates Inc., 1983.

Cox, David, ed. *By GABB & By GIBB*

Cyert, Richard M. and James G. March. *A Behavioral Theory of the Firm.* Englewood Cliffs, N.J.: Prentice-Hall, 1963.

David, Fred R. "How Do Companies Define Their Mission?" *Long Range Planning* 22, no. 1 (1979).

David, Fred R. *Concepts of Strategic Management*, 3d ed. New York: Macmillan, 1990.

David, F. R., D. Cochran, and K. Gibson. "A Framework for Developing an Effective Mission Statement." *Journal of Business Strategy* 2, no. 2 (Fall 1985).

David, F. R., D. Cochran, J. A. Pearce II, and K. Gibson. "An Empirical Investigation of Mission Statements." *Southern Management Association Proceedings* (1985).

David, Keith, William Frederick, and Robert Blomstrom. *Business and Society: Concepts and Policy Issues.* New York: McGraw-Hill, 1980.

Deal, T. and A. Kennedy. *Corporate Cultures.* Reading, Mass.: Addison-Wesley, 1982.

DeGeorge, Richard. *Business Ethics.* New York: Macmillan, 1982.

DeGeorge, R.T. and J. A. Pitchler. *Ethics, Free Enterprise, and Public Policy.* Oxford, England: Oxford University Press, 1978.

Demb, Ada, Danielle Chouet, Tom Lossius, and Fred Neubauer. "Defining the Role of the Board." *Long Range Planning* 22, no. 1 (1989).

Desjardins, J. and J. McCall. *Contemporary Issues in Business Ethics.* Belmont, Calif.: Wadsworth, 1984.

Diamond, Michael A. "Organizational Identity: A Psychoanalytical Exploration of Organizational Meaning." *Administration & Society* 20, no. 2 (August 1988).

Donaldson, Gordon and Jay Lorsch. *Decision Making at the Top.* New York: Basic Books, 1983.

Donaldson, Thomas. *Corporations and Morality.* Englewood Cliffs, N.J.: Prentice-Hall, 1982.

Donaldson, Thomas. *Case Studies in Business Ethics.* Englewood Cliffs, N.J.: Prentice-Hall, 1984.

Donaldson, T. and P. Werhane. *Ethical Issues in Business: A Philosophical Approach.* Englewood Cliffs, N.J.: Prentice-Hall, 1983.

Donnelly, R. M. "The Interrelationship of Planning with Corporate Culture in the Creation of Shared Values." *Managerial Planning* 32 (May-June 1984).

Drucker, Peter F. *The Age of Discontinuity.* New York: Harper, 1968.

Drucker, Peter F. "Management's New Role." *Harvard Business Review* (November-December 1969).

Drucker, Peter F. *Management: Tasks, Responsibilities, Practices.* New York: Harper & Row, 1973.

Dyke, C. *Philosophy of Economics.* Englewood Cliffs, N.J.: Prentice-Hall, 1981.

Ellul, Jacques. *The Technological Society.* New York: Random House, 1964.

Epstein, Edwin M. "Business Ethics, Corporate Good Citizenship and the Corporate Social Policy Process: A view from the United States." *Journal of Business Ethics* 8 (1989).

Estes, Ralph. *Corporate Social Accounting.* New York: Wiley, 1976.

Etzioni, A. and E. W. Lehman. *A Sociological Reader on Complex Organizations*. New York: Holt Rinehart & Winston, 1961

Evans, William A. *Management Ethics: An Intercultural Perspective*. Dordrecht (Netherlands): Martinus Nijhoff, 1981.

Ewen, Stuart. *Captains of Consciousness: Advertising and the Social Roots of the Consumer Culture*. New York: McGraw-Hill, 1976.

Ewing, David. *Freedom inside the Organization: Bringing Civil Liberties to the Workplace*. New York: Dutton, 1976.

Ewing, David. *Do It My Way or You're Fired!* New York: Wiley, 1983.

Fisher, Kim. "Managing in the High-Commitment Workplace." *Organizational Dynamics* 17, no. 3 (Winter 1989).

Frankl, Viktor E. *Man's Search for Meaning*. New York: Pocket Books, 1959.

Frederick, W. "Toward CSR-3: Why Ethical Analysis is Indispensable and Unavoidable in Corporate Affairs." *California Management Review* 28, no. 2 (1986).

Freeman, Edward and Daniel Gilbert. *Corporate Strategy and the Search for Ethics*. Englewood Cliffs, N.J.: Prentice-Hall, 1988.

Freeman, E., D. Gilbert, and E. Hartman. "Values and the Foundations of Strategic Management." *Journal of Business Ethics* (1988).

Freeman, E. and W. Evan. "Stakeholder Management and the Modern Corporation: Kantian Capitalism." in T. Beauchamp and N. Bowie, eds. *Ethical Theory and Business*. Englewood Cliffs, N.J.: Prentice-Hall, 1987.

French, Peter A. "The Corporation As a Moral Person." *American Philosophical Quarterly* 3 (1979).

Friedman, Milton. *Capitalism and Freedom*. Chicago: University of Chicago Press, 1962.

Frohman, Mark and P. Pascarella. "Creating the Purposeful Organization," *Industry Week* (June 9, 1986).

Frohman, Mark and P. Pascarella. "How to Write a Purpose Statement." *Industry Week* (March 23, 1987).

Garrett, Thomas M. *Business Ethics*. Englewood Cliffs, N.J.: Prentice-Hall, 1966.

Garrett, Thomas M. et al. *Cases in Business Ethics*. Des Moines: Meredith, 1963.

Glisson, Charles and Mark Durick. "Predictors of Job Satisfaction and Organizational Commitment in Human Service Organizations." *Administrative Quarterly* 33 (1988).

Goddard, Robert W. "Are You an Ethical Manager?" *Personnel Journal* (March 1988).

Goldsmith, W. and D. Clutterbuck. *The Winning Streak*. Harmondsworth, Middlesex: Penguin, 1985.

Goodpaster, Kenneth E. "Some Avenues for Ethical Analysis in General Management." Harvard Business School Case No. 383-007 (1982).

Goodpaster, Kenneth E. "The Concept of Corporate Responsibility." *Journal of Business Ethics* 2 (1983).

Goodpaster, Kenneth E. "Should Sponsors Screen for Moral Values?" The Hastings Center Report (December 1983).

Goodpaster, Kenneth E. "Ethics in Management." Harvard Business School Case No. 9-985-001 (1984).

Goodpaster, Kenneth E. "The Moral Agenda of Corporate Leadership: Concepts and Research Techniques." Paper delivered at D. S. MacNaughton Symposium Proceedings, 1986.

Goodpaster, Kenneth E. "Ethical Imperatives and Corporate Leadership." Ruffin Lecture in Business Ethics (April 1988).

Goodpaster, Kenneth E. and John B. Matthews, Jr. "Can a Corporation Have a Conscience?" *Harvard Business Review* (January-February 1982).

Goodpaster, Kenneth E., and K. Sayre. *Ethics and Problems of the 21st Century.* Notre Dame, Ind.: University of Notre Dame Press, 1979.

Goold, Michael and Andrew Campbell. *Strategies and Styles: The Role of the Centre in Managing Diversified Corporations.* Oxford, England: Basil Blackwell, 1987.

Goold, Michael with John J. Quinn. *Strategic Control: Milestones for Long-Term Performance.* London: The Economist Books/Hutchinson, 1990. U.S. edition forthcoming, Economist Books/Addison-Wesley, Reading, Mass., 1993.

Gould, R. *The Matsushita Phenomenon.* Tokyo: Diamond Sha, 1970.

Guth, William D. and Renato Tagiuri. "Personal Values and Corporate Strategy." *Harvard Business Review* (September-October 1965).

Hahn, Frank and Martin Hollis, eds. *Philosophy and Economic Theory.* Oxford, England: Oxford University Press, 1979.

Hamel, Gary and C. K. Pralahad. "Strategic Intent." *Harvard Business Review* (May-June 1989).

Hampshire, S. *Public and Private Morality.* Cambridge, England: Cambridge University Press, 1978.

Handy, Charles B. *The Gods of Management.* London: Pan, 1979.

Handy, Charles B. *Understanding Organizations.* New York: State Mutual Books, 1985.

Harrison, Roger. "Towards the Self Managing Organization: Releasing and Focusing Personal Energy with Organizational Mission Statements." Berkeley, Calif.: Harrison Associates, Prepublication draft, 1986.

Harrison, Roger. "Harnessing Personal Energy: How Companies Can Inspire Employees." *Organizational Dynamics* 16, no. 2 (Autumn 1987).

Hayes, R. & W. Abernathy. "Managing Our Way to Economic Decline." *Harvard Business Review* 58, no. 4 (1980).

Heilbroner, Robert L. *The Worldly Philosophers*. New York: Simon & Schuster, 1967.

Heilbroner, Robert L. *Business Civilization in Decline*. New York: Norton, 1976.

Herzberg, Frederick. *Work and the Nature of Man*. Antioch, Tenn.: World Publishing, 1966.

Herzberg, Frederick. "One More Time: How Do You Motivate Employees?" *Harvard Business Review* (January-February 1968).

Herzberg, Frederick. "Where Is the Passion and the Other Elements of Innovation?" *Industry Week* (November 11, 1985).

Hessen, Robert. *In Defense of the Corporation*. Stanford, Calif.: Hoover Institution Press, 1979.

Hill, C. P. *Towards a New Philosophy of Management*. London: Gower Press, 1971.

Hoffman, W. Michael and Jennifer Moore. *Business Ethics: Readings and Cases in Corporate Morality*. New York: McGraw-Hill, 1983.

Hoffman, W. Michael, Jennifer Moore, and David Fedo. *Corporate Governance and Institutionalizing Ethics*. Lexington, Mass.: Lexington, 1984.

Hunt, John W. *The Restless Organization*. New York: Wiley, 1972.

Hunt, John W. *Managing People at Work: A Manager's Guide to Behavior in Organizations*. New York: McGraw-Hill, 1981.

Hunter, Jairy C. "Managers Must Know the Mission: 'If It Ain't Broke Don't Fix It'." *Managerial Planning* (January-February 1985).

Jones, D., ed. *Business, Religion and Ethics*. Weston, Mass.: Oelgeschlager, Gunn and Hain, 1982.

Jones, D., ed. *Doing Ethics in Business*. Weston, Mass.: Oelgeschlager, Gunn and Hain, 1982.

Kanter, Rosabeth Moss. *Commitment and Community*. Cambridge, Mass.: Harvard University Press, 1972.

Kanter, Rosabeth Moss. *The Change Masters*. New York: Simon & Schuster, 1983.

Katz, D. and R. Kahn. *The Social Psychology of Organization*. New York: Wiley, 1966.

Kindleberger, Charles P. *Social Responsibility of the Multi-National Corporation*. Lanham, Md.: University Press of America.

Kobayashi, S. *Creative Management*. American Management Association, 1971.

Kotter, J. F. *The Leadership Factor*. New York: Free Press, 1988.

Kotter, John P. and Leonard A. Schlesinger. "Choosing Strategies for Change." *Harvard Business Review* (March-April 1979).

Ladd, John. "Morality and the Ideal of Rationality in Formal Organizations." in *Morality and Corporations*.

Lawler, Edward E. *High Involvement Management: Participative Strategies for Improving Organizational Performance.* San Francisco: Jossey-Bass, 1986.

Lawrence, P. R. and J. W. Lorsch. *Organization and Environment.* Homewood, Ill.: Irwin, 1967.

Leavitt, Harold J. *Management Psychology.* Chicago: University of Chicago Press, 1978.

Leavitt, Harold J. *Corporate Pathfinders: Building Vision and Values into Organizations.* Homewood, Ill.: Dow Jones–Irwin, 1986.

Lemaitre, Nadine. *In Search of Belgian Excellence.* Brussels: Université Libre de Bruxelles, 1984.

Levering, Robert. *A Great Place to Work.* New York: Random House, 1988.

Levinson, Harry. *The Exceptional Executive.* Cambridge: Harvard University Press, 1971.

Levinson, H. *Psychological Man.* Cambridge, Mass.: Levinson Institute, 1976.

Levitt, Ted. "Marketing Myopia." *Harvard Business Review* (July-August 1960).

Liedtka, Jeanne M. "Value Congruence: The Interplay of Individual and Organizational Value Systems." *Journal of Business Ethics* 8 (1989).

Likert, Rensis. *The Human Organization: Its Management and Value.* New York: McGraw-Hill, 1967.

Litschert, R. and E. Nicholson. *The Corporate Role and Ethical Behavior: Concepts and Cases.* New York: Van Nostrand, 1977.

Lorsch, Jay. "Managing Culture: The Invisible Barrier to Strategy." *California Management Review* (Winter 1986).

Lundberg, Craig C. "Zero-in: A Technique for Formulating Better Mission Statements." *Business Horizons* (September-October 1984).

Luthans, Fred, Richard Hodgetts, and Kenneth Thompson. *Social Issues in Business.* New York: Macmillan, 1976.

Lyons, N. *The Sony Vision.* New York: Crown, 1976.

Maccoby, Michael. *The Leader.* New York: Simon & Schuster, 1981.

McGinnis, Vern J. "The Mission Statement: A Key Step in Strategic Planning." *Business* (November-December 1981).

McGregor, Douglas. *The Human Side of Enterprise.* New York: McGraw-Hill, 1960.

Machiavelli, Nicolo. *The Prince.* Translated by Luigi Ricci, revised by E. R. P. Vincent. New York: Mentor Press, 1962.

McKay, Gilly and Alison Locke. *The Body Shop: Franchising a Philosophy.* Harmondsworth, Middlesex: Penguin, 1986.

Mackie, K. A. "Managing Change: How Dayton Hudson Meets the Challenge." *Journal of Business Strategy* 4 (Summer 1983).

McLelland, David C. *Power: The Inner Experience.* New York: Irvington, 1979.

March, J. G. and H. A. Simon. *Organizations*. New York: Wiley, 1968.

Marshall, Sir Colin. "British Airways." In *Turnaround: How Twenty Well-Known Companies Came Back From the Brink*, ed. Rebecca Nelson. London: Mercury Books, 1988.

Maslow, Abraham H. *Motivation and Personality*. New York: Harper & Row, 1970.

Matsushita, Konosuke. *Not for Bread Alone: A Business Ethos, A Management Ethic*. Tokyo: PHP Institute, Inc., 1984.

Matsushita, Konosuke. *As I See It*. Tokyo: PHP Institute, Inc., 1989.

Matthews, John B., Kenneth E. Goodpaster, and Laura L. Nash. *Policies and Persons: A Casebook in Business Ethics*. New York: McGraw-Hill, 1985.

Miles, Robert. *Coffin Nails and Corporate Strategies*. Englewood Cliffs, N.J.: Prentice-Hall, 1982.

Miller, Paul. "Managing Corporate Identity in the Diversified Business." *Personnel Management* (March 1989).

Milter, Danny and Peter Friesen. *Organizations*. Englewood Cliffs, N.J.: Prentice-Hall, 1984.

Mintzberg, Henry. *The Structuring of Organizations: A Synthesis of Research*. Englewood Cliffs, N.J.: Prentice-Hall, 1979.

Mintzberg, Henry. *Power in and around Organizations*. Englewood Cliffs, N.J.: Prentice-Hall, 1983.

Mishima, Kasuo. "Corporate Identity Programs in Japan." Ph.D. diss. 1988.

Missner, Marshall. *Ethics of the Business System*. Sherman Oaks, Calif.: Alfred, 1980.

Molander, Earl A. *Responsive Capitalism*. New York: McGraw-Hill, 1980.

Morita, Akio. *Made in Japan*. New York: E. P. Dutton, 1986.

Naisbitt, John and Patricia Aburdene. *Re-inventing the Corporation*. New York: Warner Books, 1985.

Nash, Laura. "Ethics Without the Sermon." *Harvard Business Review* (November-December 1981).

Nash, Laura L. *Good Intentions Aside*. Boston: Harvard Business School Press, 1990.

Nash, Laura L. "Addendum to the Report on the Conference Board Ethics Network." London, 1992.

Novak, Michael. *The American Vision*. Washington: American Enterprise Institute, 1978.

Novak, Michael. *The Spirit of Democratic Capitalism*. New York: Simon & Schuster, 1982.

Ogbonna, Emmanuel and Barry Wilkingon. "Corporate Strategy and Corporate Culture: The Management of Change in the UK Supermarket Industry." *Personnel Review* 17, no. 6 (1988).

Ohmann, O. A. "Skyhooks." *Harvard Business Review* (January-February 1970).

Olins, Wally. *Corporate Identity: Making Business Strategy Visible Through Design*. Cambridge, Mass.: Harvard Business School Press, 1990.

O'Reilly, Charles. "Corporations, Culture and Commitment: Motivation and Social Control in Organizations." *California Management Review* (Summer 1989).

Ouchi, W. *Theory Z: How American Business Can Meet the Japanese Challenge*. Reading, Mass.: Addison-Wesley, 1981.

Partridge, Scott. *Cases in Business and Society*. Englewood Cliffs, N.J.: Prentice-Hall, 1982.

Pascale, Richard T. and Anthony G. Athos. *The Art of Japanese Management*. New York: Simon & Schuster, 1981.

Pascarella, Perry. "Is Your Mission Clear?" *Industry Week* 13 (October 1986).

Pearce, John A. II. "The Company Mission As a Strategic Tool." *Sloan Management Review* (Spring 1982).

Pearce, John A. II and Fred David. "Corporate Mission Statements: The Bottom Line." *Academy of Management Executive* 1, no. 2 (1987).

Pearce, John A. II and Richard B. Robinson, Jr. *Strategic Management: Strategy Formulation and Implementation*. Homewood, Ill.: Irwin, 1985.

Pearce, John A. II and K. Roth. "Multinationalization of the Company Mission." *Sloan Management Review* (1986).

Peters, Tom and Nancy Austin. *A Passion for Excellence*. New York: Random House, 1985.

Peters, Thomas J. and Robert H. Waterman. *In Search of Excellence: Lessons from America's Best Run Companies*. New York: Harper & Row, 1982.

Pettigrew, Andrew. *The Awakening Giant: Continuity and Change in ICI*. Oxford, England: Basil Blackwell, 1985.

Phillips, J. and A. Kennedy. "Shaping and Managing Shared Values." *McKinsey Staff Paper* (December 1980).

Plant, Roger. *Managing Change and Making It Stick*. Huntington, N.Y.: Fontana, 1987.

Porter, Michael E. *Competitive Strategy: Techniques for Analyzing Industries and Competitors*. New York: Free Press, 1980.

Porter, Michael E. *Competitive Advantage: Creating and Sustaining Superior Performance*. New York: Free Press, 1985.

Porter, Michael. "From Competitive Advantage to Corporate Strategy." *Harvard Business Review* (May-June 1987).

Posner, Barry Z., James M. Kouzes, and Warren H. Schmidt. "Shared Values Make a Difference: An Empirical Test of Corporate Culture." *Human Resource Management* 24, no. 3 (Fall 1985).

Poulet, Roger and Gerry Moult. "Putting Values into Evaluation." *Training and Development Journal* (July 1987).

Quinn, B. *Strategies for Change: Logical Incrementalism.* Homewood, Ill.: Irwin, 1980.

Regan, Tom, ed. *Just Business: New Introductory Essays in Business Ethics.* New York: Random House, 1984.

Regan, Tom and Donald VanDeVeer. *And Justice for All.* Totowa, N.J.: Roman & Littlefield, 1982.

Rehder, Robert, Marta Smith, and Katherine Burr. "A Salute to the Sun: Crosscultural Organizational Adaptation and Change." *Leadership & Organization Development Journal* 10, no. 4 (1989).

Robson, Mike. *The Journey to Excellence.* New York: Wiley, 1986.

Roche, William J. and Neil L. MacKinnon. "Motivating People with Meaningful Work." *Harvard Business Review* (May-June 1970).

Rodgers, Buck. *The IBM Way.* New York: HarperCollins, 1987.

Savage, Peter. *Who Cares Wins.* Woodside, Calif.: Mercury Books, 1987.

Sayre, K. M. *Values in the Electric Power Industry.* Notre Dame, Ind.: University of Notre Dame Press, 1977.

Schein, Edgar H. *Organizational Psychology,* 3rd ed. Englewood Cliffs, N.J.: Prentice-Hall, 1980.

Schein, Edgar H. *Organizational Culture and Leadership.* San Francisco: Jossey-Bass, 1985.

Schlegelmilch, B. B. and J. E. Houston. "Corporate Codes of Ethics in Large UK Companies: An Empirical Investigation of Use, Content and Attitudes." Working Paper Series 88/16, Department of Business Studies, University of Edinburgh.

Schnyder, Klaus. "Ethical Values in Company Policy." Paper presented at Pontifical Council for the Laity, Washington (September 28,1986).

Schumacher, E. F. *Small Is Beautiful.* New York: HarperCollins, 1989.

Schumacher, E. F. *Good Work.* New York: Harper & Row, 1979.

Seidler, L. *Social Accounting: Theory, Issues and Cases.* Melville, 1975.

Selekman, Benjamin. *A Moral Philosophy for Management.* New York: McGraw-Hill, 1959.

Selznick, Philip. *Leadership in Administration: A Sociological Interpretation.* Berkeley: University of California Press, 1957.

Sethi, S. P. *Up Against the Corporate Wall.* Englewood Cliffs, N.J.: Prentice-Hall, 1977.

Sethi, S. P. and Dow Votaw. *The Corporate Dilemma.* Englewood Cliffs, N.J.: Prentice-Hall, 1973.

Sherwood, John. "Creating Work Cultures with Competitive Advantage." *Organizational Dynamics* (Fall 1988).

Shockley-Zalabak, Pamela and Donald Dean Morley. "Adhering to Organizational Culture: What Does It Mean? Why Does It Matter?" *Group & Organization Studies* 14, no. 4 (December 1989).

Sieff, Marcus. *Don't Ask the Price.* Guilford, Conn.: Ulverscroft, 1988.

Simon, Herbert A. "On the Concept of Organizational Goal." *Administrative Science Quarterly* 9.

Simon, Herbert A. *Administrative Behavior*. New York: Macmillan, 1976.

Skinner, B. F. *Beyond Freedom and Dignity*. New York: Bantam, 1984.

Sloan, Alfred. *My Years with General Motors*. Garden City, N.Y.: Doubleday, 1963.

Sober, Cyril. *Organizations in Theory and Practice*. London: Heinemann, 1972.

Staples, W. A. and K. U. Black. "Defining Your Business Mission: A Strategic Perspective." *Journal of Business Strategy* (Spring 1984).

Steckmest, F. W. *Corporate Performance*. New York: McGraw-Hill, 1982.

Stewart, Rosemary. *The Reality of Management*. London: Heinemann, 1963.

Tanaka, *Personality in Industry*. London: Pinter Publishers, 1988.

Tregoe, Benjamin and John Zimmerman. *Top Management Strategy*. New York: Touchstone Books, 1983.

Tushman, Michael L., William H. Newman, and David A. Nadler. "Executive Leadership and Organizational Evolution: Managing Incremental and Discontinuous Change." In *Corporate Transformation*. San Francisco: Jossey-Bass, 1988.

Uttal, B. "The Corporate Culture Vultures." *Fortune* (October 17, 1983).

Walton, Clarence. *Ethos and the Executive*. Englewood Cliffs, N.J.: Prentice-Hall, 1969.

Walton, Clarence. *The Ethics of Corporate Conduct*. Englewood Cliffs, N.J.: Prentice-Hall, 1977.

Walton, Richard E. "From Control to Commitment in the Workplace." *Harvard Business Review* (March-April 1985).

Wart, Jerome. "Corporate Mission: The Intangible Contributor to Performance." *Management Review* (August 1986).

Waterman, Robert. *The Renewal Factor*. New York: Bantam Press, 1988.

Watson, Thomas J. Jr. *A Business and Its Beliefs: The Ideas that Helped Build IBM*. New York: McGraw-Hill, 1963.

Watts, Reginald. *Public Relations for Top Management*. New Malden, Surrey: Croner Publications, 1977.

Weber, Max. *The Protestant Ethic and the Spirit of Capitalism*, rev. ed. New York: Macmillan, 1980.

Webley, Simon. *Company Philosophies and Codes of Business Ethics: A Guide to Their Drafting and Use*. London: Institute of Business Ethics, 1988.

Weiss, William L. "Minerva's Owl: Building a Corporate Value System." *Journal of Business Ethics* 5 (1986).

Weller, Steven. "The Effectiveness of Corporate Codes of Ethics." *Journal of Business Ethics* 7 (1988).

White, Bernard J. and Ruth B. Montgomery. "Corporate Codes of Conduct." *California Management Review* 23, no. 2 (Winter 1980).

Wickens, Peter. *The Road to Nissan*. London: Macmillan, 1987.

Wilkins, Alan L. and Nigel J. Bristow. "For Successful Organization Culture, Honor Your Past." *Academy of Management Executive*, 1, no. 3 (1987).

Wille, Edgar. "Ethics at the Heart of Business—An Integrative Approach." Paper presented at the Second European Business Ethics Conference, Ashridge Management Research Group, Barcelona, September 1989.

Williams, Oliver and John Houck. *Full Value*. New York: Harper & Row, 1978.

Williams, Oliver and John Houck, eds. *The Judeo-Christian Vision and the Modern Corporation*. Notre Dame, Ind.: University of Notre Dame Press, 1982.

Wright, J. Patrick. *On a Clear Day You Can See General Motors*. New York: Avon, 1979.

Yankelovich, David. "The Work Ethic Is Underemployed." *Psychology Today* (May 1982).

Zaleznik, Abraham and Manfred Kets de Vries. *Power and the Corporate Mind*. Boston: Houghton Mifflin, 1975.

Zoll, Allen A. "The Dilemmas of Developing and Communicating Strategy." Harvard Business School Case No. 9-387-044, 1986.

Zoll, Allen A. "Institutional Leadership." Harvard Business School Case No. 9-385-108, 1986.

Index

Disney company, 65, 90
Dist, Inc., 14, 16
    Albert company, 187, 188, 193–201
    behavioral standards, 190
    case study, 187–201
    communication of mission, 190–91, 201
    customer service policy, 189, 192–93
    decentralized structure, 188–89
    diversification, 188, 193–94
    employee adaptation to culture, 63, 200–201
    employee policies based on mission, 191, 192, 201
    employee/shareholder balance, 20–21
    employment security as value, 189, 198–200
    growth of, 187–90
    intellectual approach to mission, 87, 89, 90
    leadership, 106, 109
    management response to mission, 191, 192–93
    mission statement, development of, 79, 189–90
    Our Principles mission statement, 190–93, 197, 200–201
    profitability, 198
    quality theme of mission, 95, 96
    shareholders, 20–21, 190
    strategy, 22
    team-building events, 192
    time frame for mission development, 104–5, 201
    trust as mission goal, 109
Diversified companies, mission in, 185–86, 193–94, 279–82
Draper, Gerry, 116
Drucker, Peter, 3, 11
Dunlop, Gordon, 116, 118, 119

Egon Zehnder company, 14
    behavioral standards, 71–72
    employee loyalty, 7, 69
    founder approach to mission, 90
    mission, 28, 77
    policies, 24
    purpose, 21
    recruitment, 62
    sense of mission, 5, 6, 71–72, 289
    strategy, 18, 22–24
    values, 17, 18, 25–26
Ellsworth, Richard, 41–42, 44
Elswick company, 270
Emery, F.E., 222–23
Emotional logic, 24–27, 34

Employees. *See also* Behavioral standards; Sense of mission
    adaptation to culture, 62–63, 200–201
    appraisal, 63–64, 103, 125, 191–92
    Johnson & Johnson and. *See* Johnson & Johnson personnel policies
    based on mission, 61–63, 121, 189, 191, 192, 201
    recruitment, 61–62, 191, 197
    as stakeholders, 248, 250–51, 257
    training, 64–65, 191
    values. *See* Values, corporate
Employee values, 6
Esso, 222
Ethical behavior, 66, 72, 167, 171–76
Etzioni, A., 54

Ferranti, 274
F.I. Group, 256
Firestone Tire and Rubber Company, 166
First Chicago Bank, 63
Ford Motor Company, 33, 87
Founders of companies, 91, 94, 105, 256
France, companies in, 58
Freeman, Edward, 50–51
Friedman, Milton, 50

Garton, John, 118
GEC, 274
Georgiades, Nick, 103, 124, 126, 128
Gilbert, Daniel, 50–51
Giordano, Dick, 291–92
Goals, 32, 33
    of managers, 65–67, 100
Goldsmith, James, 282
Goold, Michael, 4, 6
Grand Metropolitan, 279
Great Britain, business climate of, 290–92

Hamel, Gary, 31, 33
Hanson company, 20, 248, 279–81
Hanson, Lord, 20, 21, 248, 280
Harris, Jim, 117
Harvey-Jones, John, 71
Heldrich, John, 142
Herzberg, Frederick, 37, 52–53
Hewlett, Bill, 77, 91
Hewlett-Packard
    behavioral standards, 26, 77, 260–64, 281
    founder approach to mission, 90, 105
    mission, 28, 77, 279, 281–82
    mission statement. *See HP Way, The*
    sense of mission, 29, 34–35
    strategy, 60–61
    values, 26, 60–61